INTRODUCTION TO CONVICT CRIMINOLOGY

Jeffrey Ian Ross

First published in Great Britain in 2024 by

Bristol University Press
University of Bristol
1–9 Old Park Hill
Bristol
BS2 8BB
UK
t: +44 (0)117 374 6645
e: bup-info@bristol.ac.uk

Details of international sales and distribution partners are available at bristoluniversitypress.co.uk

© Bristol University Press 2024

British Library Cataloguing in Publication Data
A catalogue record for this book is available from the British Library

ISBN 978-1-5292-2119-0 hardcover
ISBN 978-1-5292-2120-6 paperback
ISBN 978-1-5292-2121-3 ePub
ISBN 978-1-5292-2122-0 ePdf

The right of Jeffrey Ian Ross to be identified as author of this work has been asserted by him in accordance with the Copyright, Designs and Patents Act 1988.

All rights reserved: no part of this publication may be reproduced, stored in a retrieval system, or transmitted in any form or by any means, electronic, mechanical, photocopying, recording, or otherwise without the prior permission of Bristol University Press.

Every reasonable effort has been made to obtain permission to reproduce copyrighted material. If, however, anyone knows of an oversight, please contact the publisher.

The statements and opinions contained within this publication are solely those of the author and not of the University of Bristol or Bristol University Press. The University of Bristol and Bristol University Press disclaim responsibility for any injury to persons or property resulting from any material published in this publication.

Bristol University Press works to counter discrimination on grounds of gender, race, disability, age and sexuality.

Cover design: Hayes Design and Advertising
Front cover image: Gwenelle Moalic

Dedicated to the numerous people who have helped
to make Convict Criminology a reality.

Contents

List of Exhibit Boxes	ix
About the Author	x
Acknowledgements	xi
Foreword: Finally an Introduction to Convict Criminology by Francesca Vianello	xiii
Preface: Getting Started with Convict Criminology	xvii

PART I Introduction and Scholarship

1   Getting Up to Speed with Convict Criminology   3

Introduction	3
What is Convict Criminology?	4
Why is it important to integrate the lived experience of incarceration into scholarship on corrections?	5
Why is a realistic picture of life behind bars necessary to have?	7
What have been common misconceptions about Convict Criminology?	8
What language debates has Convict Criminology been involved in? Distinguishing among inmates, prisoners, and convicts	11
What term/s should we use to refer to people who have been formerly incarcerated?	12
Why was the label Convict Criminology chosen for this diverse collection of ideas and objectives?	13
Is Convict Criminology a collective, discipline, field, framework, group, method, movement, network, organization, perspective, school, theory, or approach?	14
In which scholarly fields is Convict Criminology located?	15
What is the difference between Convict Criminology and similar sounding approaches?	17
What are the theoretical assumptions of Convict Criminology?	22
Who is considered to be a convict criminologist?	23
What is the relevance of imposter syndrome to Convict Criminology?	24
What policy recommendations does Convict Criminology advocate?	25
Conclusion	26

INTRODUCTION TO CONVICT CRIMINOLOGY

2	**What Is the History of Convict Criminology?**	**27**
	Introduction	27
	The prehistory of Convict Criminology	27
	Convict Criminology 1.0 (Convict Criminology takes shape)	29
	Convict Criminology 2.0 emerges	34
	Later stage global expansion of Convict Criminology	38
	What has Convict Criminology accomplished?	42
	What have been the major criticisms of Convict Criminology?	43
	What has been Convict Criminology's response to these criticisms?	44
	Conclusion	45

3	**What Kinds of Scholarship Have Been Conducted on Convict Criminology and by Convict Criminologists?**	**47**
	Introduction	47
	What is scholarship?	47
	What is scientific research?	48
	What is peer review?	49
	Why might formerly incarcerated individuals with doctorates in Criminology/Criminal Justice or allied subject areas not engage in scholarly research?	49
	Why might formerly incarcerated individuals with doctorates in Criminology/Criminal Justice or allied fields not engage in Convict Criminology research?	49
	Peer-reviewed research on Convict Criminology	50
	How did Ross and Copes conduct their research?	50
	What did Ross and Copes find?	51
	From autoethnography to quantitative research	56
	The *Journal of Prisoners on Prisons*	58
	Conclusion	59

PART II Teaching and Mentoring

4	**Teaching Convicts and Formerly Incarcerated Individuals: The State of Post-Secondary Undergraduate Education in Correctional Facilities**	**63**
	Introduction	63
	University-level instruction behind bars	64
	Why is it important to provide college education to convicts?	64
	Why do most correctional facilities typically fail to provide formal education beyond high-school instruction?	65
	Why is it difficult to provide adequate college education to convicts?	65
	What are the best solutions to dealing with the inadequate provision of post-secondary formal education in prison?	70
	Teaching convicts behind bars in the United States	73

CONTENTS

	Teaching convicts behind bars in the United Kingdom	77
	Teaching convicts behind bars in Italy	81
	Conclusion	84

5	**Mentoring Convicts and Formerly Incarcerated Students**	**85**
	Introduction	85
	What is mentoring?	86
	Why some individuals are not amenable to being mentored	87
	Pathways to mentoring in Convict Criminology	88
	What duties are beyond the scope of mentoring incarcerated and formerly incarcerated individuals?	89
	What duties are appropriately performed by academic mentors of incarcerated or formerly incarcerated individuals?	90
	Searching for a suitable graduate mentor	91
	Helping formerly incarcerated people get accepted into respectable graduate programs in Criminology/Criminal Justice	92
	Challenges with Convict Criminology mentoring	96
	How to best address the challenges of Convict Criminology graduate school mentoring?	96
	Other problems with mentorship	98
	Conclusion	99

6	**How Has Convict Criminology Engaged in Mentoring? Collaboration with Convicts and Formerly Incarcerated People on Scholarly Research**	**101**
	Introduction	101
	Literature review	102
	Why should educated convicts write for scholarly publications?	105
	Constraints to conducting scholarly research and publishing in scholarly venues while incarcerated	107
	Strategies to overcome the constraints	109
	Conclusion	111

PART III Activism and Public Policy Work

7	**What Is Prison Activism?**	**115**
	Introduction	115
	The history and scope of prison activism and prisoner movements in the United States	115
	Who are the prison activists and organizations?	116
	History of prison reform	120
	Prison abolition	121
	Distinguishing between prison reform and prison abolition	121
	Sentencing reform	122
	Conclusion	122

8	**How Has Convict Criminology Engaged in Activism?**	**123**
	Introduction	123
	What is activism? Why is it essential for Convict Criminology?	124
	Challenges for instructors and professors who engage in activism	130
	Conclusion	132
9	**What Does the Future of Convict Criminology Look Like?**	**133**
	Introduction	133
	Why is it important to have a sense of where Convict Criminology is now and the future of the network?	135
	How might the future of Convict Criminology be determined?	135
	Strengths, weaknesses, opportunities, and threats analysis	136
	Suggestions for the future of Convict Criminology	141
	Conclusion	144

Appendix: Chronology of the History of Convict Criminology	147
Keywords	151
Notes	167
References	173
Index	195

List of Exhibit Boxes

1.1	Famous movies that take place in prison settings	8
2.1	Frank Tannenbaum	28
2.2	Gwynne Nettler	28
2.3	John Keith Irwin	29
2.4	James L. Burnett	33
2.5	Glen David Curry	34
3.1	Liz Elliott	59
4.1	Prisoners' Education Trust	78
5.1	Benefits of having formerly incarcerated students in university classrooms	93
5.2	Ban the Box	95
5.3	Project Rebound	97
6.1	Victor Hassine	103
6.2	Jon Marc Taylor	103
6.3	Thomas J. Bernard	111
7.1	Prominent lawyers who have attempted to change prison conditions in the United States	117
7.2	Citizens United for Rehabilitation of Errants	119
8.1	Examples of activities considered to be political activism	125
9.1	Jennifer Marie Ortiz	139

About the Author

Jeffrey Ian Ross, Ph.D., is Professor in the School of Criminal Justice, College of Public Affairs, and Research Fellow in the Center for International and Comparative Law, and the Schaefer Center for Public Policy at the University of Baltimore. He has been a Visiting Professor at Ruhr University in Bochum, Germany, and University of Padua, Italy.

Ross has researched, written, and lectured primarily on corrections, policing, political crime, state crime, crimes of the powerful, violence, street culture, graffiti and street art, and crime and justice in American Indian communities for over three decades. His work has appeared in many academic journals and books, as well as popular media. He is the author, co-author, editor, or co-editor of several books, including most recently the *Routledge Handbook of Street Culture* (2021) and *Convict Criminology for the Future* (2021), with Francesca Vianello.

Ross is a respected subject matter expert for local, regional, national, and international news media. He has made live appearances on CNN, CNBC, Fox News Network, MSNBC, and NBC. Additionally, Ross has written op-eds for *The (Baltimore) Sun*, *The Baltimore Examiner*, *The (Maryland) Daily Record*, *The Gazette*, *The Hill*, *Inside Higher Ed*, and *The Tampa Tribune*.

From 1995 to 1998, Ross was Social Science Analyst with the National Institute of Justice, a division of the U.S. Department of Justice. In 2003, he was awarded the University of Baltimore's Distinguished Chair in Research Award. Ross is the co-founder of Convict Criminology, and the former co-chair/chair of the Division on Critical Criminology & Social Justice (2014–2017) of the American Society of Criminology. In 2018, Ross was given the Hans W. Mattick Award, which honors "an individual who has made a distinguished contribution to the field of Criminology & Criminal Justice practice," from the University of Illinois at Chicago. In 2020, he received the John Howard Award from the Academy of Criminal Justice Sciences' Division of Corrections. The award is the Academy of Criminal Justice Sciences' Corrections Section's most prestigious award, and was granted due to his "outstanding research and service to the field of corrections." In 2020, Ross was honored with the John Keith Irwin Distinguished Professor Award from the American Society of Criminology's Division of Convict Criminology. During the early 1980s, Jeff worked for almost four years in a correctional institution.

Acknowledgements

Numerous people assisted with this project. To begin with, thanks to Rebecca Tomlinson, Commissioning Editor, Freya Trand, Publishing Assistant, Grace Carroll, Senior Editorial Assistant, and Angela Gage, Marketing Coordinator, at Bristol University Press. I would also like to thank Gail Welsh, who copy-edited the book, and Dawn Preston, of Newgen Publishing, who managed its production.

Kudos to Rachel Reynolds for initially editing selected chapters of this book.

I also want to extend my appreciation to several research assistants, who, over the years, tirelessly tracked down publications that I asked them to find, sometimes with only a few cryptic details on my part.

I'm grateful to Francesca Vianello for writing the excellent Foreword and to Gwenelle Moalic for taking an engaging cover photo and giving the publisher and I permission to use it. Thanks to Clifford Hayes, of Hayes Design and Advertising for a great cover design and layout.

Anonymous reviewers of the book proposal and draft also helped me to improve the focus of this work.

That being said, over the years, many individuals, some who are no longer alive, have shaped my thinking about crime, criminals, corrections, and the criminal justice system. They include, but are not limited to: Andy Aresti, Gregg Barak, Barbara Barraza Uribe, James Binnall, Jessica Bird, Stefano Bloch, K.C. Carceral, Lukas Carey, Heith Copes, Francis T. Cullen, Sacha Darke, Thomas Feltes, Seth Ferranti, Jeff Ferrell, Larry French, David O. Friedrichs, Ted Robert Gurr, Mark S. Hamm, Keith Hayward, Irving Lois Horowitz, Jonathan Ilan, Michael Irwin, Rick Jones, Victor Kappeler, Elton Kalica, Daniel Kavish, Ronald L. Kramer (University of Western Michigan), Ron Kramer (Auckland University), Sebastian Kurtenbach, John F. Lennon, Mike Lenza, Peter Manning, Shadd Maruna, Gary Marx, Ray Michalowski, Greg Newbold, Jennifer Ortiz, Susan A. Phillips, Nathan Pino, Suzanne Reich, Stephen C. Richards, Dawn L. Rothe, Michael Rowe, Marty Schwartz, Tobias Shingelstein, Richard Tewksbury, Grant Tietjen, Austin T. Turk, Francesca Vianello, Loic Wacquant, Robert Weide, Frank (Trey) Williams, Aaron Z. Winter, Benjamin S. Wright, Barbara Zaitzow, and Miguel Zaldivar.

From my childhood to my multiple work experiences, I also recognize the debt I owe to many friends, co-workers, bosses, instructors, contributors to my edited and co-edited books, students, acquaintances, and strangers too numerous to list.

Thanks to the multitude of incarcerated and formerly incarcerated individuals, correctional professionals, volunteers, and activists who shared with me their perspectives on the field of corrections and experience of incarceration.

As always, I want to acknowledge the big part played by Natasha J. Cabrera, Ph.D., my wife, and Dakota Ross-Cabrera, MA (Ph.D. Candidate), and Keanu Ross-Cabrera, MA, our children, who patiently came along on this long, interesting, and mostly fun journey with me.

Foreword: Finally an Introduction to Convict Criminology

Francesca Vianello

Almost two decades ago, when I was preparing my first Prison Sociology module and deciding what literature to make available to students, I was introduced to the book *Convict Criminology* (Ross & Richards, 2003). In the field of Critical Criminology, the lack of scientifically recognized narrating voices coming from the subjects who animated the qualitative research was discussed at the time. The debate, already introduced at the end of the 1960s by Becker, questioned that hierarchy of credibility (Becker, 1967) which denied citizenship to the voices of those who inhabited total institutions and led to sociologists of deviance criticized for being on the side of marginalized subjects.

Convict Criminology was an interesting read, because until that point in time even most of the academic work about the American prison system that I read was primarily conducted by scholars who appeared to have little personal experience with the criminal justice system. The reconstructions, even quite detailed, of the prison system and the description of the prison population, its codes and its culture, did not use or deal with the first-hand experience of those who had lived the experience of detention. Even the use of so-called privileged witnesses, mediators between inside and outside, translators of otherwise incomprehensible languages, was limited to the interview, which was too often extemporaneous and out of context, but above all translated in form and substance by the researcher. The well-known difficulties in accessing correctional facilities – and, even when permission was granted, it was next to impossible for researchers to move freely within the penitentiary – resulted in static and fragmented photographs, formally selected by the so-called gatekeepers.

This prompted Teresa Degenhardt and I to co-author the very first review of the emerging field of Convict Criminology (CC), that was eventually published in *Studi sulla questione criminale*, the most important Italian Critical Criminology journal (Degenhardt & Vianello, 2010). It was written as a tribute after the death of John Irwin (1929–2010), considered the initial inspiration behind CC. Our article introduced the *New School of Convict Criminology* to Italian researchers by analyzing its main manifesto and some of the more recent articles published on the subject. We suggested that CC lay on a continuum with the established tradition of Critical Criminology, albeit without arriving at its most radical consequences. Degenhardt and I also underscored how the school endeavored to launch a "realistic criminology" capable of changing prisoners' conditions and facilitating their re-entry in society, starting from the consideration of their personal needs rather than from legislative issues.

Over the years, I was introduced to the British side of CC. Sacha Darke and Andy Aresti, from University of Westminster, invited me to take part in a session on "Developing Insider Perspectives and Research Activism towards an Abolitionist Stance" at the 41st Annual Conference of the European Group for the study of deviance and social control held in Liverpool in 2014. The convict perspective was invited to measure itself against the more radically abolitionist approach of Thomas Mathiesen, who had just published his *The Politics of Abolitionism Revisited* (2015). Subsequent academic exchanges led to Darke and Aresti coming to Italy several times to present the experiences of the British CC. They were in Padua in 2015, as part of the Master's course in Critical Criminology which I direct, and in Bologna in 2017 at the conference on "University and Prison: A Way for Learning, Equity and Democratization." I also went to the UK to visit the prison sections where Darke and Aresti teach and mentor their detained students (in London, 2018 and 2023).

During the last ten years, I was fortunate to supervise a number of inmates or formerly incarcerated individuals who were working on their Bachelor's, Master's, and Doctoral degrees. It was the period in which university study in Italy opened up to prisoners, with the birth of the newborn experience and subsequent dissemination of penitentiary university poles. Among my detained students was Elton Kalica, who was very interested in sociological research, and excelled in his studies while he was incarcerated. His scholarly works were the first in Italy to deal with a genuine convict experience. Once released, Kalica started and completed a Ph.D. at the University of Padua, and came to focus on the connections between the various ethnographic views on prison. The explicitly CC-based publication edited by Kalica and Simone Santorso, *Farsi la galera. Spazi e culture del penitenziario* [*Doing Time: Penitentiary Spaces and Cultures*] (2018), can be considered the first CC experiment in Italian.

Some years later, in 2018–2019, Jeff and I, along with the assistance of Dr. Kalica, decided to hold the very first international conference specifically on CC at the University of Padua. While Jeff was a Visiting Professor at the University of Padua in the spring of 2019, we held the international conference on "Convict Criminology for the Future" (Padua, May 30 to June 1, 2021) with the participation (mainly in person, some via Skype) of the principal convict criminologists on the international scene. The conference gave birth to the collection of writings published in the book *Convict Criminology for the Future* (Ross & Vianello, 2021) which garnered several highly supported reviews in scholarly journals.

Until now the scholarly growth of CC has been developed through a series of relatively disconnected articles and chapters in books, and there has not been any book that pulled together the diverse threads into a standalone book. Thus it is with great pleasure and anticipation that I introduce this groundbreaking book on CC. Within these pages lies a wealth of knowledge, insight, and perspectives that integrates the published work on CC, draws connections among this work, and has the power to transform our understanding of crime, punishment, and rehabilitation. In short it is a meaningful and focused introduction to the subject matter of CC. It can be used by all those who want to measure themselves with this perspective and, perhaps, make it their own in the future or promote it to students, with or without the formal experience of incarceration, and whether they are currently incarcerated or not.

The book is not simply as a systematic reconstruction of what the school has produced so far, but it is as a toolbox to make one's own to interrogate mainstream reconstructions on corrections. One of the book's key strengths lies in its ability to bridge the gap between academic discourse and the realities of prison life. The bulk of the book focuses indeed on reviewing and analyzing the three main pillars of CC – scholarship, mentorship, and activism – and attempts to place this information into a wider context. Ross not only systematically reviews the history of CC, but confronts the numerous misinterpretations it has received. In sum, this serves as a basis for CC to challenge preconceived notions about jails and prisons, the men and women who are incarcerated in correctional facilities, and the challenges of criminological research devoted to jails and prisons.

But there is more. CC emerges at a critical juncture in our collective pursuit of justice. As we grapple with the ever-increasing complexities of crime, punishment, and societal reintegration, this book provides a timely and indispensable contribution to the discourse. It is important that we challenge long-held assumptions and question the prevailing narratives surrounding the lives of those who have experienced incarceration. Through CC, we have the opportunity to gain insights from the lived experiences of the individuals who have traversed the arduous path of confinement and emerged as scholars, researchers, and advocates. Their stories, their failures, the pains suffered, and the successes achieved restore complexity to identities too often flattened on single events, demonstrating the ability to recover and reintegrate into society. This book serves as a beacon, guiding us beyond the conventional boundaries of criminology and criminal justice. By amplifying the voices of those who have been systemically silenced, we are granted access to the hidden realms of human resilience, transformation, and redemption. By grounding scholarship in lived experience, CC offers a profound testament to the power of education, scholarship, and knowledge in dismantling the cycles of crime and punishment. Through the work of CC scholars, we witness the transformative potential of higher education within the criminal justice system, illuminating the paths toward rehabilitation, personal growth, and social reintegration.

Before delving into the book, it is important to acknowledge that Ross, one of the co-founders of CC, brings a wealth of expertise and personal experience to the table. He is one of the few scholars who is able to combine both his practical experience and scholarship with others into a meaningful whole. The CC writing has always been authentic and accessible. Ross' tireless dedication to understanding the intricacies of CC, his mentoring of formerly incarcerated people, and the human journey within the confines of incarceration shines through in these pages. The author's authority is combined with his willingness to listen and compare, constitutive dimensions of the approach explored here. The clear and accessible language makes the text usable on several levels, both as a methodological manual and as a teaching tool.

In conclusion, *Introduction to Convict Criminology* is a seminal work that challenges the prevailing narratives of crime, punishment, and retribution, and most importantly the field of corrections. Through its pages, we are invited to witness the power of knowledge, compassion, and transformation in the lives of those who have experienced incarceration. Prepare to be enlightened, challenged, and inspired as you delve into the pages that follow. The words you are about to read hold the potential to reshape our perceptions, reframe the discourse, and ignite a collective commitment to furthering CC.

References

Becker, H.B. (1967). Whose side are we on? *Social Problems*, 14(3), 239–247.

Degenhardt, T. & Vianello, F. (2010). Convict Criminology: Provocazioni da Oltreoceano La ricera ethnographia in carcere. *Studi sulla questione criminal*, 5(1), 9–23.

Kalica, E. & Santorso, S. (2018). *Farsi la galera. Spazi e culture del penitenziario*. Verona: Ombre Corte.

Mathiesen, T. (2015) *The politics of abolitionism revisited*. Abingdon: Routledge

Ross, J.I. & Richards, S.C. (Eds.) (2003). *Convict criminology*. Belmont, CA: Wadsworth Publishing.

Ross, J.I. & Vianello, F. (Eds.) (2021). *Convict criminology for the future*. New York, NY: Routledge.

Preface: Getting Started with Convict Criminology

The academic fields of Criminology and Criminal Justice are mostly interesting, but often complicated to understand. Due to a variety of factors, these subjects are broken down into several subdisciplines. In Criminology, the domain is basically divided into explanations (or more formally, theories) about the causes and effects of crime, while in Criminal Justice, the divisions are closely connected to the major branches of the criminal justice system (i.e., corrections, courts, policing/law enforcement, and juvenile justice).

In the academic discipline of Corrections, the typical focus is on institutional corrections (i.e., jails and prisons)[1] or on community-based corrections (i.e., probation, parole, etc.).

The development of scholarship in these areas of inquiry is predictably uneven, being shaped by important questions of the day, fads, availability of grant funding, and the respective interests and skills of individuals who conduct research in these areas. Scholarship also grows out of the relevant divisions of the major learned societies (e.g., American Society of Criminology [ASC], Academy of Criminal Justice Sciences, British Society of Criminology, etc.) that have supported the growth of their respective disciplines.

Meanwhile, over close to three decades, a small, dedicated, and growing (in importance, relevance, and in number of people) collective, discipline, field, framework, group, method, movement, network, organization, perspective, school, subdiscipline, or theory (hereafter approach) has coalesced around the subject and mission of Convict Criminology (CC or ConCrim).

In general, CC is predicated on the belief and knowledge that the convict voice has been traditionally marginalized in scholarship and policy debates on corrections, crime, and criminal justice, and that this failure to include the lived experiences of convicts and ex-convicts has limited the growth of the academic fields of Criminology/Criminal Justice and policy making in this area (Ross & Richards, 2003: 6–9).[2] CC is also based on the contention that individuals who have been incarcerated or criminal justice system-contacted, involved or impacted,[3] and who also hold Ph.D. degrees (or are in the process of earning one) are in a good position to make contributions to the academic fields of Criminology, Criminal Justice, and Corrections, and public policy related to these areas.

In spring 2020, the executive of the ASC, the largest scholarly society dedicated to the study of Criminology, approved the establishment of an official CC division within the organization. This pivotal decision provided CC with increased visibility, credibility, and formal access to a respected organizational platform.

The balance of this preface provides the rationale for the researching, writing, and publishing of this very first comprehensive book on CC.

Why is an introductory book on Convict Criminology not simply useful, but necessary?

Four reasons are paramount. First, since the mid-1990s, a large body of academic research has been conducted and published on the subject of CC (Ross & Copes, 2022). This content has been made available as papers presented on panels at learned society conferences, published as articles in peer-reviewed journals, and released as chapters in scholarly books. Also noteworthy are three books (i.e., Ross & Richards, 2003; Earle, 2016; Ross & Vianello, 2021, all of which are discussed in greater detail in the book) that present diverse threads of CC scholarship.

Second, to date, no broader studies organize, clarify, and explain the body of work and information about CC in an easily accessible manner for advanced undergraduate and graduate students. Third, since CC is a relatively new division of the ASC, it would be useful to have a foundational comprehensive book that both current and prospective members and leaders can consult as they determine if and how they may want to fit into and shape this field. Fourth, the subject of CC is of increasing interest to instructors, students, convicts and ex-convicts, prison activists, practitioners, and members of the news media.

Clearly missing is the publication of a well-researched and written book that assembles, organizes, reviews, and synthesizes both the global and most essential component parts of CC in a comprehensive and accessible manner, that is current in terms of coverage, and that has pedagogical value. Furthermore, a book of this nature can be revised and updated every few years by integrating new research and developments in the field of CC and its related domains of Critical Criminology and Corrections.

The most prominent books that have laid the foundation for the *Introduction to Convict Criminology*

As previously mentioned, three English-language books have been published on CC. First, *Convict Criminology* (2003), edited by Jeffrey Ian Ross and Stephen C. Richards, the primary co-founders of CC, was the first book-length treatment of the subject. It consisted of 16 chapters written by a relatively diverse group of scholars, half of whom had done time. In addition to setting the stage for CC, the chapters primarily focused on the personal experiences of ex-convicts during incarceration or their post-prison experiences and subsequent pathways to academia. The conclusion outlined a plan of action for individuals who wanted to do more work in the CC field.

This book generated many favorable reviews in respected venues. Over time, however, the purchase price of the book increased, the range of the CC subject matter expanded, and new people published in this field. Thus, not only are elements of the book out of date, but it is also out of print.

Second, *Convict Criminology: Inside and Out* (2016), by Rod Earle, a previously incarcerated British criminologist, is the first and to date the only sole-authored book on the subject. It consists of eight chapters, and provides an intellectual history of many of the concepts that went into the founding of CC. The book traces the relevance of selected writing by Saul Alinsky, Angela Y. Davis, Michel Foucault, Peter Kropotkin, and Karl Marx, and the activist movements that were the basis of CC. The book is punctuated with brief accounts of Earle's time behind bars.

Third, *Convict Criminology for the Future* (2021), by Ross and Francesca Vianello, is another edited book that features 13 chapters written by an international team of scholars, a third of whom were formally incarcerated and the majority of whom were justice-impacted. Growing out of a conference that was held in May/June 2019 in Padua, Italy, the book covers seven major aspects of CC: the historical underpinnings of CC; adaptations to prison life; long-standing challenges for prisoners and formerly incarcerated people; post-secondary education while incarcerated; the expansion of CC beyond North America; conducting scholarly research in correctional settings; and future directions in CC. The book is interdisciplinary and international in scope, signaling the expanding global audience for this subject matter.

These monographs are crucial building blocks in the development of CC. They were great reference tools for the emerging field, and have been the basis of important discussions held by men and women interested in and identifying with CC. However, there are noticeable shortcomings with each of these books, particularly from a pedagogical point of view. These drawbacks mainly revolve around the fact that they address narrow perspectives on the subject matter of CC.

Introduction to Convict Criminology, on the other hand, is the first comprehensive book on the subject that reviews the topic, integrating current developments in the fields of Corrections, Criminology, Criminal Justice, and Critical Criminology with the basic pedagogical elements one would find in a book of this nature, including exhibit boxes, and end-of-book keywords. Test questions (e.g., multiple choice, short answer, and essay), and recommended readings are available through the publisher's website. Although some observers may feel that a book of this nature is too premature, it has the advantage of being the first to inclusively deal with the subject matter of CC. It also has the potential to shape the knowledge of the field. Moreover, *Introduction to Convict Criminology* can also serve as the first book in a long line of revisions. Furthermore, the author is duly qualified to write this book as he is a co-founder of the CC discipline and has been intimately involved in its growth from its inception until now. In order to sharpen this book's analytical focus, the publisher sent both the proposal and the draft of the book out for review to appropriately qualified scholars in the CC tradition.

Organization of the book

The book is divided into three major sections (i.e., research/scholarship; teaching/mentorship; and activism/policy work), each one dealing with a major branch of CC activities. These parts range in length from two to five chapters. Thus, in addition to the introductory chapter, the book consists of nine chapters. This number of units means that instructors can conveniently assign approximately one chapter a week for their students to read during a typical 13- to 14-week semester, interspersed with alternative activities like movies, tests, or visits to correctional facilities, etc. Beyond the content of the book, *Introduction to Convict Criminology* includes a number of additional features.

Additional features of the book

Introduction

Introduction to Convict Criminology integrates current scholarship in the field of Corrections, Criminology, and Criminal Justice in general, and CC in particular. The book reviews the multifaceted complexities of the CC approach, including established and current debates. (Other important matters are discussed in the following sections in alphabetical order.)

Ancillary pedagogy

In addition to keywords, included at the end of the book, the publisher will host and maintain a companion website for *Introduction to Convict Criminology* that includes a basic PowerPoint of the contents of the book, end-of-chapter questions, consisting of multiple choice, short answer, and essay questions, as well as recommended readings.

Audience

Introduction to Convict Criminology will generally appeal to students and instructors who are part of the CC network, and experts in the fields of Corrections and Critical Criminology. The book can be adopted for university courses in this subject. Instructors who teach a course about CC at the upper and graduate levels in universities may choose to assign the book to their students. The book will have appeal not only in the United States and United Kingdom, but also in Australia, Canada, New Zealand, and the European continent, where a strong interest in CC has developed.

Although there is considerable discussion of CC in the United Kingdom, Italy, and Australia, CC has *unintentionally* emphasized the US experience and the major reason for this is because the lion's share of CC scholarship has been produced by American convict criminologists. In general, it is also important to keep in mind that the "disproportionate focus on the American experience" is less because American CC writers are poorly informed or misinformed about what is happening in the other countries, but has more to do with empirical reality.[4]

Courses where this book might be used

This book can be used in courses specifically titled "Convict Criminology."[5] Although a rare course offering, at least three such classes have been offered in American universities using that title and two in which the primary text was *Convict Criminology* (2003).[6] Also noteworthy is the fact that the author has twice taught a graduate-level course at University of Padua, titled "Convict Criminology," while an undergraduate-level class on CC has been taught at Wisconsin correctional facilities (Rose et al., 2010). Now that CC is an official division of the ASC, the number of classes on this particular subject is bound to increase. That being said, *Introduction to Convict Criminology* can be used in upper-division classes that concentrate on "Special Topics in Corrections" or "Key Issues in Corrections," as well as classes on "Critical Criminology," which are a frequent offering at many universities. The book can also be used in graduate classes focusing on "Corrections" or "Critical Criminology," and in specialized courses taught in correctional facilities used a bridging mechanism for inmates who will be released relatively shortly and may be considering full- or part-time studies at a university.

Disciplinary boundaries in the study of Convict Criminology

The book tackles CC in as comprehensive a manner as possible, and reviews causes, reactions, and proposed and actual solutions to challenges identified by CC scholarship, mentorship, and activism. *Introduction to Convict Criminology* integrates research that uses a variety of analytical methods. Discussion of relevant current events are integrated into the narrative where necessary. In addition to the previously mentioned classes, the book would be most relevant to classes in the fields of Criminology, Criminal Justice, Psychology, Social Work, and Sociology. This may include: "Critical Criminology," "Sociology of Prison," and "Sociology of Law and Deviance."

Foreword written by a prominent scholar

The foreword is written by Francesca Vianello (University of Padua). She is a well-respected Italian scholar of Convict Criminology, Corrections, and Critical Criminology. Dr. Vianello and Dr. Ross were the co-organizers of the "Convict Criminology for the Future" conference, held May 30 to June 1, 2019, at the University of Padua, Italy, which led to the publication of the edited book, *Convict Criminology for the Future* (Ross & Vianello, 2021).

Exhibit boxes

Although the book does not include photos or illustrations, it features a series of exhibit boxes. The author has attempted to have at least one exhibit box per chapter. Not only does this information break up the flow of the text, but it provides an additional way to illustrate the material discussed in each chapter and reflects on a deeper level the content of the subject matter being discussed.

Reading level

The reading level is targeted toward upper-level undergraduate university students (i.e., typically referred to as juniors and seniors at US institutions of higher education) and graduate students. The book (or selected chapters) will appeal to students enrolled in core general education courses too. These classes are useful to first-year students, who are in the process of transitioning and integrating into university studies. These courses usually attempt to expose students to interdisciplinary and contemporary subject matter. *Introduction to Convict Criminology* has a nuts-and-bolts approach, similar to most typical textbooks. The book is easy to read and designed to answer common questions asked by senior-level undergraduate and graduate students about the subject matter. *Introduction to Convict Criminology* should also be relatively accessible to practitioners (i.e., individuals working, or aspiring to work, in the fields of Criminal Justice, Law Enforcement, Urban Studies, etc.) and policy makers in these subject areas, as well as members of the news media covering stories on elements of prisons and jails. The audience will be international in scope.

All in all, *Introduction to Convict Criminology* consolidates the most essential scholarship that has been written about the field to date, thus reinforcing CC's strong position in the subject matter of Corrections and Critical Criminology.

Summary

In sum, this book sets the stage for the next generation of CC scholarly research, mentorship, and activism. It also serves as a tool that can be used to facilitate discussion among interested parties, and thus an opportunity to network, and to discuss matters that are of utmost concern to CC scholars, students, and observers.

PART I

Introduction and Scholarship

1

Getting Up to Speed
with Convict Criminology

Introduction

Every so often, new ways of approaching traditional subjects are developed and disseminated. One of these topics is Convict Criminology (CC) (Ross & Richards, 2003). Originally conceptualized in the 1990s as a reaction to and a way to combat inadequate scholarship in the field of Corrections, CC was also designed to address the perceived reluctance identified by its founders to sufficiently include the convict voice in relevant policy debates and developments. Over the years CC has matured, morphing by 2020 into an official division of the American Society of Criminology (ASC), the largest academic organization that represents the interests of scholars and instructors in this field.

In order to provide a brief, but relatively comprehensive introduction to CC, this comparatively lengthy chapter reviews the discipline's growth and answers 14 basic interrelated questions that people unfamiliar with this subject may have about its origins and significance. These questions are as follows:

- What is CC?
- Why is it important to integrate the lived experience of incarceration into scholarship on corrections?
- Why is a realistic picture of life behind bars necessary to have?
- What have been common misconceptions about CC?
- What language debates has CC been involved in? Including distinguishing among inmates, prisoners, and convicts?
- What term/s should we use to refer to individuals who have been formerly incarcerated?
- Why was the label CC chosen for this diverse collection of ideas and objectives?
- Is CC a collective, field, framework, group, method, movement, network, perspective, school, theory, or approach?
- In which scholarly fields is CC located?

3

- What is the difference between CC and similar sounding approaches?
- What are the theoretical assumptions of CC?
- Who is considered to be a convict criminologist?
- What is the relevance of imposter syndrome to CC?
- What policy recommendations does CC advocate?

What is Convict Criminology?

In the mid-1990s, a few scholars, most of whom were previously incarcerated, formed a loose group under the label of CC. Some of them initially met at the 1997 ASC conference in San Diego, where they participated on a panel and delivered papers about their experiences in prison, with the criminal justice system, and with the academic fields of Criminology and Criminal Justice in general.[1] Shortly thereafter, these people organized around a handful of principles and adopted the name CC. They recognized that the convict voice was typically ignored in scholarly research and policy making in the fields of Criminology and Criminal Justice in general, and in Corrections in particular (Ross & Richards, 2003).[2]

These individuals argued that the failure to include the lived (or direct) experiences of convicts and ex-convicts into the discourse of the academic fields of Criminology/Criminal Justice, and Corrections and policy making, was not only short-sighted, but also paternalistic and disingenuous. Moreover, omitting the convict voice stunted the growth of these academic domains (Ross & Richards, 2003: 6–9).[3] They also believed that academic criminology did a poor job of providing a realistic and authentic portrait of incarceration. The original members contended that individuals who have been *incarcerated*, or *criminal justice system-contacted* (i.e., people who have come into direct contact with law enforcement or the criminal justice system, either as victims, witnesses, or suspects, but their involvement might be incidental or peripheral to the main case or investigation), *criminal justice system-involved* (i.e., individuals in the criminal justice system who are more actively engaged with the legal process, including defendants, accused individuals, and offenders who are undergoing investigation, trial, or serving a sentence), and *criminal justice system-impacted* (i.e., people who experience the effects of the system without necessarily being direct participants in criminal activities or legal proceedings – including families of victims, communities affected by crime, and individuals who may face collateral consequences from the criminal justice process),[4] who also hold Ph.D. degrees (or are in the process of earning one), may be in a good position to make important contributions to the academic fields of Criminology, Criminal Justice, and Corrections. In order to correct this imbalance, these people, along with some non-con professors, including prison activists,[5] created a body of scholarship conducted by convicts or formerly incarcerated individuals and their allies who had a doctorate or were in the process of earning one.[6]

The initial members further understood that in many respects, CC was also a mutual-help group, similar to numerous organizations that ex-convicts formed or have been part of over the years (e.g., Eglash, 1958; 1977; Cressey, 1965; Maruna & LeBel, 2003; Irwin, 2005). For example, many convicts and formerly incarcerated people participate in prison- or community-administered substance abuse programs, including Alcoholics or Narcotics Anonymous. They may also receive training in alcohol and drug counseling programs, and earn recognized certifications that enable them to assist others with their addictions both inside correctional facilities and upon release. Through these efforts, incarcerated and formerly incarcerated individuals have been able to transform the lives of several men and women similar to themselves. Moreover, CC was and has always been a way to assist others, in similar positions, by providing a sense of belonging, and through informal mentoring to survive and flourish in academia.[7]

Lastly, members of CC wanted to participate in current public debates on Corrections, Criminology, and Criminal Justice. This includes writing op-eds, participating in public panels, and being available to the news media when issues about Crime, Criminal Justice, and Corrections are being discussed (more about this in Chapter 5). Many CC members enjoy doing these kinds of activities as part of a network that meets on a regular basis (Ross & Tietjen, 2023).

One final aspect deserves to be mentioned here. Throughout its history, though not always successful, a collective attempt was made by people who adopted the CC approach to avoid privileging or stigmatizing specific crimes that members had engaged in or were convicted of, the amount of time served, and the correctional institutions where individuals were incarcerated.

Why is it important to integrate the lived experience of incarceration into scholarship on corrections?

Occasionally comments about the importance (or neglect) of the lived experience are discussed not only in the scholarly field of Criminology/Criminal Justice, but in other academic disciplines (e.g., Anthropology, Education, Healthcare, Medicine, Philosophy, Psychology, Social Work, Sociology, etc.), and activist circles too.[8] Although lived experience is difficult to define, this term generally refers to the knowledge and skills one may acquire as a result of spending a significant amount of time living in, working in, or being exposed to an institution, setting, or environment. Thus scholars may be considered an expert on a particular subject (e.g., criminal victimization, discrimination, mental illness, poverty, etc.),[9] but they are criticized because they lack a lived experience of something (e.g., a problem, situation, series of events, etc.) or have not been significantly impacted by some relevant event. They are, therefore, often considered unqualified to understand the problem in question; their perceptions are considered suspect, invalid, or useless. (We can also see this phenomenon on a continuum.) Thus, possessing lived experience is seen as an asset rather than a liability, because it may provide a person with more credibility than knowledge and insights disproportionately achieved simply through academic learning (e.g., Doyle et al., 2021). However, once this topic is raised, the question often becomes what type of lived experience is necessary, and how much lived experience is sufficient?

More damning is the claim held by some people who subscribe to the "Nothing about us without us" perspective is that the solutions and changes advocated by so-called outside "experts" (those without lived experience) should neither be trusted nor embraced (Nichols, 2018). Thus, in many academic domains, such as Criminal Justice, Disability Studies, Gender Studies, Racial and Ethnic Studies, Social Work, etc., some individuals advocate the dismissal of expert opinions, because they do not have the accompanied lived experience.

A further complicating factor is the complementary principle that argues that "those who are closest to the problem are in the best position to solve it" (e.g., Martin, 2017; Sturm & Tae, 2017). This is often considered the remedy to past failures to involve people who have lived experiences in the shaping of agendas and solutions for groups or constituencies that are or have been negatively impacted/marginalized. This premise (i.e., those who are closest to the problem are in the best position to solve it) is based on the assumption that lived experiences unequivocally imbue individuals with specific knowledge and insights, which will make them qualitatively "better" than experts (without lived experience) to lead or advise relevant initiatives or organizations. This phenomenon, sometimes labelled *proximate leadership* (Jackson et al., 2020), is worth examining more closely.

These arguments might be convincing if only they were universally true. But they beg a number of questions, including what an expert is and who is doing the labelling?[10]

Why are the approaches summarized here questionable? There are many individuals with lived experiences who are oblivious to the situations to which they were exposed, lack the ability to adequately analyze and communicate what they saw or experienced to a wider audience, or who do not have original insights. In other words, they do not or rarely contribute anything new to add to our knowledge of a situation (or series of events).[11]

This last factor is often the reason why we are frequently exposed to the recycling or repackaging of so much information – the recounting of the same or very similar experiences shared by others, with no new insights to garner. How do we protect ourselves from this old-wine-in-new-bottles phenomenon? That is where peer-reviewed research, when properly conducted, is supposed to help.

With respect to the belief that those who are most affected are in the best position to solve a certain problem, one need not look further than the long history of numerous grassroots social movements, both in the United States and elsewhere, to see how several organizations have stumbled and fallen, a problem that had nothing to do with the meddling of outside leadership.

Often referred to as authenticity politics, many essential social causes are grappling with issues of credibility and leadership. In some circles, there has been a reification and romanticization of lived experiences, and this has led to group and movement conflict, paralysis, and dissolution. In other words, organizations, big and small, are sometimes prevented from carrying out their mission because of this preoccupation. Although difficult to balance, the perspectives of lived experiences and the approach of those who lack them can work synergistically to create stronger research, mentorship, and activism (including public policy).

All told, CC recognizes the importance of lived experience in gaining insights into the prison and post-prison situation, but tries not reify it in any manner. Failing to take this approach will lead to an unnecessarily biased perspective and one that will provide few original ideas and insights.

Why is a realistic picture of life behind bars necessary to have?

Lots of obstacles frustrate the reform of correctional facilities, exacerbate the controversial practices that occur inside them, and bring unnecessary hardship to the people who live inside or work there. This situation is not due, however, to a lack of accumulated respectable peer-reviewed research to provide advice on all manner of ways to improve jails and prisons, and community-based correctional policies and practices.

Nor does this problem exist simply as the result of powerful correctional officer unions lobbying against change, the ossification of the bureaucracies that manage jails and prisons, or a lack of resources. Although these are important challenges, these factors alone are not the main reasons why correctional institutions, practices, and policies are so difficult to change.

One of the primary reasons behind the difficulty in reforming jails, prisons and other correctional facilities, on the other hand, is the fact that many members of the general public have punitive opinions, believe that incarceration serves as a deterrent against crime, and have a limited understanding of what goes on in correctional institutions. This is largely because their opinions about this branch of the criminal justice system are based upon the information and myths they derive from popular culture portrayals of convicts, correctional facilities, and the process of incarceration (Ross, 2003).[12]

For example, few commercials, movies, or television series set in a correctional facility, including the deluge of contemporary "shock-umentaries" like *America's Toughest Prisons* (Ross & Sneed, 2018), seems complete without some physical confrontation on the yard, tier, or cell block, somebody being shivved, a prison rape, or intimidating-looking gang members. Often, this is simple pandering to prison voyeurism (Ross, 2012a) (see Exhibit Box 1.1 on famous commercial movies that take place in prison settings).

The reality is that life inside jails and prisons is mostly boring for both the inmates and the correctional officers who work there. Opportunities for

Exhibit Box 1.1: Famous movies that take place in prison settings

I Am a Fugitive from a Chain Gang (1932)

Each Dawn I Die (1939)

Birdman of Alcatraz (1962)

Cool Hand Luke (1967)

Papillon (1973)

Escape from Alcatraz (1979)

Brubaker (1980)

American Me (1992)

Shawshank Redemption (1994)

Green Mile (1999)

Dead Man Walking (1995)

The Rock (1996)

Con Air (1997)

The Last Castle (2001)

rehabilitation are sparse, and most individuals who are sentenced to a correctional facility come out worse than when they went in.

When proposals, policies, practices, and laws are introduced to reform the correctional facilities in their jurisdictions, concerned members of the public frequently do a mental check on what they believe about jails and prisons. If their notions are out of sync, and if they are suitably motivated, they reject the reforms. These sentiments eventually seep back to the elected politicians who make legislative decisions.

That is why, if we are going to make a meaningful dent in changing corrections-related policies and practices and the laws connected with their operation, and maybe even abolish prisons altogether, we need to examine and reform the way correctional institutions are presented to the public. Scholarly research is important, but of equal significance is the introduction of more effective programs and policies combined with a systematic public education campaign and increased efforts by the news media to cover what happens behind bars in a thoughtful manner.

What have been common misconceptions about Convict Criminology?

Over the years, there has been considerable confusion about what CC is and is not.[13] Embedded in this discussion are numerous misconceptions about incarceration, prisons, prisoners, and correctional professionals (Ross, 2003). Moreover, some of the terms (like the name CC itself) and arguments often used by CC can be quite contentious (Ortiz et al., 2022). To better understand CC, we might start with a discussion of what CC is not.

CC is *not* simply applicable to the United States or other Anglo-American countries. The fact that CC has not been adopted in many countries does not mean that it has been rejected in those geographical entities, but is more a reflection either of a lack of interest or enough motivated people who would like to utilize this approach.

CC is *not* mainly an American-based network. Although CC originated in the United States, two members of the initial group (i.e., Ross and Newbold) were not American. Shortly after the crystallization of the American efforts in 2004/ 2005, a British CC organization emerged (Aresti, 2012). Furthermore, because the issues that CC deals with are universal in nature, groups of men and women interested in CC also formed in Scandinavian countries, Italy (Vianello, 2021), South America (Ross & Darke, 2018; Veigh Weis, 2021), and Australia (Carey et al., 2022) (Ross et al., 2014).

CC is *not* a marketing slogan or technique. Unfortunately, some inmates (or formerly incarcerated individuals) who are hawking a new book or course will occasionally invoke the CC label without really understanding it. Or they may include the words "Convict Criminology" (including the CC hashtag) in their social media posts or advertising copy, hoping to capture the attention of people interested in CC, assuming that most readers will not know the difference.

CC is *not* just a focus on the narratives of articulate incarcerated or formerly incarcerated individuals reflecting on their prison or post-prison experiences or on important issues in the fields of Corrections, Criminology, or Criminal Justice (e.g., Copes & Pogrebin, 2012; Bernasco, 2020). Although numerous accounts (largely autobiographies and memoirs) by correctional officers (e.g., Ross et al., 2021), convicts, and ex-convicts, and victims of crime may provide alternative views of correctional facilities, the criminal justice system, and the people who are affected by these institutions and processes, they are rarely scholarly in nature. Moreover, there is a long tradition of memoirs and autobiographies by convicts and ex-convicts (Franklin, 1982; 1988; Ross & Richards, 2003: 4), and these are often written by individuals who do not hold an academic degree.

Additionally, CC is *not* simply the lived experiences of educated convicts and ex-convicts. The term "lived experience" is often misinterpreted to include not only the experiences of prisoners, ex-convicts, justice-contacted, justice-involved, and justice-impacted men and women, but anyone ranging from victims of crime to criminal justice practitioners. The use of this label may unnecessarily confuse people who would like to join the CC initiative. In Australia, for example, because of the negative connotations that the terms *convict* and *ex-convict* have, particularly when pertaining to the mistreatment of aboriginal peoples, some individuals (especially political activists) prefer using the term *lived experience* when referring to the effect that a prison sentence may have on an individual (Carey et al., 2022). In reality, several incarcerated/formerly incarcerated people, however, prefer to be called convicts or ex-convicts. These people will frequently state something like, "I didn't do all this shit to be called formerly incarcerated." Thus, the ex-convict who takes this approach adopts the *convict* (or *ex-convict*) label as a badge of honor.

CC is also *not* a bunch of disgruntled well-educated, White, ex-convict males complaining about prisons, the unfairness of the criminal justice system, or trading war stories about their time behind bars. Why? Not everyone associated with CC is White and male; in fact, over the past few years the group has grown into a diverse organization of individuals who are actively working to change corrections and prisoner re-entry through their scholarship, mentorship, and activism. Their primary goal is to not to create an additional forum to vent their anger or frustration, but a means to improve the ways through which people who are incarcerated reform themselves and create new lives once they are released.

CC is *not* exclusively designed for formerly incarcerated or system-impacted individuals. It is easy to understand why some people have garnered this impression. Periodically someone interested in the CC approach may have been rebuffed (or turned off) by one or more people connected to the CC network. The men and women whom prospects encounter, however, are often on the periphery of CC, not really knowledgeable about CC, nor the entire membership, and do not speak for the whole. In fact many individuals claiming to be part of the network have only attended one or two CC panels, and have never presented nor published any scholarship that directly mentions CC. In reality CC has traditionally had quite a few non-cons as members, Moreover, there have always been "members" who were bad ambassadors for CC. During the history of CC many people have explored both the subject matter of CC and attempted to form personal and/or professional bonds with members of the organization, but have been turned off by the statements and actions of some individuals in the network. Regrettably these potential future contributors have negatively judged the entire group based on this limited negative contact.

Although occasionally labelled as such, CC is *not* a social movement. A social movement consists of numerous people who are united to change an essential social or public policy issue (Curtis & Zurcher, 1974). Although selective members may want CC to become a social movement, none of those people have taken steps in that direction. Moreover, at no time has the "membership" of CC been larger than a couple of hundred people.

Despite occasional rhetoric to the contrary, CC does *not* argue that the corrections and post-release experience is the same for everyone who is or has been incarcerated (Richards, 2009). Most people who are associated with CC recognize that the prison experience is personal, mediated by the type of crime an individual was convicted of, the length of time they were incarcerated, the kind of institution/s they were housed in, and salient issues of gender, class, ethnicity, and race.[14]

Likewise, despite some idle chatter or the personal belief of selective proponents of CC, there is no widespread agreement among adherents to the CC position that deprivation, incarceration, or punishment (important components of incarceration) fails to deter crime, criminality, or recidivism. CC is, in fact, relatively quiet on this issue. Moreover, empirical evidence on the deterrent effect of incarceration indicate some moderate effects for incarceration.

Lastly, a period of incarceration does *not* necessarily endow a person with new intellectual insights. Although one can find examples of people who may fit this description, their situation is unique. The perception that incarceration imbues people with some sort of intellectual advantage stems from the fact that periodically widely respected writers and theorists (e.g., Jack London, Jean Genet, etc.) have been incarcerated, but they are the exception rather than the rule. The belief that being locked up provides individuals with superior insights about the world or human nature often reflects a combination of simplistic and wishful thinking and a superficial or limited knowledge about corrections. Most individuals who are incarcerated are poorly educated, and jail or prison rarely provides them with appropriate resources to further their education. In general, a low proportion of convicts have an education beyond a high school diploma, a GED, or similar levels of academic achievement found in other countries. In short, the adoption of these beliefs demonstrates that the individual (or organization) does not really understand CC.

What language debates has Convict Criminology been involved in? Distinguishing among inmates, prisoners, and convicts

Over the past few decades, many fields have debated the terms they use to refer to various actions, individuals, and institutions. The academic and practical subject areas of corrections are no different and are also participating in these discussions.

To begin with, at least in the United States, and among people who are incarcerated, there is a semantic distinction among the terms *inmate*, *prisoner*, and *convict* (Austin, 2003; Zoukis, 2013). In this context, calling someone an *inmate* could be construed as a sign of disrespect. In the world of jails and prisons, an inmate is considered as not simply obedient and a follower of rules, but an informant or snitch. The term *prisoner* is usually reserved for people who basically "do their own time" (i.e., don't get involved in petty disputes), and they follow the Convict Code (Clemmer, 1940; Ross & Richards, 2002, chapter 5). Then there are the *convicts*. They are "those who feel that they rule the roost. Convicts are the prisoners who are gruff, violent, and demand respect. Convicts feel that they are in charge of whatever goes on inside a certain prison or a certain cellblock" (Zoukis, 2013).

Just because there has been prior discussion about these three principal terms does not mean that there is consensus among people who have adopted the CC approach (e.g., Bartley, 2021). Even in the CC scholarship there is confusion, debate, and lack of agreement about the meanings and implications of the terms *convict*, *inmate*, and *prisoner*. Take for example the following statement: "Convict Criminologists suggest that authors in the field change the terms *inmate* to *prisoner*, *convict*, *men*, or *women* and *offender* to *person convicted of a crime* or *previously incarcerated person*" (Jones et al., 2009: 166). Needless to say, when this idea was originally presented, there was no rationale presented for changing terms from *inmate* to *prisoner*.

Not only do several CC members embrace the *convict* term (Ortiz et al., 2022), but many highly respected, formerly incarcerated individuals do too. For example, Reginald Dwayne Betts (2018), a formerly incarcerated, well-regarded poet, Harvard-trained lawyer, and MacArthur "Genius Grant" recipient states:

> I am an ex-convict. A felon. Formerly an inmate. When people call me formerly incarcerated or a returning citizen, I do not feel like they are less likely to deny me employment, or housing, or to shake my hand. When the occasion is right, when the need is sufficient, when it has to come up, there is no sanitized way to tell that story. The crimes I committed, intentionally and with enough blasé to make it all cruel, belong to me. (2020: 30)

Likewise, Paul Wright, (also formerly-incarcerated) editor of the well-respected *Prison Legal News*, after cogently opposing recent efforts to change the word convict to something more sanguine, states:

> Editorially, *PLN* will continue to refer to prisoners and detainees, guards, prisons, etc., unless we are quoting someone who uses a different term. The people who have referred to themselves as prisoners include Vladimir Lenin, Fidel Castro, Ho Chi Minh, Malcolm X, Assata Shakur, Jack London and many others. If prisoner was good enough for them, it's good enough for me. (Wright, 2021: 18)

What term/s should we use to refer to people who have been formerly incarcerated?

In the field of Corrections, there are lots of labels, names, and terms that the public frequently applies to individuals who are housed in, live in, and are processed by jails and prisons. These terms are frequently used in a simplistic and dehumanizing manner. Take, for example, the word *offender*. I think we can agree that many of the things that people who have been convicted did were offensive, but not all actions that they may have engaged in rise to this label, and as we know, some people who are incarcerated are wrongfully convicted (Mays & Ruddell, 2018: chapter 10).

Moving forward, when it comes time to choose the suitable labels for someone who is released from a corrections-related setting, sufficient nuance should be observed. Over the past decade numerous individuals have emphasized the need to utilize person-first or humanizing language, which advocates the use of labels such as *formerly incarcerated person* or *returning citizen* in place of the label *ex-convict* (Cox, 2020).

But caution should be exercised in this regard. Well-meaning academics, activists, liberals, progressives, including individuals working in the field of restorative justice, and in some cases perpetual bomb throwers, who voice their concerns during these discussions (Ross, 2020), occasionally appear to be short-sighted in their criticism of the CC group's use of the word convict (including felon, inmate, and prisoner). Worse, sometimes (and similar to issues raised in the previous discussion about lived experience) there is an implicit suggestion that the scholarship that has been done to date using the terms *convict* (including felon, inmate, or prisoner) or *ex-convict* is somehow suspect. Other examples exist.

Let's start with the expression *returning citizens*. Citizens are granted special rights in jurisdictions to which they belong. These include, but are not limited to the ability to vote, work, and live in that polity, access to government services and legal protections. When a formerly incarcerated person is released from jail, prison, or halfway house custody, only a limited number of their rights are restored, including, but not limited to, serving on a jury (Binnall, 2021), voting, and owning a gun. Thus, to call such a person a *returning citizen* may be aspirational, but it does not accurately reflect their status.

Next, the mere act of altering terminology does not change, blunt, or erase the stigma or objectification society gives to people who have criminal records (Denver et al., 2021). There are innumerable collateral consequences of a criminal conviction (also known as carceral citizenship) that go beyond the label we ascribe to individuals who have spent time behind bars (Kirk & Wakefield, 2018). For instance, criminal records hurt the chances for many men and women to secure adequate housing or to gain appropriate employment (Jones, 2003).

Finally, several in the "we don't call them convicts and ex-cons anymore" crowd rarely ask convicts, or ex-convicts, which labels they prefer. And in those instances in which incarcerated (or formerly incarcerated) people have been surveyed on what terms they like, the studies have not used rigorous social scientific methods, and the results were inconclusive.

Why, then, does anyone (or any organization) insist on using the labels *formerly incarcerated* or *returning citizen*? Some of these individuals may be attempting to draw a distinction between old terms and new ones in an effort to effect change. However, in light of the lack of consensus among formerly incarcerated people on how they want to be referred to, policing this language seems like virtue signaling. Thus, insisting that we must change the label of *ex-convict* to *formerly incarcerated* or *returning citizen* seems like a misguided effort.

Changing terminology does not materially improve the more pressing and important issues at hand. It fails to improve the lives of prisoners, formerly incarcerated men and women, or their loved ones, ameliorate inhumane prison conditions,[15] or solve the problems of mass incarceration. These label changing efforts neither address the pressing challenges that people who are released from correctional facilities face, nor do they improve the lives of those individuals.

Why was the label Convict Criminology chosen for this diverse collection of ideas and objectives?

There were a handful of reasons why the co-founders of CC chose the label "Convict Criminology." To begin with, the relationship between language and personal identity is very complex and personal. The founders of CC were not like a bunch of advertising executives sitting around a boardroom table poring over market research data derived from surveys and focus groups, carefully considering what the name of the new organization should be. Ross and Richards needed a name to get started, and there was not a lot of discussion, nor push-back about alternative terms or labels. Nonetheless, four reasons can be loosely offered as explanations why the CC label was adopted. First, *the founders embraced the notion of claiming or reclaiming a label*. Almost all of the formerly incarcerated people who came to the group were content to be called ex-convicts, and thus it was a way of saying, "Yes, I was a convict, and if you don't like it, then too bad." Another reason why *convict* was used in the name was a belief that *it might carry, in some sectors, a bit of a shock value*. It was hoped that those unaccustomed to seeing the words *convict* and *criminology* in the same expression might pay more attention to what this group had to say. Over time, just like a brand, the CC label was preserved because of its recognition factor. Many organizations (whether they are for-profit or nonprofit) still hold on to names over time despite changes in mission or the audience they serve. For example, the Hewlett Packard Corporation started out as a car manufacturing company, but it still retains this name despite the fact the business no longer makes cars. In general, although some members of and outsiders to the CC organization were eventually concerned about the appropriateness of using the word or label *convict* for this collection of individuals and objectives, the name still remains today.

Although there has been considerable discussion on the use of the word *convict* in the label for the group, the main governing perspective is that using the word *convict* is a way of *reclaiming its meaning*. In some respects, this is like LGBTQIA+ people using the word *queer*. For years, *queer* was a derogatory label used to identify people who were gay. In the fullest expression of reclaiming the term convict, Ortiz et al. (2022) argues that the word *convict* was never intended to be a negative term, and many who adopt the CC approach are comfortable with the term as is. One further clarification should be made and that is that formerly incarcerated people are accustomed to collateral consequences of corrections, and the policing of language choices by more influential or well-known scholars, activists, etc. can be perceived by convict criminologists as another attempt to minimize or strip them of their autonomy and perhaps shame them in the process. Moreover, this policing of language can be interpreted as another example of mainstream criminologists using their position and power to further stigmatize formerly incarcerated people.[16]

Is Convict Criminology a collective, discipline, field, framework, group, method, movement, network, organization, perspective, school, theory, or approach?

Over its nearly three-decade history, CC has variously been called or referred to as a collective, discipline, field, framework, group, method, movement, network, organization, perspective, school, theory, or approach. These labels can be a little confusing. Why? These terms are not all synonyms for the same thing. And these designations are not necessarily interchangeable, reflecting as they do both members' and observers' perceptions of and beliefs about what the CC body does, represents, and aspires to be.

Undoubtedly, these labels have led to some confusion and disagreement not just by outsiders, but by insiders and advocates too. Why? Principally, many people, including those who have adopted the CC perspective, often do not know what CC does. Unfortunately, some of them are poorly informed. Alternatively, some adherents want CC to be something it is not. Thus, there is wishful thinking embedded in their labeling. The challenge of settling on a single label is also compounded by the fact that, among its members and adherents, complete unanimity regarding a shared vision of CC does not exist.

In reality, CC is a little bit of each of the previously mentioned frameworks. In other words, it fits into each one of these categories just a bit, and that is why CC is a little difficult to classify and, for those not familiar with it, to understand. Also, over the years, individuals affiliated with CC have changed their thoughts about the appropriate label to classify CC and several now believe that CC is best understood as an approach to a number of complex ideas. This perspective feels like the most inclusive and least offensive way of viewing what CC does.

In which scholarly fields is Convict Criminology located?

Although CC does not align exclusively with a single theory, it shares some commonalities with several criminological perspectives. These include, but are not limited to, labeling theory, life course theory, desistance theory, corrections research, and critical criminology.

To begin with, CC connects with labeling theory, which suggests that individuals who are labeled as criminals or deviants may internalize and accept that label, leading to further criminal behavior. Convict criminologists often explore the effects of stigma and labeling associated with criminal records, highlighting the challenges faced by formerly incarcerated individuals in reintegration and reducing recidivism.

Additionally, CC also aligns with life course theory, which explores how individuals' life experiences, transitions, and trajectories influence their criminal behavior. Convict criminologists often emphasize the importance of understanding the complex life histories of individuals involved in the criminal justice system, including the social, economic, and environmental factors that contribute to their involvement in crime (Becker, 1978).

Moreover, desistance theory focuses on the process of individuals stopping their involvement in criminal behavior. CC incorporates desistance theory by highlighting the personal transformations and efforts of formerly incarcerated individuals to break the cycle of crime and reintegrate into society. It emphasizes the potential for rehabilitation and the need for supportive re-entry programs (Ross & Richards, 2009).

As a scholarly discipline, however, CC is principally anchored in the fields of Corrections and Critical Criminology. The connection with Corrections should be self-explanatory. In most advanced industrialized countries, Corrections is basically "a broad encompassing term for the institutions/facilities, policies, procedures, programs, and services we associate with jails, prisons, inmates, correctional officers, administrators, and other correctional workers" (Ross, 2016: 12). Similar to the academic subject areas of Corrections, CC adds to what we know about prison conditions, rehabilitative (especially educational) programs, and the challenges of prisoner re-entry. On the other hand, CC does not really deal with the academic study of prison administration, nor prison law.[17]

Conversely, CC is more rooted in the intellectual discourse of Critical Criminology. Although there are conflicting definitions and conceptualizations of Critical Criminology, it is generally understood to be a theoretical approach that primarily recognizes that crime and responses to it are

> rooted in economic, social and political inequalities, along with social class divisions, racism, and hate and other forms of segmented social organization, reinforced and rationalized by culturally derived relativistic definitions of conforming, deviant, and criminal actions, which separate, segregate, and otherwise cause governments at all levels everywhere to differentially and discriminately enforce laws and punish offenders. (Donnermeyer, 2012: 289)

Critical Criminology is mainly interested in identifying and analyzing the underlying causes and reactions to crime, including the dynamics that see crime as primarily a reaction to socioeconomic inequality and power imbalances, and why a disproportionate number of poor and powerless individuals come into contact with and are processed by the criminal justice system (Ross, 1998/2009). This is accomplished by looking below the surface at the prominent criminal justice actors, such as the police, courts, correctional facilities, victims, and mass media, and the stories and myths that support them. This includes, but is not limited to, a long-standing critique of the criminal justice industrial complex in general, and the correctional/ prison industrial complex in particular.[18]

In sum, Critical Criminology incorporates an interest in understanding and helping marginalized people – the dispossessed, the powerless, etc. – who have been negatively affected by the criminal justice system (e.g., Ross, 1998/2009; DeKeseredy & Dragiewicz, 2018). Most convicts and ex-convicts clearly fit under this umbrella (Ross et al., 2012). This also explains, in part, why, up until the creation of a separate ASC Division of Convict Criminology, with few exceptions, CC panels were recognized, if not sponsored by, the Division of Critical Criminology & Social Justice of the ASC.[19]

Additionally, CC is built upon progressive critical inquiry (Ross, 1998/2009). This element is often lacking when it comes to understanding Corrections, which predominantly has a managerial/administrative orientation (Ross, 2008b).

Lastly, the CC approach attempts to avoid political correctness. Although CC recognizes the importance of language, debates surrounding labeling, stigma (MacLean, 1991), and the role of political activism, despite the trauma that incarceration brings to people and their loved ones, CC privileges a cool, rational, and scholarly approach to the subject matter it covers rather than knee-jerk reactions to the challenges of corrections, criminology, and criminal justice.

What is the difference between Convict Criminology and similar sounding approaches?

Some of the aims, theories supporting, and methods of CC are similar in some respects to six movements in the field of Corrections and Criminology/Criminal Justice. These include, but are not limited to:

- Critical Carceral Studies
- Critical Prison Studies
- The prison abolition movement
- Narrative Criminology
- Co-production/Participatory Action Research
- Thug Criminology

Critical Carceral Studies

Starting in and around 2017 a group of critical criminologists who were interested in jails, prisons, and the practices surrounding incarceration coined the term *Critical Carceral Studies*. They suggested that Critical Carceral Studies is "an interdisciplinary location home to inspiring and insurrectionary work against police and imprisonment, for guidance in materializing criminology's abolitionist and radical potential" (Brown & Schept, 2017: 441). Its proponents argue that Critical Carceral Studies is not simply limited to analyzing, critiquing, and protesting the use and expansion of correctional facilities and practices, but covers situations in which marginalized individuals are punished. They also claim that compared to other social sciences, "Criminology has been slow to open up a conversation about decarceration and abolition" (p. 440). Although profound in its objectives, whether we date this back to the influence of Marxist or Radical Criminology, or the rise of Critical Criminology, the adoption of abolition and other progressive leanings in the field of Criminology has existed for many years. Thus it is unclear what new ground Critical Carceral Studies is attempting to cover.

Critical Prison Studies

The term Critical Prison Studies has been used as a label attached to a handful of books that examined the historical and current practice of corrections and criminal justice from a critical perspective (Seigel, 2018). Similarly, the Critical Prison Studies term has also been used in the title of a collection of papers (e.g., Turnbull et al., 2018) concerned with critiquing jails, prisons, and sentencing. That being said, neither a singular article nor book outlines a distinctive separate and unique field of studies.

Critical Prison Studies is also the name of a caucus, formed in 2009 as part of the American Studies Association. The web page indicates that:

> As a community of activist scholars, we consider research, teaching, and activism as mutually informing and intersecting activities. To that end, we seek to align our knowledge production with grassroots social movements. As an interdisciplinary network, we bring together and encourage work across academic disciplines, recognize the value of scholarship and analysis produced by people who have been criminalized and imprisoned, and invite new perspectives and new research in this area. (https://www.theasa.net/communities/caucu ses/critical-prison-studies-caucus)

As of 2023, however, no new events have been listed on this web page since 2017.

Peacemaking Criminology

Originally advanced by criminologists Hal Pepinsky and Richard Quinney (1991), Peacemaking Criminology is built on four major pillars: mediation, conflict resolution, reconciliation, and the reintegration of individuals who have been convicted of a crime back to society. Pepinsky and Quinney argue that the dominant way that crime and criminal justice in the United States is handled is similar to a war and produces more harm than good. Instead they advocate peace among perpetrators, victims of crime, criminal justice practitioners, and the wider community. Although there are several strains of Peacemaking Criminology, the principal architects of these ideas argue that we must concentrate our efforts at improving interpersonal cooperation and understanding, grassroots activities, and then integrate peacemaking techniques such as victim–offender mediation into our organizations and institutions. Some of the ideas advanced by Peacemaking Criminology, especially finding alternatives to an overreliance on criminal sanctioning, including sending individuals convicted of crimes to correctional institutions, dovetail with the CC approach.

The prison abolition movement

Soon after the first prison in the United States was constructed, calls for its reform were made. One of the most radical positions has been the prison abolition movement that "want[s] to either eradicate whole elements of the current punishment system or bring an end to it entirely. They also advocate for a variety of alternatives" (Greene, 2005: 2). In the forefront of this movement are "activists, ex-prisoners, academics, religious actors, politicians, inmates and their families" (Greene, 2005: 2). The modern origins of prison abolition started during the 1960s in Scandinavia, and soon spread to other western countries. In the United States, the prison abolition movement began in 1976 with the help of Quaker and prison minister Fay Honey Knopp, who established the Prison Research Education Project, and later authored the well-known book, *Instead of Prisons: A Handbook for Abolitionists* (1976). In 1981, the Canadian Quaker Committee for Jails and Justice started advocating for prison abolition, and in 1983, the very first International Conference on Prison Abolition was held in Toronto (Ross, 1983). Since then, the organization has evolved, including a name change, substituting the words "circle" for "conference" and "prison" for "penal," so that the organization is now called the International Circle on Penal Abolition (e.g., Piché & Larson, 2010; Ruggiero, 2010; Mathiesen, 2015). Some people who adopt the CC approach also believe in prison abolition and the practices that it advocates like victim–offender mediation (Carrier & Piché, 2015; Kalica, 2018).

Narrative Criminology

Pioneered by Lois Presser, Narrative Criminology "adopts a constitutive approach to the relationship between stories and crime." This includes every method "that posits stories as antecedents and other harmful action qualifies as narrative criminology" (Presser, 2017).[20] This theoretical and methodological approach shares some intellectual space with CC, largely because most individuals who are incarcerated or formerly incarcerated have stories about their time behind bars. In order to draw connections between Narrative Criminology and CC, Earle outlines how ethnographies and autoethnographies are the mainstay of prison research. He also reviews the notion of not simply narratives of prison lives, but counternarratives (Earle, 2019; 2021). Earle states that "[p]erhaps unsurprisingly, counternarratives have a tendency to reveal prisoners as neither the mutes nor the brutes of popular imagination but as people fashioning themselves to their circumstances with the usual distinguishing features of human agency; dignity, humour, intelligence and integrity" (2019: 66).

Co-production/Participatory Action Research

Although co-production of research and Participatory Action Research (PAR) involve the participation of stakeholders in the research process, there are subtle differences between the two approaches. In the first case, co-production of research generally refers to a process where researchers and stakeholders (e.g., policy makers, practitioners, community members, or service users) work together (as equal partners with shared decision-making) throughout the entire research process, from designing the research question to interpreting the results and disseminating findings. The aim is to ensure that research is relevant, meaningful, and applicable to the needs of the stakeholders involved (e.g., Weaver, 2011). In the second case, PAR is an interdisciplinary approach to conducting research that involves the assistance of affected people as part of the research process. This can include not just individuals, but organizations, and communities too (Dupont, 2008; Chevaliar & Buckles, 2019). PAR engages the affected community or participants directly in identifying research questions, collecting and analyzing data, and implementing interventions or actions based on the research findings. The main purpose of PAR is to address social issues and promote social justice through collective action and change. It often takes place within marginalized or vulnerable communities and aims to empower participants by giving them a voice and active involvement in the research process. Both approaches to research have operated in a number of different domains, including healthcare, local economies, higher education, and the criminal justice system. Its most direct connection to CC is the realization that research conducted with the involvement of incarcerated people can serve to ameliorate their conditions of confinement, empower them with the tools of academic research, and better prepare them for a life outside of prison (e.g., Fine et al., 2003; Sturm & Tae, 2017; Haverkate et al., 2020).

Thug Criminology

Building on his lived experience as gang member, criminologist Adam Ellis, with the assistance of sociologist Olga Marques, who has worked with marginalized individuals, advanced the term Thug Criminology (Ellis & Marques, 2022), which they also categorize as a new branch of Critical Criminology. This "platform," which the authors claim is "inspired by indigenous and feminist standpoint theory," rests on three arguments. To begin with they believe that gang research is biased. Additionally they argue that "the voices of insider/insider (formerly street or gang-involved scholars who have obtained employment within academia) and insider/outsider gang researchers (formerly street or gang-involved academics working outside of academia) have not been privileged within academia" (Ellis & Marques, 2022: 35). Finally, they maintain that scholars of gangs are outsiders to the subject matter they study. Although acknowledging that CC calls attention to the importance of lived experience, they appear to minimize its contribution to the field of Criminology/Criminal Justice, and Critical Criminology.[21]

Conclusion

There is always a constant ebb and flow of ideas in any subject area. And the proliferation of subtopics and approaches in scholarly fields is to be expected. However, it is somewhat disconcerting when scholarship tied to the previously reviewed theories, approaches, and movements fails to recognize how certain elements of their core ideas are similar to the methods and goals of CC. It is not clear why this is the case, but it creates the impression that these scholars either did not do a comprehensive scan of the field of Criminology, Critical Criminology, Corrections, and/or do not understand CC very well. It is also incumbent on journal and book editors and reviewers, selected to evaluate and peer-review these materials, to have the appropriate domain knowledge and take their jobs seriously enough to point out omissions and errors when they arise.

One more thing: addressing fake allies

An interesting development has been noticed by some individuals involved with CC and this is the presence of people and organizations who might be considered to be fake allies. These entities are typically on the periphery of CC activities, speak up once in a while, but do not, and/or are reluctant to reference or acknowledge CC scholarship despite full well knowing that it exists.

Fake allies are not limited to the CC approach, but are evident in other parts of academia and among progressive social movements. They may claim to support marginalized communities, and/or social justice or diversity initiatives, but engage in performative actions (e.g., virtue signaling) without genuine commitment or substantive change. These entities may espouse progressive values publicly, however fail to take meaningful steps to address systemic issues or actively perpetuate oppressive dynamics within academic spaces.

One example of fake allies in academia is when institutions of higher education or colleagues participate in tokenism. Tokenism occurs when a superficial effort is made to include a few representatives from marginalized groups, often as a means of symbolic diversity, without actually addressing broader systemic inequalities. These gestures can give the illusion of progress while allowing the underlying oppressive structures to persist.

Moreover, fake allies may engage in performative activism. This refers to actions or statements made solely for the purpose of appearing socially conscious or politically correct without a genuine commitment to social justice. They may engage in surface-level activities, such as organizing or attending diversity events or sharing supportive posts on social media, without actively challenging or transforming the discriminatory practices and policies in academia.

Fake allies in academia can also exhibit microaggressions or subtle forms of discrimination. They may engage in dismissive or condescending behavior, make biased assumptions, or perpetuate harmful stereotypes. Despite claiming to be allies, their actions reveal a lack of understanding or empathy toward the marginalized communities they claim to support.

Addressing fake allies in academia requires a shift toward authentic allyship. This involves engaging in self-reflection, actively listening to marginalized voices, and taking concrete actions to challenge and dismantle oppressive systems within academia. Genuine allies must continuously educate themselves, actively advocate for marginalized communities, and work toward creating inclusive spaces that foster equity, respect, and meaningful change.

What are the theoretical assumptions of Convict Criminology?

Despite its frequent identification as a theory, scholarship on this aspect of CC is thin. As Richards pointed out, "it is not yet a theory. … Despite our progress, the Convict Criminology Theoretical Perspective requires more formal development if it is to become operational as a theory that can be empirically tested. A formal theory requires research hypotheses that can be discussed at length" (2013: 5). Richards then posited a handful of hypotheses amenable to testing. Although these could be examined in detail here, that is not the purpose of this chapter. It is safe to say, however, that, although the lived experience of incarceration is central to any understanding of the field of Corrections, a dominant argument articulated by Irwin (1929–2010) (e.g., Irwin, 1970; 1980), it is not by itself a sufficient explanation.

More recently, Tietjen (2019: 118–119), while acknowledging that CC has made significant strides in theoretical development, also recognized that a considerable amount of additional work needs to be done for CC to become more developed and widely accepted. He outlined a three-part explanation that is important in the development of that model. To start with, the insider perspective may provide ex-convict scholars with better access to specific information, which may not be available to traditional criminologists. Formerly incarcerated academics may also be more attuned to the verbal and nonverbal behavior displayed in correctional institutions than researchers without this kind of experience. Moreover, people behind bars may feel more comfortable with formerly incarcerated outsiders who come into jails and prisons to conduct research than with those without that kind of background (Richards & Ross, 2003a). In turn, mentorship and collaborative experiences inside CC enable some prisoners to make connections between their lived reality and existing scholarship. Finally, both the experience of prison and the stigma encountered as ex-convicts may supply these budding scholars with more reflexivity, which might provide additional insights into the fields of Corrections and Criminal Justice (Tietjen & Kavish, 2021).

As CC evolved, the network determined that it would strive to make three essential contributions: scholarly research, mentorship, and policy work/activism (e.g., Ross et al., 2012). It was also understood that not everyone who is involved in CC activities has an equal interest and expertise in participating or contributing to each of these components. Some members are more interested, committed, or effective at devoting their resources to one area over another. According to Tietjen et al., "one need not engage in all three and many people who identify with CC concentrate on one or two of the three components at a given time; many change their focus over time as circumstances or opportunities arise or present themselves" (2021: 2). Decisions to invest one's resources in one sector of CC is a purely personal decision and neither requires permission nor approval from anyone involved in the group, organization, or network.

Who is considered to be a convict criminologist?

Over the years, there has also been considerable confusion over who can legitimately be considered a convict criminologist (Ross et al., 2016). Although numerous individuals have identified with CC, until recently, there has neither been a formal organization dedicated to furthering the interests of the approach, nor any kind of test that would lead to a licensure, or similar widely recognized level of membership. Thus, the natural question is what qualifies someone to be a convict criminologist? Ostensibly, a convict criminologist is an individual who:

- has spent a significant amount of time in jail or prison;[22]
- possesses or is in the process of earning a Ph.D. in Criminology/Criminal Justice or a related field;
- self-identifies as a convict criminologist;
- believes that the convict voice is underrepresented in scholarly research and policy debates; and
- participates in corrections-based research/scholarship, mentorship, and activism.

If a person meets all of these criteria, but does not self-identify as a convict criminologist, it is disingenuous to label them as one (e.g., Warr, 2021).

Likewise, in general, if a person meets these criteria but does not possess or is in the process of earning a Ph.D. in Criminology/Criminal Justice or a related subject area, it is not appropriate to call them a convict criminologist. Why is possession of a Ph.D. or being on the way to earning one important? Clearly, there are a lot of articulate convicts and ex-convicts, who have unique insights and a lot of interesting and relevant things to say, but earning a Ph.D. from an accredited university in the field of Criminology, Criminal Justice, or an allied subject area basically means that you have been trained in social scientific research, and that you are capable of critically analyzing scholarship in the field of Corrections or Criminology/Criminal Justice in a social scientific manner.

Another type of individual who may be part of CC are those who are referred to as "non-con" members. This includes anyone who is currently or formerly *criminal justice system-contacted*, *criminal justice system-involved*, or *criminal justice system-impacted*. What exactly do these three terms mean? Easily confused and misused, these expressions refer to the following things:

- *System-involved* refers to individuals who are actively participating or engaged in the criminal justice system. It includes individuals who have been accused, arrested, charged, or convicted of a crime and are going through various stages of the legal process, such as investigation, trial, or serving a sentence. (This also includes criminal justice practitioners.)

- *System-contacted* is used for individuals who have had direct contact or involvement with the criminal justice system. It generally implies that a person has encountered law enforcement, been arrested, detained, or had some form of official interaction, such as appearing in court or being incarcerated. The term "contacted" suggests a more direct and personal engagement with the criminal justice system.
- *Justice-impacted* refers to individuals or communities who have been affected or influenced (typically negatively) by the criminal justice system. It encompasses a wide range of experiences and consequences resulting from interactions with the criminal justice system, such as being a victim of a crime, being accused or convicted of a crime, or having a family member or loved one involved in the criminal justice system. The impact can include emotional, social, economic, and psychological effects.

Again, in general, because of the previously mentioned criteria, these individuals must be either a Ph.D. student or a Ph.D. holder.

Further, other non-cons include critical criminologists/activists who have *not* been incarcerated, but who possess a Ph.D. and are committed to the goals of the CC network. Such members are actively involved in CC scholarship, mentoring, and activism, some since the group's inception. So, what does this mean? It is inappropriate to label someone as a convict criminologist unless they have met the criteria outlined here and have self-identified as a CC (Ross et al., 2016).

This brings us to the concept and practice of disclosure or coming out. Not unlike individuals who are gay, lesbian, or transgender, there is an understanding that the wider society is not always smitten by people who are convicts and ex-convicts. That is why there has been a significant amount of discussion among convict criminologists on the importance of disclosure (Ross et al., 2011a).

In the past, some vocal members believed that it was important to disclose one's identity as an ex-convict to others, while almost 99 percent of those who were affiliated in one shape or form with the CC network believed that it was a purely individual decision, recognizing the real-world negative implications of doing so. Most people closely connected to the CC approach also understood the contextual and relational issues which might impact a decision to reveal one's ex-convict identity to academic colleagues, but not to one's students.

What is the relevance of imposter syndrome to Convict Criminology?

Many ex-convicts who apply to, enter, take classes, and graduate from university suffer from imposter syndrome. They feel intimidated, like fish out of water, that they are not entitled to this achievement, kind of role (i.e., undergraduate or graduate student), and that others students know more than they do. This kind of feeling may start at the bachelor level, and can extend throughout a formerly incarcerated student's graduate program and beyond, as tenure-track assistant professors, if they chose to take that path. This is often because most formerly incarcerated people come from poor or working-class backgrounds where their public school educational experience may have been inadequate. Additionally, they are often the first people in their families to get a university degree. Unlike middle-class kids, who may have graduated from a high school with an effective guidance counsellor, or parents or relatives who could assist them, they may not be able to distinguish between a college (as in a community college) and a private college (like Dartmouth), and think that all universities are the same because they have the name university in their title. Issues of accreditation may be foreign to them too. The imposter syndrome may be exacerbated by issues of race and ethnicity too, particularly when African-American and Hispanic men and women seek education in predominantly White institutions (Strayhorn et al., 2013).

What policy recommendations does Convict Criminology advocate?

Despite an abundance of scholarship, and numerous panels held at academic meetings, the articulation of formal explicit CC policy recommendations is rare. One of the most concrete statements embodying a CC policy agenda, however, was jointly authored in 2011. In "Convict criminology: Prisoner re-entry policy recommendations," the authors (Richards et al., 2011) argued that 12 initiatives must be taken or expanded upon by politicians, activists, etc.:

- reduce the US prison population;
- increase the scope and rage of restorative justice programs;
- end the "War on Drugs";
- demilitarize the criminal justice system;
- end punishment packages;
- restore voting rights to felons and prisoners;
- close old prisons;
- restore federally funded higher education to all prisons;
- prepare inmates properly for release;
- improve medical services;
- provide more community resource centers; and
- provide more residential treatment centers.

Although there was no attempt to rank order these initiatives, nor who or what organization should bear responsibility for their implementation, it was the first attempt at this nascent kind of thinking. That being said, if a close examination of the CC scholarship is conducted (Ross & Copes, 2022) then one can identify policy recommendations that include, and build upon, those outlined by Richards et al. (2011). Also, although most individuals who adopt the CC approach would probably agree with these policy recommendations, because of the diverse nature of many members of CC there is bound to be lots of disagreement too.

Conclusion

This chapter has provided an introduction to the field of CC and produced a contextual understanding surrounding the more crucial questions that people may have about this approach. Understanding CC requires one to dig below the surface and closely examine the ongoing debates that have emerged as part of the group's activity. This kind of activity, among other factors, makes studying CC interesting and engaging. The next chapter provides a detailed history of the formation of the CC organization starting from the beginning to the present.

It is important to note that CC is a relatively new perspective, and it continues to evolve as more research, activities, and discussions take place. Its primary objective, however, is to provide an alternative viewpoint that challenges conventional criminological theories and practices, scholarship on corrections that disproportionately focuses on managerialism, by placing a strong emphasis on the lived experiences and voices of those directly affected by the correctional system.

2

What Is the History
of Convict Criminology?

Introduction

The history of Convict Criminology[1] (CC) can be divided into approximately three distinct phases: the prehistory era (1920–1999); the early founding period (1990–1980) (sometimes called CC 1.0) (Jones et al., 2009); and the present stage, that some people associated with CC call Convict Criminology 2.0 (Ross & Tietjen, 2022). In addition to reviewing these periods, this chapter also covers the later stage global expansion of CC. What has CC accomplished? What have been the major criticisms of CC? And what has been CC's response to these challenges?

The prehistory of Convict Criminology

In some respects, the history of CC predates the establishment of the CC network during the mid-1990s (Earle, 2016; Ross, 2021a). Elements of CC discourse are dominant in the writings and activities of formerly incarcerated individuals like Frank Tannenbaum (1893–1969), Gwynne Nettler (1913–2007), and John Irwin (1929–2010), who later became professors and scholars of Criminology and Criminal Justice. (see Exhibit Boxes 2.1–2.3).

Core messages of CC can also be traced to the work of political activists operating in the decades before CC's more formal establishment. Not only does Earle (2016) acknowledge the contributions of former labor leader, convict, and university professor Frank Tannenbaum, but he sees merit in the work of community activist and political theorist Saul Alinsky, African-American sociologist W.E.B. Du Bois, political activist Angela Davis, and gas station robber/convict turned scholar John Irwin.

Ross (2021a), in a complementary fashion, argues that CC is also the result of larger structural trends in society. He states that "[s]everal tertiary and immediate/proximal factors (variables, influences and mechanisms) in the wider society

Exhibit Box 2.1: Frank Tannenbaum

In 1914, labor activist Frank Tannenbaum, Ph.D. (1893–1969) was arrested, and spent a year incarcerated at New York State Prison in Sing Sing (Yeager, 2015). Upon release Tannenbaum enrolled in and completed his bachelor's degree in 1921 at Columbia University. He was also involved with early efforts in the prisoner rehabilitation movement. In 1927, he earned his doctorate from the Brookings Institution. After close to a decade working in Mexico, Tannenbaum returned to the United States in 1932 and taught criminology at Cornell University. He then transitioned to a position as a professor of Latin American History (with a cross appointment in Sociology) at Columbia University. During this time, he wrote extensively about crime and prisons; in his ten books, three of them focused exclusively on crime and prisons.

Exhibit Box 2.2: Gwynne Nettler

In 1947, Gwynne Nettler, Ph.D. (1913–2007), after jobs that included being a stuntman in Tarzan movies and earning his Ph.D. from the University of California at Santa Barbara, became a cat burglar (i.e., a stealthy and agile thief, who is able to scale walls and break into houses or businesses undetected). He was eventually arrested and spent time in a California prison. Nettler later became a professor of Criminology at the University of Alberta (Canada) and published extensively in the field of Criminology. In addition to numerous peer-reviewed articles, Nettler was the author of a handful of important books (e.g., Nettler, 1970; 1974; 1982; 2003) (Gillis et al., 2008).

contributed to the rise of Convict Criminology" (Ross, 2021a: 13). By *tertiary influences*, he means mechanisms that were permissive, that existed in the general public and assisted or facilitated the creation of CC. Under this category Ross includes: the rediscovery of prison ethnography, academic fads, prominent social movements, pedagogical movements, and a concern for mentorship. By *immediate* factors, Ross refers to precipitant or triggering mechanisms. Under this list he includes: Critical Carceral/Prison Studies, the scholarly field of Corrections, Critical Criminology, Peacemaking Criminology/Restorative Justice, the prison abolition movement, the *Journal of Prisoners on Prison*, the increasing importance of prisoner re-entry in American society, and the rise of mass incarceration.[2]

The modern history of CC, however, goes beyond these individuals, and structural trends, and begins with the establishment of a number of panels at academic conferences, scholarly papers presented at these venues, articles published in peer-reviewed journals, chapters included in edited books, and the publication of a handful of books.

WHAT IS THE HISTORY OF CONVICT CRIMINOLOGY?

Exhibit Box 2.3: John Keith Irwin

John Keith Irwin, Ph.D. (1929–2010) grew up in Southern California, was a surfer and a heroin user, who later turned to crime. During the 1950s, after robbing a gas station, he was arrested, convicted, and incarcerated for five years. Upon release from Soledad Prison, Irwin earned a bachelor's degree in 1961 from the University of California, Los Angeles, and a doctorate in 1968 in Sociology from the University of California, Berkeley. During graduate school he was supervised and worked with Donald Cressy, a well-known and respected criminologist. Irwin taught at San Francisco State University (SFSU) for most of his career, and authored or co-authored seven books on jails, prisons, and the field of corrections (Irwin, 1970; 1980; 1985a; 2005; 2009; Irwin & Austin, 1994; Austin & Irwin, 2012). His scholarship primarily focused on "developments in convict culture, prisoner typologies, convict perspectives on how they are treated, conditions of confinement, political manipulation of the public's fear of crime to expand the reach of the criminal justice system, and the unintentional creation of a felon underclass in the United States" (Richards, 2010: 175). Irwin was also a prison activist, and in 1967 established Project Rebound, an organization designed to assist ex-cons enter university. He retired from SFSU in 1994. Irwin was a central member of the CC approach, and participated in the early CC panels held during American Society of Criminology (ASC) meetings (Fagen, 2010; Richards, 2010; Richards et al., 2010). Irwin's life and career was an inspiration for several members of the CC network (Irwin 2003). Richards adds that "Irwin's work is quintessentially American and particularly focused on California, the state with the largest prison system, the one he knows best, the place where he 'did time'" (2010: 178).

Convict Criminology 1.0 (Convict Criminology takes shape)

The formation and development of CC starts with several panels held at a variety of Criminology conferences in the United States. These venues functioned as crucial stepping stones in the history of the network. Not only did these settings provide formal situations where academic papers were presented and critiqued, but they also included numerous informal opportunities (i.e., coffee breaks, meals, and occasional receptions) where panelists met and interacted with each other. Additionally, individuals in the audience (including students), and other like-minded people gave and received feedback, exchanged information, and networked with each other.

The first Convict Criminology panel

In the mid-1990s, one of the first CC panels was held at the annual meeting of the ASC in San Francisco. Shortly thereafter, Jeffrey Ian Ross and Stephen C. Richards coined the term "Convict Criminology," and fleshed out the intellectual rationale, objectives, and practical contours of this approach. Almost immediately, the two of them decided to edit a scholarly book on this subject. They did this by encouraging people they knew who were either formally incarcerated or sympathetic to the goals of CC and who had doctorates or were in the process of earning a Ph.D., to present papers on panels on CC at several ASC conferences. Early CC panels included, but were not limited to, the participation of William G. Archambeault, Bruce Arrigo, James Austin, Marianne Fisher-Giorlando, John Irwin, Richard S. Jones, Alan Mobley, Daniel S. Murphy, Greg Newbold, Barbara Owen, and Charles "Chuck" M. Terry. Some of the papers delivered at these venues were eventually included in *Convict Criminology* (Ross & Richards, 2003).

After the publication of this edited book, many articles in peer-reviewed journals, chapters in scholarly books, and a series of entries in encyclopedias and handbooks were published, that advanced the ideas supported by the CC network. Many elements of this approach were accepted by the mainstream academic fields of Criminology and Criminal Justice. Also important, shortly after these developments, Bob Grigsby assisted the group to establish a CC website.

Another step has been the slow global expansion of CC, including representation by individuals in Europe, Australia, and New Zealand (Newbold, 2003; Ross et al., 2014; Aresti & Darke, 2016; Earle, 2018; Carey et al., 2022). For example, scholars such as Andreas (Andy) Aresti, Sacha Darke, and Rod Earle in England, Ikponwosa (Silver) O. Ekunwe in Finland (Ekunwe, 2007), Greg Newbold in New Zealand (Newbold, 2017), Francesca Vianello and Elton Kalica in Italy (Kalica & Santorosa, 2018; Vianello, 2021), and Lukas Carey in Australia (Carey et al., 2022) helped to promote CC in their countries and among their professional networks. Meanwhile, since the mid 2010s Darke and Aresti have visited Argentina and Brazil numerous times and developed an expanding network of country partners (including scholars, prison activists, and inmates) who are not only interested in CC, but are holding panels and publishing on this topic. Moreover, there also appears to be some interest in the Czech Republic (Dirga, 2017), France (Salle, 2007), Germany (Graebsch & Knop, 2023; Graebsch & Ross, 2023), and Russia (Shchukina, 2021) too. This engagement has been expressed through the writing of papers, delivering of lectures, and the organization of panels, workshops, conferences, and symposia specifically devoted to CC, and the publication of articles, chapters in scholarly books, and books in whole or in part dealing with CC.

The Tampere conference

In June 2010, a conference titled "An International Scientific Conference on Global Perspectives on Re-Entry" was held in Tampere, Finland. It was organized by Ikponwosa (Silver) Ekunwe (University of Tampere) and Richard S. Jones (Marquette University), both of whom had long-time associations with the CC group. In addition to Ekunwe and Jones, members of the CC network in the United States, including Annette Kuhlmann, Mike Lenza, Barbara Zaitzow, Richards, and Ross, attended and presented papers. Over the course of three days, attendees discussed the challenges of reentry both in the United States and in Finland. The meeting also included a visit to Vilppulan Vankila open prison. The conference proceedings were eventually turned into an edited book, *Global Perspectives on Re-Entry* (Ekunwe & Jones, 2011).

The development of the British Convict Criminology group

In 2011, Aresti and Darke (University of Westminster) and Earle (Open University), established a CC panel at the British Society of Criminology (BSC) conference in Newcastle, England. They started their own CC group (referred to as British Convict Criminology or BCC for short) modeled on the U.S. CC one. These scholars also recognized both the contribution of the academic field of Corrections to the movement in general, and the value of the Critical Criminological orientation. Since 2011, Aresti, Darke, and Earle have periodically held panels at annual BSC conferences and have served as a catalyst by helping to draw together a number of British criminologists, graduate students, incarcerated individuals, and formerly incarcerated people who are sympathetic to and have been encouraged by the CC mission.

The KROM and European Group annual conferences (2014)

In the late 1960s, Norwegian criminologist Thomas Mathiesen (1933–2021) facilitated the establishment of KROM (The Norwegian Association for Penal Reform), a grassroots movement where critical scholars, prisoners, former inmates, and practitioners collaborated on radical criminal justice reform. Their annual conferences bring together critics of the penal system. Beginning in 2014, Aresti and Darke presented papers on BCC at three of KROM's annual conferences in sessions dedicated to exploring parallels between the two groups. At the 2014 annual conference of the European Group of the Study of Deviance and Social Control in Liverpool, a number of KROM members joined BCC and Italian colleagues working within the CC perspective on a panel entitled, "Developing Insider Perspectives in Research Activism." KROM's delegation included Mathiesen and one former prisoner activist. The Italian delegation included Francesca Vianello (a professor at the University of Padua) and Elton Kalica (a former prisoner who was studying under Dr. Vianello for a Ph.D.). Mathiesen and Kalica were not physically present at the conference, but were able to deliver their papers via Skype.

Ross and Darke's Convict Criminology work in South America

Beginning in 2013, Ross made a series of trips to Argentina, Chile, and Ecuador (more specifically in Buenos Aires, Santiago, and Quito), where he made connections with local criminologists and Criminal Justice practitioners, gave papers on CC, and visited correctional facilities. Meanwhile Darke conducted research in Brazilian prisons (e.g., Darke, 2018) and made connections with prisoners and ex-convicts in the process of earning social science degrees in Brazil and Argentina (e.g., Darke et al., 2020). In 2016, 2017, and 2020, Darke, along with Aresti, followed a similar path of giving lectures about CC in Brazil and (in 2019) in Argentina. In 2016, Ross and Darke attempted to organize a CC conference in São Paulo or Santiago. Although this did not materialize, it did result in an article arguing for the expansion of CC in that region (Ross & Darke, 2018; see also Vegh Weis, 2021). In 2019, Aresti and Darke assisted Dr. Karina Biondi and former prisoner Francisco Lopes de Magalhães Filho in their efforts to establish the first CC education initiative in South America, at APAC de São Luís prison, in the state of Maranhão (in northern Brazil). In 2021, Darke was invited to write the foreword to a book by a former prisoner who had started studying undergraduate social science from open prison conditions and had recently earned a master's degree at the State University of Rio de Janeiro (Lourenço, 2022).

Convict Criminology starts to falter

Starting around 2010, however, CC, at least in the United States, appeared to falter. After creating an official summary of the first 15 years of CC, including the founding history, scholarship, and attempts to lay the groundwork for a formal theory of the discipline, Richards (2013) indicated that CC was struggling, stating "our ranks of ex-convict professors remain thin" (2013: 384). In another article that discussed the state of CC, Tietjen (2019) identified the development of some important ideological debates within CC:

> over 20 years later, there is discussion within CC circles that cultural shifts within society and criminal justice have altered how the world perceives the term, "convict," and many people find the term offensive, potentially deterring some FI [formerly incarcerated] students and professors from affiliating with the CC field. This is an ongoing discussion that has the potential to reshape CC's impact on justice reform and reach a wider spectrum of justice-impacted people. (Tietjen, 2019: 110)

Reform and rehabilitation had, over time, become more popular, while mass incarceration and, in some circles, the "tough-on-crime" mentality of the 1980s and 1990s fell out of favor (e.g., Matthews, 2017; Kirk & Wakefield, 2018). While struggling with some internal concerns and continuing to work on many issues vital to furthering equality for system-contacted, involved, and impacted individuals, CC failed to widen its focus to the more humanistic social perceptions of criminal justice of the current era. The inability to account for these cultural shifts potentially hampered the progressive development of CC.[3]

Meanwhile, because of the academic space that CC occupied, the group experienced organizational challenges. It needed to establish and implement formal mechanisms to enable its continuation, and to change and adapt to new circumstances. The group additionally found itself the focus of some academic critiques (e.g., Larsen & Piché, 2012; Newbold & Ross, 2012), including Belknap (2015) who stated in an ASC presidential address (and accompanying article in *Criminology*, the flagship journal of the ASC), that CC had ignored many formerly incarcerated people and was not doing enough to promote diversity and inclusion within its ranks. A 2016 special issue of the journal *Critical Criminology* responded to these criticisms, arguing that CC's struggles over the decades had been much more complex than both Belknap and some others commonly understood.

For example, Ross et al. (2016) pointed out that CC had long attempted to be inclusive, while at the same time respecting and protecting the identities of individuals who were formerly incarcerated. Few men and women who have a felony conviction are comfortable sharing this information with others, and in some cases, disclosing this identity could have harmed the lives and careers of various individuals who fit the criteria of Convict Criminologists, but wished to remain anonymous. Thus, actively recruiting and potentially publicly exposing people with criminal convictions or who were formerly incarcerated is inappropriate and unethical. Ross et al. (2016) also highlighted how CC has always welcomed and included individuals, regardless of criminal justice background,[4] and at several points in time, people without any criminal record comprised close to 50 percent of CC's members. By tracking participation in CC sessions held at the annual meetings of the ASC, Ross et al. (2016) further demonstrated that female, minority, and international (i.e., foreign-born) representation in CC increased from 1999 through 2015. Female and minority representations, in particular, more than doubled during this time period. Needless to say, these criticisms of CC further motivated the organization to redouble its efforts to support the active participation of women and broaden the diversity of people interested in CC activities (see Exhibit Box 2.4).

Exhibit Box 2.4: James L. Burnett

James L. Burnett, Ph.D. (1961–2021), was one of the few formerly incarcerated African-American professors allied with the CC network. During his academic career Dr. Burnett was a visiting Assistant Professor of Sociology, Social Work, and Criminal Justice at Idaho State University, Department of Criminal Justice, Minnesota State Mankato, and later Assistant Professor of Criminology at Urbana University. Burnett made research contributions to the *Journal of Prisoners on Prison* (Williams & Burnett, 2012) and *Critical Criminology: An International Journal* (Williams et al., 2014).

Besides the previously mentioned reasons, why else did CC seem to falter? Four interrelated things happened: some close allies passed away; the health and commitment of some of the original founders declined; other organizations that seemed (on a superficial basis) to provide some of the same benefits as CC emerged; and a strong leadership structure had not yet been established (Ross & Tietjen, 2022) (see Exhibit Box 2.5).

Exhibit Box 2.5: Glen David Curry

(Glen) David Curry, Ph.D. (1949–2015). During the 1960s, Curry "was drafted and sent to Vietnam as an intelligence officer during the war. He was promoted to captain" (Sorkin, 2015). He served in the military from 1969 to 1972 (https://umsl.edu/ccj/faculty/curry. html). When Curry returned to the United States, and suffering from post-traumatic stress disorder, "he was speaking out against the war. He served as a state coordinator of Vietnam Veterans Against the War. He became a regular expert witness for the local NAACP and the Southern Poverty Law Center" (Sorkin, 2015). During this time Curry earned a Ph.D. in Sociology in 1976 from the University of Chicago. In 1982, a government informant testified that he "was a regular supplier of cocaine for other veterans. A jury found him guilty on two of three counts of distribution, plus conspiracy to distribute, and one count of using a telephone to facilitate a felony" (Sorkin, 2015). Curry was sentenced to 34 years in prison. After exhausting most of his appeals, Curry got an unexpected break. "The judge resentenced Professor Curry to five years in prison plus six years special probation and another six years regular probation – again, to run consecutively" (Sorkin, 2015). In 1994, after work as a professor at University of South Alabama and West Virginia University, Curry became a professor of Criminology at the University of Missouri Saint Louis (UMSL). Over his three-decade-long career, he conducted a significant amount of research on street gangs, domestic violence, military service, and youth violence. This was translated numerous scholarly articles, chapters in books, and books. In addition to "bringing in more than $800,000 in external funding as a principal or co-principal investigator ... in 2004 he received the Chancellor's Award for Excellence in Service" (https://umsl. edu/ccj/faculty/curry.html). Professor Curry also served on the "national boards of the Boys and Girls Clubs of America, winning its Advocacy Award in 2001, and the Vietnam Veterans Against the War" (https://umsl.edu/ccj/faculty/curry.html). In 2000, President Bill Clinton granted him a pardon. Although Curry did not write specifically on CC, he called himself a "convict-criminologist" (Sorkin, 2015), and worked in the background of the CC network and attended many CC panels and socials. He retired from UMSL in 2011 (https://umsl.edu/ccj/faculty/curry.html).

Convict Criminology 2.0 emerges

Introduction

Given the previously reviewed challenges to the long-term health and survival of the CC network, Ross and Richards, the original CC co-founders, and other members of the old guard knew that one day they would have to hand over the reins of the organization to others. The group needed a more formal organizational structure and an individual or preferably a team that would be willing to provide timely information to its members, plan for future events, and respond and recruit like-minded individuals.

The first Convict Criminology constitution

Despite some confusion over how to proceed, it was determined that in order to maintain the organization and to more efficiently divide up tasks, the group needed a constitution that authorized the appointment of an identifiable executive who could oversee an equitable division of power/responsibilities. So, in advance of the 2017 annual ASC meetings, with the assistance of Denise Woodall, a graduate student (at the time) who was very active in CC's organizational efforts, and Dr. Grant Tietjen, an assistant professor (at the time), also closely connected to CC (both formerly incarcerated individuals), Ross drafted a constitution. At the meeting, the CC network held its very first business meeting, and with minor modifications, the constitution was ratified. Both Woodall and Tietjen were chosen to be the co-chairs of the CC organization. Additionally, the assembled group talked about how to best resurrect the fledgling CC website. Also essential was a collective desire to do more posting on the CC Facebook page. After the constitution was ratified and an executive was chosen, the reins of the organization were transferred to the hands of the people who represented the best interests of the collective organization.

The 2018 American Society of Criminology Atlanta meeting

The second CC business meeting was held at the 2018 ASC conference. Those assembled started to do the kinds of bureaucratic things most learned groups do, such as drafting an agenda, distributing it in advance, recording meeting minutes, sending these out to members after the meeting, electing people for positions, and outlining tasks that needed to be accomplished, forming committees, and choosing individuals who could complete the work over the coming year. There was also considerable discussion over changing the name of the organization from CC to something else. CC was now struggling with its evolution into a more formally structured group, and it became clear that CC needed to function in a more efficient and productive capacity. Numerous ideas were suggested about the future of CC as a more efficient and organized group.

Several members argued that more people would join CC if the name were different (Ortiz et al., 2022). They claimed that the CC title somehow excluded individuals who had been harmed by incarceration from being open and participating in CC activities.[5] Other people in attendance mentioned that there were many justice-involved, justice-contacted, and justice-impacted individuals who hold or were working on doctorates in Criminology/Criminal Justice, but they were not sure that the CC group was reaching them.

Per the suggestion of several CC members concerned about the use of the term "convict" within CC's name, an online survey was sent out on two separate occasions, and the largest group each time voted in support of keeping the name as Convict Criminology.

One of the questions that was discussed with some frequency and with greater seriousness in the fall of 2018 was whether CC should be a formal division of the ASC. Support for this proposal increased after this time.

Convict Criminology considers becoming a division of the American Society of Criminology

In November 2018, shortly after the annual ASC meeting, Ross reached out to Dr. Chris Eskridge, the Executive Director of ASC, about the possibility of the CC group becoming a division within the larger ASC organization. Subsequently, as a means to begin the division-building process, Ross introduced the then-current leadership of CC to Eskridge, who explained the process that the CC network needed to follow in order to become an official division of the ASC. Eskridge diligently worked with CC, generously providing guidance on the division's development until the organization was ready to submit its materials to the ASC executive board.

The electronic vote

In spring 2019, an online vote regarding a group name change was administered to the membership. In preparation for this step, the members were informed about the implications of this change, which required the creation of forums for discussion, the holding of a vote, and using of a free and fair method to record this vote. This process took about a year. In the end, the majority of people who voted decided against a name change. Some of the members believed that changing the name of CC would not result in any major effect on the group in terms of membership, increased participation, or broader acceptance among individuals on the periphery of the CC movement. All in all, the vote involved an immense amount of work, yet it generated a clearer picture of the group's position on the name change issue. Further, this process allowed CC to move forward with other important issues which needed attention.

Convict Criminology for the Future conference and book

In fall 2018, Ross and Vianello started organizing a conference on CC that would be held at the University of Padua. There were a handful of reasons why a project of this nature made sense. To begin with, this type of event was long overdue. The interest in CC in continental Europe and Italy, in particular (e.g., Kalica & Santorosa, 2018; Vianello, 2021), was growing, and many of these scholars had neither come to the United States, nor the United Kingdom to participate on CC panels, and recognized that a conference and new book on CC could continue to shape the field. Along with the assistance of Dr. Elton Kalica (University of Padua), the conference was held between May 31 and June 1, 2019. Over two days approximately 15 papers were delivered.

The meeting started with a visit to Casa di Reclusone Due Palazzi, a local prison where some of the conference panelists gave presentations and afterwards talked with incarcerated people, correctional officers, and administrators. The meeting continued with the traditional lectures and discussions that these functions typically have. Over the space of two days, the number of individuals who attended the panels fluctuated. At its height, there were close to a hundred people in the audience, and the conference included not only in-person sessions, but also Skype and Zoom presentations too. In attendance were a small group of long-established CC members, as well as some activists, instructors, scholars, and students new to the organization. Several of those who attended were European scholars who study the carceral system from both a critical (as in Critical Criminology) and CC lens. Those in attendance exchanged ideas, and got to know each other better. The conference played an crucial part in the development of CC 2.0, especially with the publication of *Convict Criminology for the Future* (Ross & Vianello, 2021). Selected papers presented at the conference were included in the book. The conference and book encouraged the development of a new generation of CC scholarship at a global/international level, as a culturally, ethnically, and racially diverse organization.

Further attempts to revise the Convict Criminology website

After the *Convict Criminology for the Future* conference, a dedicated effort to rebuild the official CC website started. The old website, which had been created and maintained through the dedicated generous efforts of some early CC members, had become outdated. It was decided that a new online platform was needed, along with a fresh update of the content that this resource provided. Through the immense efforts of CC member Dr. Daniel Kavish and with the support of a few other CC members, a new website was constructed that included updated CC scholarship and an online space to support the soon-to-be-formed Division of Convict Criminology. This new website (https://www.concrim.org/) brought the CC organization firmly into alignment with the current organization's mission and exhibited a respectable online presence.

The 2019 San Francisco American Society of Criminology meeting and the establishment of Convict Criminology as an official division of the American Society of Criminology

During the CC business meeting at the 2019 ASC meeting in San Francisco, a spirited and productive discussion occurred. The advantages and disadvantages of CC becoming an official ASC division were discussed among those present. One of the most important issues was how to structure CC as a more formal division within the ASC. These conversations continued via email in the months following the 2019 ASC conference. Various members of CC who had been active in group-related business when CC was still an informal network reached out to Eskridge again about the steps necessary to formally establish the organization as a division of ASC. The CC leadership at the time drafted an ASC-sanctioned CC constitution for their division, established basic guidelines, and determined how CC wanted to structure committees and the division administration body. In order to demonstrate adequate ASC membership support for the formation of a Division of Convict Criminology (DCC), the members of CC were required to collect the signatures of at least 3 percent of the active ASC membership in the form of a petition. A handful of committed members of CC canvassed at the 2019 ASC conference in San Francisco, sent out emails to ASC members, and were able to collect far in excess of the required number of signatures required by ASC. This also included a large number of signatures from student members of ASC and from outside parties supporting the formation of an official CC division.

Once the petition signatures for the formation of the DCC were collected, they were officially confirmed by the ASC administrative staff. Next, CC submitted drafts of the CC constitution and guidelines, along with the certified petition signature list to the ASC executive office. The next step was the approval of the CC application by the ASC executive board. In April 2020, the board voted to approve the CC division application, and CC officially became the ASC Division of Convict Criminology (Ross & Tietjen, 2022).

Later stage global expansion of Convict Criminology

CC has emerged in several countries beyond the United States. In each context, it has taken a slightly different path. What follows is a quick review of some of the highlights of the development of Convict Criminology in each of these settings. It is essential to keep in mind, however, that just because one or more scholars, or currently or formerly incarcerated individuals, who were interested in CC reached out to selective members of the network, it did not mean that the movement caught on in that country. It often required a unique blend of expertise, salesmanship, and tenacity in each context. That being said, CC is still underrepresented in Africa, Asia, Eastern Europe, and the Middle East.

The challenges of establishing Convict Criminology in New Zealand and Australia

Given its historical origins as a penal colony; the fact that one of the original old-school CC members (i.e., Greg Newbold) originated from New Zealand; periodic communications between formerly incarcerated Australian and New Zealand scholars and CC members around the world about CC; the relative size of the prison population in both countries; a thriving community of criminologists who publish widely and attend international Criminology/Criminal Justice conferences; and the ease of pursuing post–prison education upon release from prison in New Zealand and Australia, it is a little puzzling that few New Zealander and Australian criminologists adopted the CC approach (Carey et al., 2022).[6]

The penal origins of the two countries

The penal origins of Australia (and to a lesser extent New Zealand) have played a prominent part in the history of these countries. It was only after various stages of self-government, the suppression of their respective indigenous communities (i.e., Aboriginals, Torres Strait Islanders, and Maoris), and massive waves of immigration, both countries have evolved from settler colonies to become the advanced industrialized democracies that these states are today. Over the years Australia and New Zealand developed their own correctional systems and facilities modelled on both British and American penal institutions (Newbold, 2013). These were distributed through each country.

The role of Greg Newbold

One of the original members of CC was New Zealander criminologist Greg Newbold. Although he attended ASC conferences in the United States, presented papers on CC panels, and authored or co-authored articles and chapters on CC, and had considerable contacts within New Zealander and Australian Criminology circles, he did not initiate a local "chapter" of CC. As a reminder, CC is a loose collection of people and each CC member is free to choose how they want to invest their resources, including evangelizing CC to anyone. Moreover, Newbold lives in New Zealand. And New Zealand is not Australia.

Interest from Australians and New Zealanders in the Convict Criminology perspective

Over the years, although members of the CC network periodically received correspondence from convicts and ex-convicts in Australia and New Zealand who were interested in CC, it was not until 2020–2021 that Dr. Lukas Carey, a formerly incarcerated person from Perth (Australia) with a Ph.D. in Education, reached out to some individuals in the CC network in the United States and in the United Kingdom, and attempted to organize a formal Australian CC group. He tried to do this through the Australian and New Zealand Society of Criminology (ANZSOC, "devoted to promoting criminological study, research and practice in the region and bringing together persons engaged in all aspects of the field," https://anzsoc.org/), but was met with considerable challenges at that time from the leadership of this organization.

The prison population of Australia and New Zealand is moderate

Given that, as of this writing, the United States has about 1,675,400 adults incarcerated in different facilities (and an incarceration rate of 505 per 100,000 individuals), both Australia and New Zealand have comparatively moderate prison populations. In the case of New Zealand, for example, Newbold (2017) notes that "expansion [of CC] into New Zealand has been less successful. The principal reason for this is that the prison population—although high per capita and rising rapidly—is still quite small with only about 9400 inmates in total" (Newbold, 2017: 609). In current numbers there are 7,964 individuals that make up New Zealand's prison population; an incarceration rate of 155 per 100,000 individuals. Australia, which has a considerably larger population than New Zealand, has 43,403 people who make up the prison population, with an incarceration rate of 165 per 100,000 individuals.[7] By comparison, the United States ranks first in the world in terms of the number of people it incarcerates, Australia is in 45th position and New Zealand 109th.

The internationalization of Australian and New Zealander criminologists

Both Australia and New Zealand have a number of criminologists who are originally from the United Kingdom, United States, Canada, and Europe, where CC is more widespread. Alternatively, many of the Australian and New Zealander criminologists went abroad to study for and complete their doctorates and return to these countries. Both countries boast a thriving ANZSOC group that publishes a well-respected journal.

Despite easier access to education few ex-convicts pursue doctorates in Criminology/Criminal Justice

Given that higher education in Australia and New Zealand is better funded than in the United States, one might assume that a larger proportion of Australian and New Zealander ex-convicts would pursue doctorates upon release, and a higher percentage of them would enroll in and graduate from Criminology/Criminal Justice programs. Regrettably this is not the case. Doyle et al. (2021), building on Newbold (2017), point out that, "[t]here has been a small number of Australians who have served prison sentences and then proceeded to university studies" (Doyle et al., 2021: 7). Their article identifies four Australians with doctorates (i.e., Lukas Carey, Craig Minogue, Anu Singh, and Kerry Tucker), who have served time behind bars, that publish on the topic of corrections. Needless to say, each of these individuals have different approaches to dealing with their convict past. More specifically, at the time of writing this book, only one has a university appointment.

The convict label is seen as a pejorative term in the Australian context

Another reason why CC may have had a more difficult time taking root in Australia (and perhaps New Zealand) is because the label "convict" is perceived to be offensive in those countries (Carey, et al., 2022). This argument was raised when in 2020, under Carey's direction, approximately 15 individuals signed a petition to support the creation of an ANZSOC thematic CC group.

Not only was this process very effortful, it failed to gain the required numbers of supporters to get formally established, and ultimately didn't gain traction with the ANZSOC executive. According to Doyle et al. (2021), "there are concerns about using 'convict' criminology in the Australian context given Australia's history of colonization." This state of affairs motivated Carey et al. (2022) to argue that if CC ideas want to thrive in Australia, they might necessitate a name change. They also acknowledge that, "along with a new name, comes a possibility of disconnection from the roots of the idea and the ideals Convict Criminologist mainstays … but something I believe they would not begrudge due to the complexities of the Australian setting" (Carey et al., 2022: 81).

While CC ideas persist in the Australian and New Zealand context, the possibilities of developing a more formal organization, at least for the time being, appear to be placed on hold.

Putting the brakes on bifurcation

Meanwhile, starting in and around 2020, despite scholarship from Earle (e.g., 2016), Davies (e.g., Davies & Nichols, 2016), and Honeywell (e.g., 2015; 2021), Aresti and Darke, two of the three co-founders of BCC, came to believe that having a BCC group that was distinctly separate from the wider CC movement was counterproductive. This was demonstrated by their disinclination to participate in BCC writing projects, including a chapter in the *Oxford Handbook of Criminology*, 7th edition (Earle et al., 2023). Their sentiments were elaborated in an article, "Against bifurcation: Why it is in the best interests of Convict Criminology to be international in scope & not a collection of individual country level organizations," where they laid out why perhaps at one time it made sense for BCC to be a separate entity but it now outlived its utility (Aresti et al., 2023).

The "Insider Prison Perspectives in Europe & the Americas" symposium

In the June 2023, Aresti and Darke, with the assistance of students affiliated with their CC program at the University of Westminster, organized a four-day symposium titled, "Insider Prison Perspectives in Europe & the Americas." The meetings occurred at four locations (i.e., Her Majesty's Prison [HMP] Coldingley, HMP Pentonville, HMP Gendron, and Westminster University). Attended by scholars (mostly criminologists) from Argentina, Brazil, England, Italy, and the United States, graduate students, and others involved with various prisoner programs, the panelists explored different themes under the CC umbrella. Selected prisoners at each of the correctional facilities were present either in person or virtually and many of them (including inmates at HMP Five Wells and APAC de Toldedo Prison, Brazil) delivered papers to the audience. As with previous meetings of this nature, symposium attendees were able to discuss multiple issues connected to CC, Corrections, research in these areas, and with academia in general. The hope is that some of these presentations can be assembled into a scholarly book and made available to a wider audience.

What has Convict Criminology accomplished?

In its relatively short history, CC has accomplished quite a few things. These include, but are not limited to (and ranked from least to most crucial), the following items. To begin with, *selected CC members have made news media appearances* where they have provided commentary on corrections-related developments and stories. These have been broadcast on regional, national, and international news media outlets. Many of these opportunities have allowed members to inform viewers and audiences about the core messages of CC.

Additionally, CC has been responsible for *organizing and participating in numerous panels* (at community forums, academic conferences, etc.) that focused on Corrections and the problems of re-entry and mass incarceration. These events have served multiple purposes, including stressing the importance of the lived experience of incarceration as a basis for knowledge, and the significance of the convict voice to scholarly and public policy debates.

More importantly, over the past three decades, scholars associated with CC have *published many articles and chapters in scholarly journals and academic books*. In these venues, CC has been able to shed light on more obscure, but no less crucial, aspects of prison life and refine the CC mission. This process has also been an important opportunity for mentoring formerly incarcerated individuals in the publication process (Ross & Copes, 2022).

Also crucial is the fact that the CC network has *mentored numerous convicts, ex-convicts, enabling them to complete bachelor's, master's, and doctoral degrees* (Ross et al., 2011a; 2015b; Ross, 2019; Tewksbury & Ross, 2019; Tietjen et al., 2021). These individuals were either ignored or marginalized (or felt this way) in their university programs or felt like they could benefit from CC members' assistance by writing meaningful letters of recommendation, conducting research with them, co-authoring academic papers together, providing feedback on job searches, and helping them acclimate to the norms of academic culture and settings (Custer et al., 2020).

Members of the CC network have *given lectures or taught classes in various correctional facilities*. In 2000, for example, Richards along with other colleagues at University of Wisconsin–Oshkosh administered a program in conjunction with the Wisconsin Department of Corrections initiated the Inviting Convicts to College Program. In England, Aresti and Darke, based at the University of Westminster, have for a number of years taught classes at HMP prisons and established a prison-to-college pipeline (Darke & Aresti, 2016). CC has also enabled formal research opportunities for various convicts and ex-convicts (Aresti et al., 2016).

Moreover, some CC members have *participated in important policy debates* (e.g., National Institute on Medicine) (Richards et al., 2011). Although a more detailed accounting of these activities is presented in Chapter 7, these initiatives have included a willingness to be interviewed by the news media, appearances on news casts, participating on community panels that address selective challenges of the criminal justice system, and writing op-eds.

Lastly, CC has *forced corrections experts and mainstream criminologists to look at the field of Corrections in a different way* (e.g., Arrigo, 2003; Sbraccia, 2021; Sterchele, 2021). One that takes into consideration the importance of the lived experience of people who not simply work in correctional settings, but are forced to live, sleep, and eat there 24 hours a day, seven days a week for numerous years of their life (Mobley, 2009).

What have been the major criticisms of Convict Criminology?

Over its close to three-decade history, CC has had its fair share of critics and critiques. Some of these arguments have been generated by individuals closely associated with CC (e.g., Larsen & Piché, 2012; Newbold & Ross, 2012), but most of the negative comments have been leveled by people outside of the group (e.g., Belknap, 2015) who possess superficial knowledge and understanding of the goals, challenges, and history of CC.[8]

The majority of the criticisms of CC have been done in informal venues, via social media, and banter at scholarly meetings, while only a handful have been published in scholarly venues.

In short, there are four primary shortcomings that have been leveled against CC.[9]

To start with, some individuals have suggested that, in terms of methodology, *CC is not sufficiently rigorous in the methods and analysis it uses.* Indeed, during the early years of CC, some of the papers delivered by ex-convicts at academic conferences resembled war stories and tended toward self-aggrandizement in their narration of all the tough times they had experienced before, during, or after incarceration. Later, once it was clear that a disproportionate number of the early research studies in CC were autoethnographies, some outsiders who had read these accounts realized that they had misunderstood the epistemological context of this type of research method.

Another problem pertained to the misperception that CC *tended to be exclusive* – that only certain types of people could be members of or affiliated with CC (e.g., convicts or ex-convicts), or that CC provided certain individuals a privileged status within the academic context. One final unfounded criticism was that CC excluded women, ethnic minorities, and members of the LGBTQIA+ community.

Although some of these criticisms might have had some merit, they also appeared to be overgeneralizations, and demonstrated a superficial understanding of CC (i.e., often those who believed these things did not do the hard and necessary work of reading and understanding the scholarship, but simply based their opinions on attending only one or two CC panels or on what they learned through word of mouth).

Despite subtle changes introduced through the growth of CC, some people, who are either loosely affiliated with CC, or know a little about CC, still believe and argue that *women, racial and ethnic minorities, LGBTQIA+ individuals, and other marginalized people are somehow excluded from CC*. Unfortunately, those supporting this "failure to include the voices of intersectional members of CC" position don't sufficiently review, know, or perhaps understand CC scholarship and activities that have dealt with this issue, academic research written by and about women or marginalized populations, who are affiliated with or draw upon the CC approach,[10] and the actions that the leadership of CC engaged in leading up to the creation of the DCC and its comparatively short history as part of the ASC. In this context, CC has had a significant number of, at the very least, women and racial and ethnic minorities in leadership positions, not to mention its current chair who is a Latinx.

A recent sophisticated analysis by Cox and Malkin (2023) deals in part with this issue. After reviewing CC's long-standing "struggle for inclusion," including the modest gains the approach has accomplished in trying to include LGBTQIA+ individuals and voices, they argue that "ConCrim should embrace feminist epistemology at the forefront of its growth as a discipline" (Cox & Malkin, 2023: 2). Cox and Malkin recommend that at least three feminist epistemologies CC should "consider utilizing in future research: feminist empiricist philosophy (Harding, 1991), feminist standpoint theory (DeVault, 1996; Harding, 1991) and situated knowledge (Haraway, 1988)" (Cox & Malkin, 2023: 4).

Although it is beyond the intent of this book to go in to greater detail on these approaches, the authors provide helpful examples from other organizations that can be applied to CC. These, and other perspectives, may be adopted in whole or in part based on the relative resources and interests of people who come into and are active in the CC network.

What has been Convict Criminology's response to these criticisms?

The CC approach has always welcomed thoughtful critiques. CC members have repeatedly and publicly stated that they believe well-founded and articulated criticisms force CC as a whole to improve its efforts and the ideas they ascribe to (Newbold & Ross, 2012). CC members have found, however, that in general, many of the external assessments are based on misinformation or a lack of understanding, while others are straw men arguments. Therefore, a large part of what members affiliated with CC continuously do is explain to others the goals and reasoning underpinning CC.

Despite criticisms that CC has either failed to engage in rigorous empirical analyses, or does not produce a sufficient amount of this kind of scholarship,

CC has encouraged individuals who are part of the network to not be content with simply presenting papers at conferences, but to submit them to journals where they would be subjected to peer review, to co-author papers so that they could learn from each other, and to avail themselves of the informal mentoring opportunities offered by selected CC members and now a formal mentoring system provided by the ASC Division of Convict Criminology mentoring program (https://concrim.org/mentorship/). This practice has also involved understanding more fully the framework of autoethnography (Gatson, 2003; Ellis & Bochner, 2005; 2006; Ellis et al., 2011; Jewkes, 2012; Newbold et al., 2014; Ferrell, 2018; Adams et al., 2022), rather than viewing it as simply a synonym for a memoir or autobiography.

CC has further tried to more effectively explain its attempts to recruit women, visible minorities, and members of the LGBTQIA+ community. These initiatives were addressed in a seminal article (Ross et al., 2016) where some of the established members of CC at the time provided empirical evidence of the group's efforts to be as inclusive as possible.

Furthermore, some members of the CC approach recognize that it is important to re-emphasize that people who claim to be convict criminologists need to have adequate/appropriate training in research methods, and to use these skills when conducting academic research. In other words, the lived experience of time spent behind bars does not necessarily mean that an individual has scholarly expertise that is typically earned through formal training in an accredited Ph.D. program.[11]

In order to address some of the criticisms, CC members increased their mentorship activity (Ross et al., 2015b; Ross, 2019). Finally, because of the efforts of selected members of CC, more than half of the executive board of the ASC DCC are women, including people of color. Furthermore, diversity and inclusion are primary goals of the DCC executive board members, who plan collaborative events with peer divisions that also represent marginalized populations in ASC (e.g., People of Color & Crime, Queer Criminology, etc.).

Conclusion

In the 1960s the popular band the Beatles wrote, performed, and recorded a song titled, "The Long and Winding Road." Although there have been multiple interpretations of the lyrics, the song emphasizes how despite occasional detours, a loving couple or relations will eventually lead to both people returning to each other. In many respects, despite different preoccupations, detours, and people coming in and out of the CC network, bringing with them new ideas and ones that were challenged, the CC journey is one that returns to its roots; a concern for critical and rigorous scholarly research, mentorship, and activism.

Or, interpreted through a different perspective, in some respects, the history of CC is similar to the classic children's book, *The Little Engine That Could*, and the more contemporary business book, *The Innovator's Dilemma.* In the first story, the little train engine encounters doubt and discouragement from other trains, but ultimately triumphs through self-belief and determination. In the second story, we see how disruptive innovation challenges established policies, practices, and organizations.

3

What Kinds of Scholarship Have Been Conducted on Convict Criminology and by Convict Criminologists?

Introduction

One of the central pillars of Convict Criminology (CC) has been the production and publication of scholarly research. The founders recognized that if they were going to be taken seriously then they needed to create a body of respected academic literature that people and organizations could refer to. In general, that meant the generation of peer-reviewed research.

This chapter begins by describing and explaining what scholarship, scientific research, and peer review are. It then considers why formerly incarcerated individuals with doctorates in Criminology/Criminal Justice or allied fields may not engage in research in general, and/or why they might shy away from conducting research on CC subject matter. Next it discusses the *Journal of Prisoners on Prison*, one of the most important scholarly journals that integrates the voices of convicts, ex-convicts, and academics. The chapter continues with a discussion of peer-reviewed research that has been conducted on CC. Subsequently it concludes with a summary of a comprehensive study, conducted by Ross and Copes (2022) that analyzed peer research on CC.

What is scholarship?

Scholarship basically consists of research and writing that involves the rigorous analysis of ideas or sets of ideas.[1] This intellectual pursuit typically includes exploration, critical thinking, and reasoning. It goes beyond the acquisition of facts, fostering a deeper understanding of complex phenomena and promoting intellectual growth. Scholarship can include examining existing knowledge, questioning assumptions, and pushing the boundaries of understanding. It also subsumes the meticulous examination of evidence, a synthesis of ideas, and the development of new insights.

This type of work is generally conducted by individuals we call scholars or academics, but not all people society labels scholars or academics engage in scholarship, and not all scholarship is done by individuals generally identified as scholars. Scholars are mainly highly educated, usually earning a Ph.D. from a respectable university. Scholars contribute to the advancement of their disciplines by generating new ideas, theories, and discoveries that attempt to shape and enrich the world.

In the CC approach, as with several disciplines and subdisciplines, not all scholarship is produced by individuals who have a Ph.D. or are in the process of earning one. Nor need the researchers be experts in the fields of Criminology, Criminal Justice, or Corrections. Scholarship, on the other hand, usually means that the written piece has been subjected to the process of peer review. Although a considerable number of articles, chapters in books, and other monographs, academic papers, podcasts, and websites mention CC, only a subset of this work can legitimately be called scholarship.

What is scientific research?

Scientific research is a systematic, rigorous, and methodical investigation designed to increase our understanding of phenomena. It is a way of "testing theories and hypotheses by applying certain rules of analysis to the observation and interpretation of reality under strictly delineated circumstances" (Manheim & Rich, 1986: 4). This can include, but is not limited to, designing and running experiments, conducting observational studies, collecting and analyzing evidence/data, and then drawing conclusions based on those patterns (Manheim & Rich, 1986: chapters 1 and 2).

Most scientific research attempts to answer essential questions, solve problems, and discover new connections. Its bedrock frame of reference is objectivity, transparency, and reproducibility. One of its core principles is that other researchers analyzing the same data will come to the same conclusions. This also encompasses the principals of verifiability and validity.

Each scientific field (i.e., ranging from the hard to the soft sciences) have different favored research methods, including laboratory experiments, field observations, computer simulations, and statistical analyses. The ultimate goal is to generate reliable and robust data that contribute to the collective body of scientific knowledge.

Scientific research is used to improve our understanding of complex phenomena, drive technological innovation, and address societal challenges. It forms the foundation for evidence-based decision-making, policy development, and the development of new technologies, medicines, and interventions that can improve the quality of life for individuals and society as a whole.

What is peer review?

Peer-review of academic research typically relies on blind review. The author/s of a scholarly paper, chapter, or book (or even a grant proposal) submits their work to an editor of a journal or editorial board, and if the manuscript *appears* appropriate for that venue, then it is sent to experts in the field who evaluate the piece on a variety of important criteria (e.g., originality, methodological rigor, quality of writing, etc.). At this stage of the publication process, only the editor and/or the editorial board know the identity of the author/s and reviewers. Conversely neither the researcher/s nor the reviewers know each other, thus the word "blind." The reviewers are expected to carefully read the paper, chapter, etc., write a brief report about the merits and shortcomings of the piece, and ultimately tell the editor/editorial board whether the work should be accepted, rejected, or encourage the writer/s to revise and resubmit their piece. The editor/s then makes a decision based on this feedback. Not only can this process take a very long time, but this is how most hard and soft sciences operate and build a body of knowledge. Peer review is the backbone of most academic research. It is the basis upon which most rational policy decisions are made.

Why might formerly incarcerated individuals with doctorates in Criminology/Criminal Justice or allied subject areas not engage in scholarly research?

Not everyone who has earned a Ph.D. conducts research after they have completed their dissertation. To begin with, depending on the country and specialization, before, during, or after completion of a doctorate many people choose, find, or settle for nonacademic jobs. These positions may be in government, private industry, or with nonprofits. Moreover, these jobs may not require individuals to do scholarly research. For example, some formerly incarcerated men and women take positions with think tanks or lobbying organizations that do not require any form of scholarship. Alternatively, if these individuals work for a college or university, they may have a position (e.g., in administration) that does not require them to do academic research to maintain or advance in their job. Lastly, some Ph.D. holders may work for an academic institution that does not value research, thus incentives to engage in this type of activity may be low.

Why might formerly incarcerated individuals with doctorates in Criminology/Criminal Justice or allied fields not engage in Convict Criminology research?

College instructors and professors have a wide latitude regarding the subjects that they chose to conduct research on, and the methods they apply to these fields of inquiry. Some scholars may encourage their colleagues or faculty (typically ones that are junior to them) to avoid CC type research or ideas. Rarely is this done explicitly. It is more likely that this advice is communicated in subtle messages. Alternatively, a formerly incarcerated academic might self-censor their research on prisons and prisoners and try to present their subject matter and findings in more liberal terms. Also, there is the prospect that formerly incarcerated individuals, with doctorates, who are also knowledgeable about CC, may be bored with conducting research on CC, Criminology, Criminal Justice, or anything that reminds them of their time served.

Peer-reviewed research on Convict Criminology

Although most peer-reviewed articles that touch on, use, or build upon the CC perspective briefly review the scholarship on this subject, few approach the task in a comprehensive manner. In an attempt to more rigorously understand CC scholarship, Ross and Copes (2022) conducted an in-depth content analysis of scholarly publications on CC.

These researchers attempted to discover "who is engaging in this type of research," "how they are doing this research," "what topics they prioritize," "the broad content of what is being published," and the impact of individual pieces of CC scholarship (Ross & Copes, 2022: 2).

Overall, Ross and Copes' content analysis of CC scholarship aimed to "provide the foundation to critically analyze this body of work to determine if they are meeting their aims and to suggest paths forward to invigorate future work in the area" (2022: 3).

How did Ross and Copes conduct their research?

Using principles based on Krippendorff (2018 [1980]), Ross and Copes began by collecting all citations of English-language publications (e.g., articles, chapters, and books) for the period of January 1, 2001, to August 1, 2022,[2] by keying in the expression "Convict Criminology" into Google Scholar. They also included chapters from the edited books *Convict Criminology* (Ross & Richards, 2003) and *Convict Criminology for the Future* (Ross & Vianello, 2021). Then they scoured the references of these publications for CC scholarship that they may have missed.

For a piece of scholarship to be initially included in the sample, it was not sufficient for it to simply use the words *Convict Criminology* in the body of the text or to make passing reference to the concept. Also, it was not enough to merely discuss correctional facilities or the convict experience. The authors had to actively engage with the CC framework by implementing its core ideas or by contextualizing a review of or findings drawn from this literature. Thus, excluded from this initial list were a handful of chapters that were published in *Convict Criminology* (Ross & Richards, 2003) and *Convict Criminology for the Future* (Ross

& Vianello, 2021), which were relevant to CC, but did not directly engage with scholarship on this theme. Ross and Copes "were more lenient with chapters in *Convict Criminology* because CC was embryonic at this stage and many of the parameters of the field had yet to be decided" (2022: 3). The researchers "included introductions to special issues and edited collections if they expanded on issues relating to CC and were not simply statements of what was included in the edited collection" (2022: 4).[3]

On the other hand, Ross and Copes excluded:

- encyclopedia entries, handbook chapters, forewords to edited books, prefaces to special issues, chapters in conference proceedings, and biographies of convict criminologists;
- reprints of articles or chapters, even if they had a different title;
- scholarship written by people associated with the CC network if they were not directly engaging with CC; and
- studies engaging in many of the things CC advocates (e.g., Participatory Action Research), but that did not specifically mention CC or utilize CC scholarship.

Consequently, Ross and Copes (2022) delimited the initial list of publications to a more manageable set of 79 items that met the inclusion criteria.

The investigators then refined their coding sheet throughout the coding process. All publications were coded by Ross and Copes (2022) and if there were disagreements in category selection, they were discussed between the two researchers to ensure unanimity in coding. This process identified four principal themes: lead author information; general manuscript information; consideration of the three tenets of CC; and manuscript impact.

What did Ross and Copes find?

To begin with, in order to gauge the periodicity and wider productivity of publications on CC, the year that a publication was printed was recorded. The first article that detailed the core ideas of CC was published by Richards and Ross (2001). In principle, this piece set the broad agenda for the field. Two years later, these same authors published *Convict Criminology*, an edited collection devoted to CC (Ross & Richards, 2003). After these early works, another CC publication did not appear until 2008. Ross and Copes determined that "[t]he highest number of journal articles published in a single year was 10, in 2012." In 2021 another edited collection was released (Ross & Vianello, 2021), substantially increasing the number of CC-related publications in circulation. All of this took place as CC scholars expanded the aims and the reach of the approach beyond North America (Ross et al., 2014), initially to the United Kingdom (Aresti, 2012; Earle, 2018), then to Italy (Vianello, 2021), Latin America (Vegh Weis, 2021), and Australia (Carey et al., 2022).

Who were the lead researchers?

Understanding who the authors of the manuscripts are can provide insights into the direction of CC. There were a total of 67 unique individuals listed as authors on one or more of the CC articles and chapters. Forty-four people were lead authors, while eight individuals wrote five or more CC manuscripts. Of the 44 lead authors, more than half (n=24) were currently or formerly incarcerated and 20 were not. The lead researchers of CC manuscripts were largely White men. The racial backgrounds of the lead authors were: 39 White, two Hispanic, two Black, and one Native American. Thirty-six were men, and eight were women. Of the men, 32 were White, two were Black, one was Hispanic, and one was Native American. Of the women, seven were White and one was Hispanic. Most of the lead authors were working in the United States (n=28), while the others were employed in the United Kingdom (n=6), Italy (n=5), Canada (n= 2), Argentina (n=1), Australia (n=1), and New Zealand (n=1).

Although the academic ranks of the lead authors changed over time (largely because they were promoted):

> the majority of lead authors were in tenure-track positions at the time of the publication: 21 were full professors, 24 were associate professors, and 16 were assistant professors. In addition, 8 were students, 6 were independent scholars, 2 were instructors, 1 was a post-doc, and in one case [Ross and Copes] … were unable to determine their official rank. (Ross & Copes, 2022: 6)

Where was the research published?

Of the 79 publications analyzed, "42 (53.2%) appeared in journals and 37 (46.8%) were in edited collections. In terms of content, the six most common subjects discussed in CC articles/chapters were Convict Criminology (n=28), prison experiences (n=20), prisons/corrections (n=11), education (n=11), scholarship (n=6), and re-entry experiences (n=5)" (Ross & Copes, 2022: 8).

What kind of approach or research methods did the investigators use?

Four classifications (i.e., empirical, normative, review, or mixed) of research approach were coded. According to Ross and Copes:

> [t]he frequency of these approaches were normative approach (n=37, 46.8%), review (n=16, 20.3%), mixed (n=16, 20.3%), and empirical (n=10, 12.7%). … For the publications that were based on empirical methods, they most often relied on qualitative methods (n=11, 73.3%), followed by mixed methods (N=3, 20%), and quantitative content analysis (n=1, 6.7%). (Ross & Copes, 2022: 8)

One of the original cornerstones of CC was the desire for the scholarship to include autoethnographies (Ross & Richards, 2003). Despite this intention, Ross and Copes discovered that "only one publication conformed to commonly accepted definitions of autoethnographies" (Ross & Copes 2022: 9). Instead, the publications were narratives anchored in "the personal experiences of the authors. These experiences were more often derived from being incarcerated, but they also include experiences working in prisons or as being family members of those who were incarcerated" (Ross & Copes, 2022: 9).

How is the subject of mentorship treated?

The second of the three pillars of CC is the promotion of mentorship for those who are behind bars and those who have been released from correctional confinement. Consequently, Ross and Copes determined if authors actively promoted mentorship of those in prison and individuals now in academia. They found that about one-fifth of the articles/chapters discussed mentorship of those in prison (n=17, 21.5%) or of those who were previously incarcerated and who are now in academia (n=10, 12.7%).

Another way to measure mentorship is to determine the number of co-authors for a publication. The assumption is that co-authors work together, often in a mentor–mentee relationship (Ross et al., 2015b). Overall, 38 (48.1%) of the publications were co-authored and 41 (51.9%) were solo-authored. Of the co-authored articles, 22 (57.9%) were led by formerly incarcerated scholars and 16 (42.1%) by non-incarcerated scholars. For the sole-authored publications, 26 (63.4%) were written by incarcerated scholars, and 15 (36.6%) were written by non-incarcerated scholars. Book chapters were more likely authored by single authors than were journal articles.

What did the researchers say about changing policies and activism?

The third stated tenet of CC is promoting progressive correctional and criminal justice system reform and activism to support this. Although it has been common for academics to critique prison and criminal justice policy, only 18 (22.8%) of the publications actively encouraged or recommended specific policies and practices. Even fewer promoted activism (n=11, 13.9%). Chapters published in edited collections were more likely to recommend policy (n=14, 37.8% of the chapters) than were articles in journals (n=4, 9.5% of the articles). Journal articles were slightly more likely to promote activism (n=7, 16.6%) than were chapters in edited collections (n=4, 10.8%).

How impactful has Convict Criminology scholarship been?

Ross and Copes noted that CC scholarship was only moderately cited in other sources. This may be explained by the fact that "[t]he articles tended to be published in specialty criminology journals" (e.g., *Journal of Prisoners on Prisons* [n=14] and *Critical Criminology* [n=6]), with few of them appearing in more traditional Criminology/Criminal Justice journals (e.g., *Criminology*, *Journal of Research in Crime and Delinquency*, and *Justice Quarterly*).

What did Ross and Copes conclude?

The authors noted that although "a unified approach to CC scholarship" does not exist, researchers adopting CC themes "tend to support three primary tenets: scholarship, mentoring, and policy/activism" (Ross & Copes, 2022: 10). Ross and Copes also stated that "in many ways CC scholars have more work to do to achieve these aims" (2022: 10). They lamented the fact that "[t]here is a large body of research on correctional facilities that covers the same content and methodological approach as convict criminology, but does not outright mention this field" (Ross & Copes, 2022: 10).

The investigators theorized that this may be a result of unfamiliarity with CC among "scholars, reviewers and editors" (Ross & Copes, 2022: 10). Another reason might be that "this group of experts may be misinformed about CC." Also, some formerly incarcerated scholars, despite doing insider research, may either feel antipathy toward CC or may worry that close association with this approach may limit their job prospects and opportunities for career advancement.

Ross and Copes also noted that that CC scholarship "has been historically a largely White, male enterprise." They acknowledged that several CC members know about this and have been actively recruiting qualified people "to address this gender and race/ethnicity issue" (Ross & Copes, 2022: 10).

To CC scholars' credit, Ross and Copes stated that "nearly half of the women lead authors published within the past two years. Women represented 6 of the 22 (27%) lead authors in 2021 and 2022. Additionally, current leadership in the Division of Convict Criminology is gender and racially diverse, to formerly address previous criticisms of the network" (2022: 11).

Convict Criminology content

Ross and Copes found that "CC scholars devote a significant amount of time reviewing and discussing the boundaries of the field" (2022: 11). They indicated that "over a third of the published work focuses on overviews" (Ross & Copes, 2022: 11). Thus, Ross and Copes argued that it is time to move past this type of scholarship and to examine more closely those who are "indirectly impacted by incarceration (family, friends, and victims of those in prison)" (2022: 11). This, Ross and Copes asserted,

> would show the reach of harm from excessive incarceration. Including more research on those in community corrections, including the harms and benefits of such programs, would reach bigger populations. In

short, CC scholars should limit the amount of reviews and increase applications of the framework to other areas within the justice system. (Ross & Copes, 2022: 11)

Ross and Copes maintained that

CC scholarship underutilizes empirical methods. CC scholars tend to use other approaches in their work, primarily reviews or normative approaches where they discuss personal experiences ... using empirical methods is also important. The broader acceptance of evidence-based practices in criminal justice supports this claim. Many in positions to implement policy look to empirical research to shape policies and programs. (Ross & Copes, 2022: 11)

Ross and Copes found "evidence of indirect mentorship through the practice of co-authoring" (2022: 11). That being said, "it was rare for CC scholarship to detail specifics about mentoring programs" or how to do this in an effective manner (Ross & Copes, 2022: 12).

Policy and activism

In the context of policy and activism, Ross and Copes explained that

less than a quarter of all publications recommended policy changes. It is common for CC scholars to critique existing policy, often from personal experiences. What is missing is the advancement and articulation of actual policy suggestions. The same is true for the promotion of activism, where less than 15%" dealt with this issue. (Ross & Copes, 2022: 12)

Meanwhile, "[d]etailing specific policies and programs and directing activism in clear ways can increase the reach of CC" (Ross & Copes, 2022: 12).

Impact of Convict Criminology scholarship

Although it is difficult to measure the impact of research, Ross and Copes note that it is crucial for CC scholars to start publishing in more mainstream Criminology/Criminal Justice journals and venues: "This singing to the choir approach may have been appropriate during the early formation of CC, where getting out the word was important, but the field is now close to 25 years old and those interested in the CC perspective should invest more time engaging with empirical research" (2022: 12).

   Ross and Copes also encourage scholars grappling with CC issues to move beyond reviews or further elaborations of CC. Such reviews and elaborations are essential, but this type of work represents a large – perhaps excessively – portion of the published works. Engaging with empirical, data-driven research will help CC scholars to publish in more prestigious journals, that include articles that are more frequently cited. More importantly, empirical research will allow CC researchers to make stronger policy recommendations and to inform effective activism.

Additionally, although the majority of CC research is based on first-hand accounts, little of this scholarship employs autoethnographical techniques in the truest sense of the term. Ross and Copes note that although it is critical to

> detail personal experiences … it is important to have clearly defined and rigorous methods. Retrospective accounts are limited in their ability to convincingly direct policy, since they can be discounted as merely anecdotes. As one of the major tenets of CC is to promote policy, having more sophisticated methods will aid in bringing this to fruition. (Ross & Copes, 2022: 12)

Although the bulk of CC research highlights the experiences of individuals who are currently or formally incarcerated, including the challenges of prisoner re-entry, this focus may also be a limiting factor. CC is also well-suited to understand the experiences of those who are indirectly affected by carceral systems. At the micro level this includes, people (i.e., parents, spouses, partners, and children) with incarcerated relatives or friends (Cox, 2021). At the macro level this may include entire communities that are negatively affected by mass incarceration (e.g., Clear, 2009). Moreover, insights from those who work in correctional institutions can be used to inform CC and to offer policy recommendations (e.g., Ross et al., 2021).

From autoethnography to quantitative research

As Ross and Copes (2022) suggest, the early CC movement emphasized ethnography and autoethnography as its core methodological framework (Terry, 2003a; 2003b; Newbold et al., 2014). This approach derived from the scholarly notion of *phenomenology*. Most comprehensive reviews of this method, however, note that there is no agreed upon definition for this term. Nevertheless, it is generally understood that phenomenology places an emphasis on how people understand or represent the environments in which they work and live. One of the best introductions to this argument was written by Irwin (1987), a former felon and professor of Criminology/Criminal Justice, who has been credited with being an inspiration to many in the CC network, in his outgoing essay as journal editor for the *Journal of Contemporary Ethnography*. He argued that "any theoretical approach that is not extremely sensitive to the categories or meanings that actual actors employ in defining their world and deciding their courses of action is a gross distortion of human behavior" (1987: 42). Irwin continued by suggesting that a large amount of the quantitative research on corrections from the 1960s (mainly using surveys based on Sykes' *The Society of Captives* [1958]) misinterpreted what was actually occurring in prisons during that decade. In other words, methodological tools should never be based on outdated scholarship. Irwin was particularly disturbed by research that emphasized the existence of a criminal typology, which was reflected in things such as the bogeyman concept.

The original decision by CC to privilege autoethnographic methods was predicated on the fact that it is difficult for most scholars to gain access to correctional facilities to conduct research (Marquart, 1986; Farkas, 1992; Apa et al., 2012; Gacek & Ricciardelli, 2021), and if they are allowed to do research when inside, the kinds of studies they are permitted is highly limited. More importantly, not only do appropriately trained incarcerated and formerly incarcerated individuals have a number of crucial experiences that were not being captured by traditional quantitative criminological research, especially that which was being done on jails and prisons, but they are in an ideal position to conduct this kind of work. The shortcomings, or more specifically the paucity of prison ethnographies during the latter part of the 20th Century was highlighted by Wacquant (2002) and by a subsequent renaissance in prison ethnographies (Drake et al., 2015).

Unmistakably, a vast literature on prison ethnography exists, and autoethnographies done by prisoners or formerly incarcerated people appears to be increasing. Autoethnography, however, is more than the telling of war stories or the writing of memoirs and autobiographies, mainly because data collection is supposed to be done in a systematic manner. Although autoethnography was chosen as the original "backbone" research method of CC, over time scholars affiliated with the CC approach have used a multitude of research methods to answer the questions they ask (Ross & Copes, 2022). Many CC members are skilled in a variety of investigative methodologies, and insights can be garnered about jails and prisons using numerous kinds of research methods. Focusing on one type of investigative strategy, to the exclusion of others, may be caused by poor training, narrowmindedness, elitism, laziness, a lack of confidence in one's research skills, etc. Several individuals have also failed to understand that both memoirs and autobiographies can have some of those elements. War stories are similarly problematic and do not qualify as autoethnographies.

Some additional points should be considered in this discussion. It is next to impossible for a prisoner, even one who has been appropriately trained, to conduct a rigorous ethnography behind bars. Why? In the United States and in most advanced industrialized countries, researchers wishing to conduct studies inside correctional facilities need to get Institutional Review Board approval from the prison or prison authority. This kind of request is typically very foreign to most correctional facilities and, among other reasons, there's a general unwillingness to grant them. Additionally, there's considerable variability among countries, prison systems, and facilities, with respect to the ease, topics, and methods that researchers can pursue inside correctional institutions. In other words, some corrections themed research is easier to conduct than others. In fact, that's why autoethnographies were privileged in the early days of CC. In the case of autoethnographies, formerly incarcerated individuals don't need human subject approval. Furthermore, despite the original objective to privilege autoethnographies, most of CC research is informed by the prison experience, rather than consisting of autoethnographies (Ross & Copes, 2022). Why? It might be that scholars claiming to use this approach, do not really understand what ethnography is and how to conduct one, and thus performing an autoethnography is beyond their current skill set. Moreover, because of the unpredictability of the environment of jails and prisons, it is almost impossible to conduct an autoethnography, because this requires a systematic approach to data collection and a secure method of data storage (Adams et al., 2022).

Regardless, since the original formation of CC, many individuals committed to the core principles of the approach recognized the importance of the autoethnographical methods to understand the prison experience, but also argued that additional types of qualitative research, including direct observation, face-to-face interviews, semi-structured interviews, and retrospective analysis could also answer some of the questions that CC was concerned with (Richards, 2013). Since then, there has been greater appreciation of the role of quantitative research in CC studies. One of many signals in this direction was in 2019, when Daniel Kavish, a professor at Southwestern Oklahoma State University, chaired the first panel of its kind on quantitative research in CC at the annual American Society of Criminology meeting.

The *Journal of Prisoners on Prisons*

It is valuable for an emerging discipline to have a scholarly journal that aligns with its core issues. Thus it is unsurprising that CC shares a natural affinity with the mission, the work published in, and the individuals connected to the *Journal of Prisoners on Prison* (JPP). This publication was established in 1988 following the third International Conference on Prisoner Abolition, which occurred in Montreal. Similar to CC, the JPP was founded on the belief that the voices of educated convicts were typically ignored and that there needed to be a formal scholarly publication that featured this work, and that it would be helpful if it had a university affiliation, to facilitate this mission.

The original editorial collective included Howard Davidson, Liz Elliott, and Bob Gaucher, and the journal was and continues to be published at University of Ottawa (Gaucher, 1988) (see Exhibit Box 3.1). In order to have a paper published in the JPP, at least one of the authors must be a convict or ex-convict. The connection between CC and the JPP has been reaffirmed three times. In 2012, Richards and Lenza edited a special edition of the journal titled "A Special Issue Commemorating the 15th Anniversary of Convict Criminology," 21(1&2), and in 2018, Darke and Aresti edited a special issue commemorating the 20th anniversary of the CC network. Another issue directly focusing on CC was published in 2024 and is co-edited by Grant Tietjen, Alison Cox, and J. Renee Trombley. Since 2010 JPP has been capably edited by Justin Piché and Kevin Walby.

Exhibit Box 3.1: Liz Elliott

Liz Elliott, Ph.D. (1957–2011) was a professor in the School of Criminology at Simon Fraser University (SFU; Burnaby, BC). In addition to working as an instructor and scholar, she was instrumental in helping to establish the *Journal of Prisoners on Prison*. Elliott earned a Ph.D. in Criminology from SFU in 1996 and rose up through the ranks to earn full professor status. In addition to her multiple publications, she spent a considerable amount of time assisting both individuals who were incarcerated and those who were released from correctional custody. She served on the boards of "the Canadian Prisoner Aid Organization, the John Howard Society of the Fraser Valley and the West Coast Prison Justice Society" (Anderson, 2015). Elliott was involved in the "restorative justice group, FAVOUR, based out of a federal minimum security institution, and taught in SFU's Prison Education Program" (Anderson, 2015). As an instructor she was notable for enabling her students to visit correctional facilities and having them lecture in her courses (Anderson, 2015). "Elliott also cofounded the Centre for Restorative Justice at SFU, a resource and research centre dedicated to promoting the values and principles of restorative justice—a practice whose roots are found in Aboriginal healing traditions and the non-retaliatory responses to violence endorsed by many faith communities. Restorative justice focuses on repairing the harm caused by criminal acts" (Anderson, 2015).

Conclusion

Scholarship has always been the foundation of the CC approach, and the content and research methods are constantly evolving. Although early research emphasized the role of autoethnography there is considerable room for other methodologies to be used. As reviewed in this chapter, Ross and Copes' sample was limited to English-language publications. "As CC has grown, scholars writing in varied languages have begun to produce important CC work. Accordingly, further iterations of this research should include foreign-language (e.g., French, Italian, Portuguese, etc.) scholarship written on CC" (Ross & Copes, 2022: 13). Ross and Copes also noted that "[f]ollow-up research might endeavor to ask the authors of this scholarship about the experience of writing in this field, including questions surrounding their motivation and the effect it had on their lives and careers" (2022: 13).

PART II

Teaching and Mentoring

4

Teaching Convicts and Formerly Incarcerated Individuals: The State of Post-Secondary Undergraduate Education in Correctional Facilities

Introduction

Although the pillar of the Convict Criminology (CC) approach is the production of relevant scholarship, it also devotes considerable resources to teaching, instructing, and mentoring currently and formerly incarcerated people (Ross, 2019; Tietjen et al., 2021).[1] In order to provide sufficient discussion of these interrelated subtopics, this book devotes three chapters to this subject. This chapter, in particular, reviews the difficulty of getting instruction behind bars, and the follow-up chapters review, respectively: methods of mentoring convicts and ex-convicts in scholarly research, assisting them in their graduate school applications, and providing advice on how to survive this training and establish productive academic careers.

More specifically, this chapter examines the difficulty inherent to teaching and learning while incarcerated. It focuses on the multiple barriers to earning academic degrees in correctional settings and on the characteristics of effective mentoring of someone behind bars (or recently released) who is entering a university course of study (Ross, 2019; Tewksbury & Ross, 2019). The chapter also explores the provision of post-secondary education while incarcerated in three countries (i.e., the United States, England and Wales, and Italy) where CC has flourished.

University-level instruction behind bars

In general, correctional facilities are supposed to accomplish approximately four major goals, including:

- punishing individuals convicted of criminal offenses;
- protecting society/keeping society safe;
- deterring both inmates and people in the wider society from engaging in crimes; and
- rehabilitating convicts (Ross, 2016: 3).

For the most part, rehabilitating prisoners includes helping them to deal with the psychological, vocational, and educational challenges that may have led to their incarceration. Despite these noble objectives, most correctional institutions typically fail to provide suitable education beyond high-school instruction (Bloom & Bradshaw, 2022).

This chapter reviews the challenges of providing formal post-secondary (also known as higher, college, or university) education in correctional facilities or institutions (interchangeably referred to as jails and prisons) in the United States. Then the chapter argues why it is important to offer college education to convicts. This is followed by outlining why most jails and prisons usually fail to deliver appropriate formal education beyond high-school instruction. After this, the chapter outlines the most crucial reasons why supplying adequate college education to convicts is difficult. This section will conclude by advancing a handful of the best solutions to deal with the inadequate provision of post-secondary education in prison.

Many readers may already be familiar with some or all of these ideas. If that is the case, please consider this chapter as a way of organizing what we already know. For those who have not heard these ideas, the ones advanced in this chapter can hopefully be useful in dealing with the essential challenge of providing undergraduate-level education in correctional institutions. That being said, this chapter draws heavily from the American experience of providing university education in jails and prisons, and this setting may not easily generalize to what occurs in other countries.

Before examining these issues, we should consider the following question: Why is it crucial to provide college education to inmates?

Why is it important to provide college education to convicts?

Most prisoners generally and desperately need to upgrade their education. In some correctional facilities, the majority of inmates are high-school dropouts. Even if a formerly incarcerated person has a high-school diploma, the fact that they have a criminal record significantly hinders their long-term career prospects, typically leaving them with limited options, often restricted to minimum-wage jobs. Earning college credits and possibly a degree may improve their ability to secure a well-paying job, support their families or loved ones, and avoid being homeless, cycling through, or being permanently in the welfare system (Lockwood et al., 2012; Davis et al., 2013).

Most rigorous research clearly demonstrates that higher education is the single most effective means of lowering criminal recidivism rates (Linden & Perry, 1983; Taylor, 1994; Tregea, 2003; Vacca, 2004; Kim & Clark, 2013; McMay & Kimble, 2020). Simply stated, convicts who complete a year or more of college courses while incarcerated are much less likely to violate parole or be returned to jail or prison on a new conviction (e.g., Dennison, 2019). Moreover, for the correctional system, educated convicts are typically easier to deal with because they may distrust rumor, and respond better to reason, facts, and empirical evidence (Curtis et al., 2021).

Furthermore, after being released from prison, one possible path for formerly incarcerated people is to go to college (Ross & Richards, 2003; Ross, 2019). As former prisoners, ex-convicts are already institutionalized (Clemmer, 1940) and are accustomed to dormitory living (if this is part of the university setting) and bureaucratic rules. Moreover, entering college may be a good path for ex-convicts because they usually emerge from behind bars without a job or any income and have not paid taxes in years. Depending on the crimes for which they were convicted, they can sometimes qualify for privately funded student loans and possible grants.

Nevertheless, formal classes, beyond high school (or General Equivalency Diploma [GED] certification, which is used in the United States),[2] with rare exceptions, are not available in jails and prisons. Most correctional systems do not offer adequate post-secondary educational opportunities (Taylor & Tewksbury, 2002).

Why do most correctional facilities typically fail to provide formal education beyond high-school instruction?

It goes without saying that most correctional settings, regardless of the country, are poor places for formal education. Why?

Although room and board are typically provided free of cost to inmates, they must contend with numerous distractions that can negatively affect their ability to read and study. Nevertheless, convicts who fail to complete a course of study while incarcerated may finish community college diplomas and college degrees at universities when and if they are released from jail or prison.

Why is it difficult to provide adequate college education to convicts?

There are about 15 interrelated reasons why the provision of post-secondary education to inmates is mostly inadequate. These are ordered from least to most important.

Opportunities for non-classroom educational experiences are limited, due to security concerns

University education is often not circumscribed to classroom instruction with an instructor standing at the front of the room, lecturing, and students diligently taking notes. Labs and field trips may be included as components of a course. Unless we are talking about open prisons, as they exist in many European countries, where inmates can leave during the day to take classes at a nearby university, most correctional institutions and programs lack this kind of opportunity.

The majority of formal post-secondary education programs offered in prison are directed toward earning an undergraduate degree

If a university-level program of instruction is offered in a correctional setting, the classes are predominately at the undergraduate level. If the inmate already has an undergraduate degree, then they will usually not be able to take a master's course or higher (instead, they usually take another bachelor's level course of study).

Many colleges and universities that offer instruction behind bars end up dropping their classes and programs

Occasionally, cash-strapped or entrepreneurial post-secondary institutions of higher learning might offer college-level courses and educational programs in correctional contexts. The classes are often dependent on the resources and the predicted/actual financial incentives that the educational institution receives, beyond what is invested by the prison administration. In any event, these educational opportunities often only serve a few dozen prisoners at a time and only those who can somehow scrape together the funds to pay the tuition. Colleges often terminate these classes and programs when they discover, or get frustrated with, the convicts who cannot afford the courses and/or when they lose patience with the bureaucratic hurdles they must negotiate with the correctional facilities or system in the jurisdiction in which the jail or prison is located. In particular, Departments of Corrections may be very slow with the payments to the schools in question, and the college or university may decide that it is not economically viable to continue (Ross & Richards, 2002).

There are few alternatives to face-to-face university instruction while incarcerated, and those outside of this teaching modality are substandard

Some colleges and universities offer self-paced (asynchronous) correspondence-type university instruction and degrees in which prisoners can enroll. Most of these programs are for-profit (not public), do not have admission requirements, and do not require a GED or high-school diploma for matriculation. The quality of these programs varies. Many of them are unaccredited, the accrediting body is weak, and thus the quality and utility of the degree once the inmate completes the program is questionable (Ross et al., 2015a). For example, a noted CC writer, whose three books were released by very respected publishers, completed his doctorate behind bars via a university that specializes in correspondence instruction. Upon release, most colleges to which he applied for a full-time job told him that because of the reputation of the educational institution from which he had earned his Ph.D., his degree was practically useless.

Many adult learners have a difficult time learning in situations where the instruction is not face-to-face

Synchronous, face-to-face instruction facilitates instruction and engagement where discussion occurs. In general, learners in these venues benefit from the group work that naturally occurs in these settings and the opportunity to ask questions and receive immediate feedback.

Outside instructors who teach in prison face numerous bureaucratic obstacles to holding their classes

Just like correctional workers, most instructors who teach behind bars are subject to several security protocols upon entering and exiting the correctional facilities. Over time, this can be unnecessarily onerous. For example, instructors may not be able to bring in their laptops, computer sticks, or USB flash drives, or they may not have access to the world wide web that they may need for pedagogical purposes.

Many capable instructors do not want to teach in correctional institutions

In addition to the previously outlined challenges, many capable educators often do not want to teach in jails and prisons. Why? Instructors may encounter numerous inconveniences that they don't face teaching in other educational settings. To begin with, several correctional facilities are located in remote areas, and thus there is the added time it takes to travel to and from the institution. Instructors may not be able to rely on public transportation and, thus, need a car or a lift to get them to the jail or prison. Additionally, instructors, like all visitors, are subjected to security protocols and require extra time to be processed in to and out of the institution. Moreover, some correctional facilities are very dangerous, prompting the most committed of all instructors to shy away from these environments as places where they want to work or volunteer their time. Finally, if an instructor has a previous criminal record or are public figures with controversial political ideas, they may be barred from entering the facility altogether.

Some correctional workers and administrators distrust outside instructors

For good reason, many correctional workers and administrators, even those who are dedicated to rehabilitation, see outside instructors as potential threats to the security and smooth running of their institutions (Ray, 2013). They worry about the instructors bringing in contraband and "brainwashing" inmates, which might eventually create havoc among the prisoners.

Some correctional workers and administrators distrust educated prisoners

Some correctional workers and administrators consider educated convicts to be a threat to their authority, since these individuals may be more knowledgeable and skilled, and may appear more credible than many of prisoners they supervise, particularly because of their communications with outsiders (e.g., the news media and with oversight agencies). In short, educated inmates may report on poor prison conditions, corruption, and incompetent prison employees. Because of this distrust, convicts taking college classes may be subject to frequent cell searches and disciplinary transfers to administrative detention (i.e., solitary confinement) or other institutions. This disrupts their ability to regularly take classes and complete their course of studies.

Security restrictions frustrate prisoners' ability to study in correctional institutions

Typically, inmates are subject to numerous security restrictions that complicate their efforts to take classes and study, including limits on the number of books they may keep in their cells; restricted use of typewriters, computers, and copy machines; and regulated mail procedures. Some mail, incoming and outgoing, is opened, read, and copied by Correctional Officers (COs). In some prison systems, books mailed to convicts from friends and families usually have their covers ripped off by prison employees to prevent or minimize the entry of contraband into the institution.[3] In other correctional systems, convicts can only receive books mailed from a reputable publisher or bookseller, and thus the price to buy books is often higher than ones purchased from a used bookseller.

Prisons have too many distractions for convicts to properly study

The speed with which it takes prisoners to complete a course of studies depends on several factors: the time limits established by the school; the inmates' funds to pay for courses, books, and stamps; scholastic ability; determination; the conditions of confinement (including access to the internet);[4] and distractions. Inmates have many preoccupations, including always having to be wary of theft and negotiating the challenges of simply surviving day-to-day.

Convicts usually have a difficult time registering for university courses offered in correctional facilities

Inmates normally need a prison case manager, counselor, or "free-world" friend to register on their behalf and pay tuition to a college/university. Convicts have to figure out how to pay for the college credit courses and which classes to take. Inmates may use the meager amount of money they earn inside the prison or ask for outside help (e.g., family or friends) to pay for courses. Alternatively convicts may need their (often cash-strapped) family or friends to pay tuition fees in advance of completion, with the promise and hope that the convict will reimburse them later, perhaps only after he or she is released.

Prison and university administrators frequently have to negotiate a considerable number of bureaucratic obstacles to provide adequate instruction

Prison and university administrators who want to offer post-secondary education for inmates must often surmount significant hurdles in order to ensure the delivery of high-quality education for the convicts who are housed in their institutions. Meanwhile, the highest priority for wardens, correctional officers, and other correctional workers is to ensure the security of the institution (that inmates have food, etc.). Education is a lower priority issue for them.

In the United States, at least, prisoners must pay for their post-secondary education

In the United States, public elementary, middle, and high school education is free. Although there are many "public" post-secondary school educational institutions, typically called community colleges and universities, students must pay for their bachelor's, master's, and doctoral education. In order to fund this education, students use their savings, or depend on loved ones, grants, and loans.

With few exceptions, in the United States, most correctional systems are only obligated to provide inmates with high-school courses. Few community colleges and universities offer classes in correctional facilities, and the ones that do require convicts to pay for the education. The programs that are free for prisoners are often run by volunteers, and operational costs are funded by donations from the private sector.

Until 1994, Federal Pell Grants were available for both state and federal convicts to help them pay college tuition for courses taught inside prisons or by correspondence. This benefit was, however, problematic. Occasionally, inmates applied for the grants but never received the support because the applicants were transferred to another correctional facility. Alternatively, prisoners sometimes applied for Pell Grants, but the education office at the prison (not the individuals themselves) actually received the funds, which could be spent by the institution on anything that could be even vaguely interpreted as educational (e.g., basketballs, pencils, and flower gardens).

Pell Grants for prisoners came to halt in 1994 when the Violent Crime Control Act (aka the Crime Bill) was passed. It cut funding for post-secondary correctional education to prisoners. During the Obama administration (January 20, 2009, to January 20, 2017), however, the Pell Grant system was reinstituted, and funding flowed to a handful of universities with programs offering courses in prisons.

Few correctional facilities and prison systems devote adequate resources to post-secondary school education

Most importantly, very few resources (e.g., staff, space, etc.) are devoted to "inmate education." Prisons may have an education section or department, which may be as small as a single classroom or as large as a wing of a building. The education section may include a small library and a few classrooms, and be staffed by teachers, COs, and convict clerks, with a range of certifications, training, abilities, and motivations (e.g., Ahmed et al., 2019).

The lack of resources is not necessarily the fault of the correctional facility, since it often originates in the municipalities, counties, states, and countries where the correctional institutions are located. In general, politicians are relatively happy to incarcerate inmates, but when it comes to the provision of meaningful rehabilitative programs, including ones that include education, the money for this kind of activity either does not exist or is inadequate.

Why? Because the majority of politicians' constituents do not want their taxes to be used to provide rehabilitative services to inmates. This sentiment is particularly true for people who come from working-class backgrounds. Although they recognize the importance of rehabilitation for prisoners, they do not want convicts to receive any special breaks, perhaps believing that they never received any special help to get to where they are in life. In other words, they think that everyone needs to pay their "fair share."

What are the best solutions to dealing with the inadequate provision of post–secondary formal education in prison?

There are at least eight strategies that can be used to introduce or maintain appropriate university classes in correctional facilities. They are listed from least to most crucial.

Correctional workers and administrators and instructors and professors should tap into the resources of the Division of Convict Criminology and the Convict Criminology network

As previously mentioned, one of CC's three main objectives is mentoring convicts and formerly incarcerated people through their bachelor's, master's, and Ph.D. degrees. Not only has some of CC's educational work been done in jails, prisons, and other correctional settings, but the group has established a large international network that can assist individuals to pursue their goals of starting and completing a college education behind bars and upon release.

Create nonprofit foundations or educational trusts that channel prisoner requests to enroll in post-secondary education while they are incarcerated

In some countries nonprofit organizations have been created to provide funding to prisoners who request this kind of assistance for post-secondary education. The granting of funds is done on a case-by-case basis. One example of this is the Prisoners' Education Trust in the United Kingdom (Clark, 2016); see Exhibit Box 4.1).

Conduct empirical research on university-level prison education

Over the past five decades, a considerable amount of scholarship has been conducted on learning in prisons. This includes three English-language scholarly journals that focus on this subject (i.e., *Advancing Corrections: Journal of the International Corrections and Prisons Association*, *Journal of Correctional Education*, and *Journal of Prison Education and Reentry*). One problem, however, is that the majority of the research that is published on this subject consists of single, descriptive case studies. These efforts are helpful, but analyses that compare different programs are needed (e.g., Lockard & Rankins-Robertson, 2011; Ludlow et al., 2019). Additionally, it is often beneficial to review and learn from the experiences of university programs that exist in other countries (e.g., Armstrong & Ludlow, 2016; Pastore, 2018; Earle & Mehigan, 2020; Borghini & Pastore, 2021; Pelligrino et al., 2021). Hopefully those analyses will assist educators, etc., with insights regarding favorable initiatives/best practices that might be applied in correctional facilities in the United States.

Thoroughly analyze existing programs

Over the last half-century, several popular university-sponsored and -led programs that provide college-level classes to inmates have been developed in various advanced industrialized democracies. Today an array of post-GED formal college educational programs are offered to men and women who are incarcerated (Tregea, 2003; Sokoloff & Schenck-Fontain, 2017). These include, but are not limited to the:

- Inside-Out Prison Exchange Program (Pompa & Crabbe, 2004);
- University of Wisconsin at Oshkosh's Inviting Convicts to College Program (Rose et al., 2010; Richards et al., 2006);
- Washington State University Program;
- Bard Prison Initiative (Condliffe Lagemann, 2011; Karpowitz, 2017);

- University of Nebraska Program;
- Prison University Project (at San Quentin);
- Project Rebound (State of California);
- Underground Scholars Program in California (Martinez, 2021); and
- State of California Initiative.

Short of reviewing each one of these efforts, it is safe to say that these initiatives have had differing objectives, histories, teaching modalities, and outcomes. Rarely, however, are these programs evaluated in a comprehensive manner or outcomes-type evaluation framework. Instead, many of the assessments are based on anecdotal evidence and conducted by the organizers of the programs. Although this is a good start, the administrators of these efforts need to have skilled outside experts evaluate these programs to minimize bias/conflicts of interest, to ensure that they are meeting their objectives, and that the findings are used to improve the delivery of instruction to inmates and convince funders of their utility. Lastly, these evaluations need to be done on a regular basis.

Provide evidence and arguments to correctional workers and administrators about the utility of university education for prisoners

Instructors, professors, and university administrators need to identify progressive correctional workers and administrators, and offer them the appropriate evidence necessary to convince them to start or continue to provide post-secondary classes and programs of study behind bars. Sometimes the repetition of the messages has a cumulative effect on convincing key supporters to take these initiatives more seriously than they currently do.

Correctional workers and administrators considering starting and maintaining university programs must identify and utilize the appropriate resources

This includes not just money, but skilled and dedicated people and organizations that can help to implement and maintain formal educational programs behind bars.

Convince politicians, the news media, and the public that university-educated convicts engage in less crime upon release

Politicians, educators, correctional workers, and administrators who believe in the provision of post-secondary education for convicts need to convince, not just other like-minded individuals, but also the news media and their constituents that providing prisoners with university-level classes (better still the completion of a university degree) will lead to a decrease in crime and recidivism. One way to do this is to show per-capita spending on university education per inmate in each jurisdiction, both in terms of rehabilitation and post-secondary education.

This information may convince some individuals who need or want this kind of data that their jurisdictions' spending is inadequate, and they are not doing enough to assist people while incarcerated. Also important is the dissemination of authentic and believable stories and anecdotes about inmates who have benefited from university education behind bars. These accounts should be collated and distributed in a systematic fashion to appropriate audiences.

Establish formal legal mechanisms to enable and protect the provision of post-secondary education for prisoners

Only a handful of countries consider the provision of higher education to be a right of men and women who are incarcerated, and some have even included it in their constitution, or through some sort of enabling legislation.

Additionally, a comparatively small number of prisoners fulfill the formal requirements for studying at university. For those who are eligible, it requires an enormous amount of paperwork and tenacity to find an appropriate program and make suitable arrangements to pay for it. Rarely do these individuals receive much assistance from the correctional facility or the institution of higher education that offers classes. Additional obstacles for convicts in this position are the prison administration and policies and practices, including rules against using a computer/the internet, the number of books allowed in a cell, etc.

Furthermore, only a minority of prisoners want to earn a bachelor's degree, and even fewer want to earn a master's and Ph.D. (Lanier et al., 1994). And if these individuals want to earn a bachelor's degree, it is often in a field unrelated to Criminology and Criminal Justice. Moreover, it is usually difficult for inmates to pursue higher education beyond a GED, which is basically the same as a high-school diploma, while they are incarcerated.

Undoubtedly there are a number of universities in the United States that offer master's and doctoral-level correspondence courses that prisoners can enroll in while they are locked up. Ones that are offered by accredited institutions are typically rare and often do not last long before funding or commitment by both the educational and correctional institution ends (e.g., Lanier et al., 1994). On the other hand, most of the post-bachelor programs accessible to inmates are mainly available from unaccredited institutions, or the accrediting body is frowned upon in the mainstream academic community (Ross et al., 2015a). Unfortunately, when formerly incarcerated people who have completed master's and doctorates from these institutions are released, their academic credentials are not taken seriously.

Teaching convicts behind bars in the United States

Introduction

Today a smorgasbord of post-GED formal educational programs are offered to individuals who are incarcerated (Tregea, 2003; Sokoloff & Schenck-Fontain,

2017). Similarly numerous educational offerings have been established to assist returning citizens on college campuses. The majority of them, however, have been directed toward earning an undergraduate degree.

What follows is a brief review of selected American-based state and private colleges and universities that have developed college-level courses for convicts behind bars. This includes, but is not limited to, the Inside-Out Program (run out of Temple University) and the Inviting Convicts to College Program (e.g., Rose et al., 2010). Later the chapter will provide a brief review of some undergraduate and graduate instructional efforts that have been conducted in England and Wales, including those offered by instructors from the Convict Criminology at Westminster program (Darke & Aresti, 2016) and Open University (Earle & Mehigan, 2020), Learning Together (Armstrong & Ludlow, 2016), and programs and courses offered in Italy to educate prisoners who may not have access to proper teaching modalities will also be covered (Borghini & Pastore, 2021; Pelligrino et al., 2021; Torrente, 2021), This chapter will also look at the difficulties inherent to earning a post-baccalaureate degree in prison (Ross et al., 2015a).

Inside-Out Prison Exchange Program

Piloted in 1997 by Lori Pompa, a licensed social worker and current instructor in the Department of Criminal Justice at Temple University, and with the support of the Philadelphia Prison System and Temple University, the Inside-Out Prison Exchange Program: Exploring Issues of Crime and Justice Behind the Walls enables college students pursuing bachelor degrees in Criminology and Criminal Justice to take university-level classes in prison alongside inmates. The program boasts cumulative statistics that include over 300 college students and 400 inmates. In 2002, Pompa received a year-long Soros Justice Senior Fellowship to expand Inside-Out nationwide. In 2004, she stated: "After relatively limited outreach, 75 instructors have expressed interest in being trained in this approach. The first Training Institute, scheduled for mid-July 2004, was attended by 20–25 instructors from a dozen different states" (www.temple.edu/inside-out/). Since then, "there have been 130 instructors from 82 colleges/universities in 32 states" who have taken the course.[5] In 2006, Inside-Out "became an established program in the College of Liberal Arts at Temple University" (www.temple.edu/inside-out/).

The program incorporates the pedagogy of community-based service learning (i.e., a kind of pedagogy that combines classroom teaching with performing some sort of valuable service). According to Pompa:

> This unique educational experience provides dimensions of learning that are difficult to achieve in a traditional classroom. At its most basic level, Inside-Out allows the "outside" students to take the theory they have learned and apply it in a real-world setting, while those living behind the walls are able to place their life experiences in a larger academic framework.[6]

According to the organization's website:

> The core of the Inside-Out Program is a semester-long academic course, meeting once a week, through which 15 to 18 "outside" (i.e.: undergraduate) students and the same number of "inside" (i.e.: incarcerated) students attend class together inside prison. All participants read a variety of texts and write several papers; during class sessions, students discuss issues in small and large groups. In the final month of the class, students work together on a class project. (http://www.insideoutcenter.org/about-us.html)[7]

All program participants are assigned a variety of Criminal Justice texts and write several papers; during class sessions, students discuss issues in small and large groups; and, in the final month of the class, students work together on a class project. Crucial to the Inside-Out pedagogy is the powerful exchange that occurs between "inside" and "outside" students. It is the reciprocity and authenticity of this exchange that makes Inside-Out unique. Like many similar programs, no comprehensive external process or impact evaluations have been conducted of Inside-Out.

The Inviting Convicts to College Program

In 2004, shortly after the publication of *Convict Criminology* (Ross & Richards, 2003), University of Wisconsin–Oshkosh, Criminal Justice professors Susan Reed, Chris Rose, and Stephen C. Richards coordinated the first "Inviting Convicts to College" program in two state prisons (Rose et al., 2010; Richards et al., 2006). On a weekly basis, pairs of undergraduate or graduate student teachers visited selected medium- and maximum-security prisons and taught classes about crime, criminals, and prisons. The university students learned to teach by developing course syllabi, giving lectures, administering examinations, grading their own class of prisoner-students, and receiving internship credits in return. The convicts got a free education relevant to not only their backgrounds, but also possible future careers.

The curriculum was composed of three free noncredit college courses that use *Convict Criminology* (Ross & Richards, 2003) as a textbook in the first two courses. The organizers hoped that this book would inspire the inmate-students to plan on attending colleges and universities upon completion of their prison sentences. Prisoner-students discuss the readings and write papers. The third course, "College Preparation and Enrollment," was devoted entirely to teaching prisoners how to transition from prison to college, including completing college admissions and financial aid forms.

Upon finishing the three courses, the prisoner-students received a certificate of completion from the university. Students would show the letters notifying them of their acceptance to college to their fellow convicts, and this, in turn, inspired more prisoners to take the course. Some convicts' "release plans" included attending college or university, where their financial aid checks were waiting.

The Inviting Convicts to College Program subsumed a number of innovative ideas. The classes were free because undergraduate or graduate students taught them. University departments that include student internship programs may find this model an attractive option for placing students as classroom instructors in prisons. Deploying students in this fashion means that universities do not incur the expense of reassigning faculty to teach these classes. The use of student interns as instructors is the key to keeping university and departmental costs to a minimum. The faculty members, in turn, supervise a number of internships, including multiple placements of student interns in different prisons. This model is relatively easy to implement, thus making it easily employed at no expense in many correctional facilities across the country.

As of July 2007, the program had deployed 13 student teachers to work with 120 convict students.[8] The program first ran in the 2003–2004 academic year (both semesters at Racine Correctional). Beginning in 2004, another program started at Oshkosh Correctional, and operated every semester until the fall of 2015, when the program came to an end. The administrators of the program stated that they were unable to find any qualified and willing students to teach in the program. Additionally, Oshkosh Correctional had recently hired a new Educational Director who has just started working. Nevertheless, the administrators at Oshkosh Correctional have expressed how much they liked the program and their desire to see it continue running.[9]

Another interesting program bears mentioning. In the early 2010s Iowa State University (ISU) professors James Burnett and D.J. Williams introduced a for-credit university-level Sociology class, based on CC principles, in the Iowa Youth Detention system. Burnett and Williams (2012) brought university students into the Bannock County facility to assist detainees complete the class, and offer a mechanism for university-level students to mentor them in their studies. The youth would get college credit for successfully passing the class, and it would provide a pathway for them to enter into ISU. The student mentors had three basic responsibilities: "a) Teach youth appropriate information and skills; b) foster pro-social and health enhancing values and beliefs, and c) create environmental supports to reinforce the real-world application of skills" (Burnett & Williams, 2012: 53).

Although a formal evaluation of the program was not publicly available, Burnett and Williams documented positive responses from "Bannock County judges and corrections officials, as well as BCYDC administrators and staff" (2012: 54), Bannock County Youth Detention Center youth and ISU student-mentors. This perception was buttressed with appropriate anecdotes supporting this general overall initiative.

Although educational initiatives, where college and university instructors taught in correctional facilities, received increased resources during the Clinton and Obama administrations., it was challenging to maintain these programs during the Bush and Trump political eras. Many constituencies hope that these programs will receive additional funding during the Biden presidency.

Teaching convicts behind bars in the United Kingdom

In the United Kingdom, it has long been understood that prisoners and society can benefit from the provision of formal education while they are locked up (Coates, 2016; Darke & Aresti, 2018; Gauke, 2018).[10] This is supported by an increasing body of important scholarship (e.g., Forster, 1996), governmental reports (e.g., Coates, 2016), and a considerable amount of this research that has appeared in special issues of the *Prison Service Journal*.

Flynn and Higdon (2022), basing their argument on data advanced by McFarlane (2019) state, for example, that "[t]here are approximately 2,000 UK prisoners enrolled in higher education (around 2.5%) – most of them in part-time, distance-learning degree courses – although the demand for distance-learning in prison is estimated to be some 30% higher" (p. 200). The authors, referring to the Coates report (2016: iii) suggest that "one fifth of prisoners would prefer to be studying at a higher level," and there are several barriers beyond the inmates' capabilities that prevent them from doing so, including the fact that "further and higher education courses are not government-funded. The cost of undertaking higher education has to be paid for by incarcerees themselves," and "inmates are prevented from studying at higher levels until they are within six years of release" (Flynn & Higdon, 2022: 200). This means that years in which they could have been studying are wasted. Flynn and Higdon also single out the less-than-ideal distance education model of university education that dominates the mode of delivery in His Majesty's Prison Service (HMPS). They emphasize that distance learning is less than ideal for inmates who have never had this kind of pedagogy and would benefit more from face-to-face instruction.

Since there is minimal government financial support, prisoner education is hosted by a number of entities including the charity, and principal funder, the Prisoners' Education Trust (PET).[11] As of 2014, "PET has given over 32,000 packages of support (currently over 2,000 a year) to prisoners who apply to study while in prison" (Clark, 2016: 3). PET's funding is not restricted to university education. According to Rod Clark, the Chief Executive:

> PET awards help with a very wide range of distance learning courses, from relatively low level NVQs or non-accredited learning to embarking on degree level study with the Open University. Courses range from those pursued purely for personal interest to academic courses or some aimed very closely at acquiring skills and knowledge for a particular vocational route. PET also funds applications for arts and hobby. (Clark, 2016: 5)

"PET has brought together a group of organizations from across the sector to form the Prisoner Learning Alliance to bring prison education issues to the attention of policy makers. PET has also actively engaged to promote, develop and disseminate research evidence on prison education" (Clark, 2016: 3; see Exhibit Box 4.1).

Exhibit Box 4.1: Prisoners' Education Trust

The PET is a nonprofit organization that helps to improve the lives of UK prisoners through education. Since its inception in 1989, believing in the power of learning to break the cycle of reoffending and facilitate successful reintegration into society, PET has been committed to providing educational opportunities to incarcerated individuals. Operating across various prisons in the UK, PET offers vocational courses, distance learning, and tutoring initiatives. By enabling prisoners to gain essential skills and knowledge, PET aims to reduce recidivism rates and enhance the prospects of ex-offenders upon release. The Trust collaborates with universities, volunteers, and funders to expand its reach and impact. The PET has not only helped improve access to education within the prison system, but also fostered a sense of hope, self-worth, and personal development among inmates. By investing in education, PET contributes significantly to creating a safer, more inclusive society for all.

What follows is a review of some of the more prominent educational initiatives that have been provided to inmates incarcerated in HMPS.[12]

Open University program

Headquartered in Milton Keynes, one of the leading educational programs that enables UK prisoners receive university instruction and earn their bachelor's degree is through the Open University (which specializes in distance education) (Weinbren, 2014). According to McFarlane and Pike:

> In 1974 HMP Wakefield celebrated the first OU prison graduate and since then thousands of students have gained a degree while in prison, with thousands more gaining certificates and diplomas or simply beginning their learning journeys. There are currently almost 1800 OU students in prisons and secure hospitals across the UK, with degree pathways in all Faculties. (McFarlane & Pike, 2020: 11)

Earle and Mehigan note that:

> While the technology and course or module titles have changed over the years, the basic principles of OU [Open University] teaching have

> remained reasonably consistent. Central academics and a wider team of advisers and external contributors design the teaching and learning materials for a module. Once they have been produced, in all their diverse and changing forms of media, they are presented to students by associate lecturers ... who support regionally based tutor groups. Students in secure environments, such as prisons, cannot participate in these groups and are allotted a dedicated tutor to support their learning. (Earle & Mehigan, 2020: 7)

How are these classes delivered?

> Tutors allocated to support a student in prison will have different levels of access to their students, depending on the distance of the tutor from the prison, the teaching requirements of the module or course, and other aspects of the learning design developed by the team. Each prison's capacity and willingness to facilitate such access is a further factor influencing the student's learning journey. (Earle & Mehigan, 2020: 7–8)

Predictably it is challenging to provide incarcerated students with "a consistent experience [which] is difficult for all forms of distance education, but it is even more complicated for prison students, given their unusual status as both student and prisoner, living for the future and suffering for their past" (Earle & Mehigan, 2020: 8).

It is important to acknowledge that some correctional institutions, administrators, and staff are more accommodating than others for university education, whether that is face-to-face, online, or correspondence-based instruction (Earle & Mehigan, 2020: 9; Irwin, 2020).

According to Aresti, Darke, Bint Faisel and Ellis, with respect to the Open University, "currently only students taking an access module are allocated a personal tutor. Further, the role of Open University regional learning support teams is restricted to advising on study choices, careers options, fees and funding" (Aresti et al., 2020: 478). One must also keep in mind that not all inmates are eligible to enroll in Open University courses. One of the stipulations is that prisoners have to be doing a long sentence, one that is in excess of six years, to qualify for admission to Open University classes. Additionally, prisoners now have to apply for funding, which they did not previously have to do.[13]

Learning Together

Over the past decade, one of the most prominent prisoner education mechanisms was the Learning Together program, started in 2014 by Dr. Amy Ludlow and Dr. Ruth Armstrong at the Institute of Criminology, University of Cambridge (Armstrong & Ludlow, 2016). The initiative began as a small reading group within the prison system, with the aim of bringing together university students and prisoners to study alongside each other. Since its inception, the program has grown and evolved, expanding its reach and impact. It received widespread recognition for its innovative approach to education and its positive influence on the lives of both university students and incarcerated individuals. Learning Together was an umbrella program funded by the UK government and had both for credit and noncredit courses.

In November 2019, however, Usman Khan, who had served a sentence for terrorism-related crimes, was out on license (i.e., temporarily released from prison), and taking part in a Learning Together event at Fishmonger's Hall (London). Shortly after the event started, Khan stabbed five people, two of whom were connected to the program, resulting in their death.[14] Consequently, Cambridge University suspended, then terminated, the Learning Together program, and the Ministry of Justice suspended or significantly decreased university–prison partnerships.

Convict Criminology at Westminster University

Starting in the early 2010s, combining both pedagogy and service activities, professors Aresti and Darke have offered undergraduate-level classes in Criminology and CC both at Westminster University and at HM Prison Pentonville (in the London borough of Islington). Since 2013, their program, now called "Convict Criminology at Westminster," has provided "an academic mentoring scheme for prisoners studying degrees in criminology and cognate disciplines such as psychology, politics and law … and, more recently, partnerships between Westminster and three prisons (HMP Pentonville; HMP Grendon; HMP Coldingley)." This agreement involves Aresti and Darke "taking small groups of University of Westminster students once a week to the prison library (Pentonville), education centre (Coldingley) or onto a prison wing (Grendon) to study critical and convict criminology courses with inmates" (Darke et al., 2020).[15]

Recent challenges

Lastly, although a significant amount of university-level courses offered in prison in the UK are through the Open University program, some instructors through their universities are also teaching in correctional facilities on an ad-hoc basis. Without question, however, as with all prison systems throughout the world, the provision of many educational services in UK prisons was interrupted because of COVID-19 (Bradley & Davies, 2021). Although the formal partnerships between the HMPS and universities administered for credit classes have been temporarily suspended, the ad-hoc ones are not. This has occurred because both the HMPS and universities are risk-averse. Moreover, the inclusion of CC content in course materials is at the discretion of individual instructors.

On top of it all, the provision of instruction, whether it is of a vocational nature or more liberal arts oriented, is operating during a time when the government is cutting back on funding not just for correctional programs, but on education too.[16]

Teaching convicts behind bars in Italy

Italian prisons present an interesting case study of the introduction of university teaching in prisons. Like most correctional systems throughout the world, there is considerable diversity in "their styles of administration and prison practices" (Vianello, 2021: 101). Italy has about 189 prisons, 60,000 inmates, 32,000 prison staff, and under 1,000 educators (Vianello, 2021: 101). Like most prison systems, the majority of individuals behind bars are men (approximately 95 percent) and there are different types of correctional systems, holding individuals awaiting trial or short sentences (i.e., *instituto circondariale*), and those incarcerating people for three or more years (*casa di reclusione*). These factors, among others, affect prison conditions, including the ability to offer education to inmates (Vianello, 2021: 101).

Why is higher education needed in Italian correctional facilities? A large number of prisoners come from lower socioeconomic status backgrounds, where they may not have had the opportunity or ability to complete a formal education (Vianello, 2021: 106).

Nevertheless, as Vianello notes:

> from a legislative standpoint, formal education has to be provided in prison as an integral part of the custodial treatment. Before the reform of 1975, when the prison population still suffered from high rates of analphabetism, education was even envisaged as compulsory, together with work and attendance at religious ceremonies. Since then, society's idea of schooling has changed and it is now seen everywhere as an opportunity for personal emancipation that cognitively and critically empowers the individual. (Vianello, 2021: 102–103)

As of 2019, approximately one-third of Italian inmates (i.e., 20,357) were "receiving formal education, especially reading and writing classes" while locked up in Italian correctional facilities. And "[p]risons now benefit from a whole array of agreements and conventions with local school authorities, and full-blown branches of the local schools are established inside a fair number of them" (Vianello, 2021: 106).

In order to assist in the provision of post-secondary education to prisoners in Italy:

> Dedicated prison sections usually have larger prison cells, more spaces available for studying and socializing, and more flexible hours

for personnel, such as lecturers, tutors and volunteers, coming from outside. The prison staff responsible for surveillance may be assigned exclusively to such dedicated sections, and consequently have a better relationship with the prisoners. Opportunities for contact with the outside world may be facilitated too, possibly through a limited use of IT communication tools such as the internet and Skype. (Vianello, 2021: 103)

Up until 2014, a broad-based "system of volunteers" assisted "students behind bars access to university studies. As part of their numerous other support and cultural activities, they helped individual students with the paperwork needed to enroll at a university, and they kept in touch with single lecturers" (Vianello, 2021: 106).

But in 2014, under the direction of the Ministry of Justice, a system of Prison University Programs (PUPs) was established (e.g., Borghini, 2018; Prina, 2018).

> Most of the PUPs developed from the efforts of voluntary workers in negotiations between lecturers (often retired professors and volunteers themselves) and single prison administrations as regards dedicated study spaces and permission for books and lecturers to be brought in. ... Over time, this gave rise to very different solutions around the country, characterized not only by a useful flexibility of practices, but also by a strong degree of precariousness. Like any other activity proposed by voluntary organizations operating inside prisons, the real feasibility of university studies while incarcerated could be heavily influenced by: the quality of the relationship between the prison management and other operators; the actual availability of single volunteers to serve as mediators between the prison administration and the university lecturers; and the availability of funds for tuition fees and reading material. (Vianello, 2021: 106)

The PUPs have been one of the most significant developments in the provision of post-secondary education in Italian prisons to date. These were developed through an agreement among "Italian universities, the Department of Prison Administration (DAP), and the Regional Prison Administration Agencies (PRAP)" (Chiola, 2021: 1).

The first one started in 1998,

> in Turin and from that date until today, 92 Prison Institutes have been set up, involving 30 Universities, 177 Departments and 269 Degree Courses for a total of 926 (897 men, 29 women) students enrolled in the academic year 2019/20. The percentage of prison university students enrolled in prisons, out of the total prison population, is about 1%. Among them, there are prisoners in external criminal execution

who have undertaken their studies in prison and who continue them when they obtain benefits, but also prisoners who are serving their sentences under special, more restrictive regimes, such as high security and 41-bis. (Chiola, 2021: 1)

Vianello adds that "[t]he recent development of a network of PUPs now provides opportunities for approximately 800 prisoners to continue their further education" (Vianello, 2021: 103).
Vianello argues that

> the gradual institutionalization of the PUPs, their acknowledgement by the central prison administration and regional education departments, and the organization of a national conference (CNUPP) which prompted efforts to develop guidelines for homogenizing these practices (see Prina, 2018), have all helped in recent years to limit the discretion of the social actors and the consequently precarious nature of these university teaching experiences. In this new scenario, the university in prison project is promoting a very different approach from those traditionally typical of prison life. (Vianello, 2021: 106)

More recently, universities are taking a more proactive role in the provision of university courses in Italian prisons, seeing education as a necessity and working to counteract education as a selective benefit for some inmates. In 2018, the National Conference of Rectors' Delegates for Prison Universities (CNUPP) was established by the Conferenza dei Rettori delle Università Italiane (a group of Italian public and private universities). This body is designed to "facilitate coordination between universities that are involved in prisons" (Chiola, 2021: 5).

That being said, there are numerous challenges with PUPs. This includes the fact that a very small percentage of the budget allocated to correctional facilities is spent on education. According to Chiola, based on 2019 funding, "funds allocated to education, recreation, and kindergartens for the children of inmates were only 2.2% of the Department of Prison Administration's budget" (2021: 4). He, among others,[17] makes a number of suggestions including, but not limited to, the "concentrat[ion] of PUPs in a few prisons larger and closer to distinguished universities for size and resources, which through agreements with other prisons adjacent to them, would solve the problem of tax relief and lead to substantial savings" (Chiola, 2021: 4). He also recommends "identify[ing] best practices that are homogeneous throughout the national territory, rather than favouring a differentiated governance that facilitates the different background and historical path of the universities participating in the PUPs' project" (2021: 4). Additionally,

> [t]he CNUPP must represent in a unified way the requests arising from the university system and the centralized and local prison administration. Since there are still many universities that have not

committed themselves to offering opportunities to students in prison, the objective is to establish at least one PUP for each Region. (Chiola, 2021: 5)

Regrettably educational services delivered to Italian prisoners are uneven. "Instead, empirical studies have shown that they are the exception, not the rule, and they are generally perceived by all the actors in the prison world as a *reward* – a destination that is seen as a better prison within the prison." More specifically, "the number of places is limited, and the conditions for gaining access to them very often have much more to do with good conduct, the type of crime committed, and the duration of a sentence than with prisoners' inclination to study or their academic results" (Vianello, 2021: 103–104).

Conclusion

Higher education is an important rehabilitative mechanism for people who are incarcerated. Whether we are talking about the United States, United Kingdom, or Italy, the provision of formal post-secondary courses and classes in correctional institutions and systems, however, is frequently not considered a high priority. Thus it is all the more challenging when the program of study offered to inmates is at the university level. Conversely there are a handful of proven ways that correctional workers and administrators, college instructors and administrators, and prison activists (including volunteers) can introduce and maintain university education to inmates. Hopefully the previously reviewed ideas have been helpful in understanding the provision of university-level education behind bars, particularly in the countries where CC has gained traction.

Finally, while mentoring and teaching currently and formerly incarcerated individuals is central to CC, for reasons previously explained, not all men and women involved in CC teach inside prisons, nor formally or informally mentor individuals who are incarcerated or released from correctional custody.

5

Mentoring Convicts and Formerly Incarcerated Students

Introduction

Although many individuals and organizations are willing and capable of mentoring incarcerated and formerly incarcerated (FI) people, considerable confusion exists regarding what mentoring entails, the aims and tasks of mentoring, and the situations where it is appropriate. This chapter[1] explores several aspects regarding mentoring in general, mentoring FI people enrolled in university education, and how mentoring has evolved in the Convict Criminology (CC) approach, including:

- What is mentoring?
- Why are some individuals are not amenable to being mentored?
- Scholarship on mentoring convicts and formerly incarcerated people.
- Pathways to mentoring in CC.
- What duties are beyond the scope of mentoring incarcerated and formerly incarcerated people?
- What obligations are suitably performed by academic mentors of incarcerated or FI individuals?
- How ex-convicts can best search for an appropriate graduate mentor.
- Helping formerly incarcerated individuals get accepted into respectable graduate programs in Criminology/Criminal Justice.
- Challenges with CC mentoring.
- How to best address the challenges of CC graduate school mentoring.
- Other problems with mentorship.

To begin with, not all mentoring is equal. There are better and worse kinds of mentoring (i.e., not all help is helpful). And providing occasional assistance to individuals (whether they are incarcerated, FI, or not) is not in and of itself mentoring. For example, writing letters of recommendation, agreeing to chair or be on master's or doctoral dissertation, etc. is not a proxy for academic mentoring. Also, the type and quality of mentoring often depends on the makeup of both the mentor and the mentee. Finally, while mentoring exists in both correctional and academic settings, it is not a main goal of either of these contexts. These issues have numerous implications.

Additionally, although the CC approach was initially designed to assist incarcerated and FI people in graduate schools, including those who had completed these academic programs, over time many of the individuals who are affiliated with the CC approach also mentor individuals who are completing their bachelor's and master's degrees too. That being said, at least in the United States, as with the general population, there are more incarcerated students attempting to complete a bachelor's degree than there are ones who are working on their master's or doctorates. Also, many of the people who are either behind bars or released from correctional facilities who want to pursue a university education do not want a degree in Criminology/Criminal Justice. Moreover, it is not CC's job to convince them otherwise.

What is mentoring?

Introduction

To start with, it is crucial to realize that there are subtle differences among coaching, counseling, facilitating, helping, training, and mentoring. In essence, mentoring is a reciprocal and voluntary professional relationship between one or more interested people (Aitken, 2014) where one of the individuals has some sort of valued knowledge or expertise/skills and attempts to direct, guide, or influence the less experienced person by providing advice, assistance, or help. And, just because a student, junior worker, or colleague seeks their advice, or FI individuals freely gives some, it does not automatically mean that FI individuals have a mentoring relationship with them. Clearly these kinds of interactions are relatively complicated and develop over time. Also, mentoring is not friendship. Although a mentor and mentee may have a friendly relationship, friendship and mentorship differ significantly on the purpose and focus; expertise and guidance; formality and structure; duration and intensity; and power dynamic of the relationship.

How does mentoring take place?

Although sharing some aspects with parenting, academic advising, and teaching, mentoring is slightly different. While parenting and teaching, for example, may include instruction and the acquisition of important information and the mastery of skills, the knowledge imparted will usually also incorporate subtle negotiations of boundaries. It is through the process of interaction that important knowledge gets transmitted, and skills both academic and nonacademic get transferred.

Where does mentoring take place?

Mentoring occurs in many settings, including the workplace, the military, and various educational environments. Mentoring is most relevant to CC when incarcerated and formerly incarcerated individuals seek assistance in improving their educational and academic opportunities, both when locked up and upon release. Mentoring may take place in an informal manner, or a more formal manner consistent with current efforts (2022–2023) of selected American Society of Criminology's Division of Convict Criminology (DCC) members that are pairing senior DCC scholars with aspiring CC scholars and monitoring their progress on a regular basis.[2]

Why is mentoring important?

Although people may learn on their own through books, videos, and trial and error experiences, having the input of a qualified and skilled mentor improves the ability of individuals to do better in their pursuits. As Walker notes:

> Mentoring may be the most important thing we do as faculty mentors. Very few of us will have research or publications that last decades. But many of us can have students or younger faculty members who go on to make a tremendous contribution to the discipline and the world. And mentors are "force multipliers" because they can mentor many others throughout a career. (Walker, 2020: 28)

Furthermore,

> [w]ithout quality mentors, many students may not have positive experiences or may even drop out. Mentoring can be as simple as quality constructive feedback on an assignment to an extended collaboration with an advanced doctoral student. While specific tasks may vary depending on the level, there are some things that are consistent for all students. ... Probably the most important element of being a good mentor is listening to the student. (Moak & Walker, 2014: 427)

Why some individuals are not amenable to being mentored

As harsh as it may sound, and the possibility that it may disturb or anger progressives, liberals, and activists, some people, regardless of how capable, friendly, needy, or smart they are or appear to be, whether they are incarcerated or FI, and the context in which they live or work, are not just difficult to mentor, but repeatedly ignore the advice of the individuals who have agreed to mentor them, or fail to implement their good counsel.[3]

At the same time, it is unrealistic to believe, think, or require students, workers, or other people with whom mentors have a mentoring relationship to follow all the "pearls of wisdom" that mentors freely bestow on them. But some mentees, for one reason or another, may discount or ignore almost all of what mentors have to say.

Not all work, career, or relationship advice potential or actual mentors may offer is helpful. And an astute mentee should judge the quality and source (i.e., expertise) of the advice and its potential ramifications. Plus the mentee may choose not to implement their advice now, but do it later on.

Actual or potential mentors, on the other hand, sometimes ignore a mentee's stories about their dissatisfaction with the mentors they left (or left them), their constant search for new advisors, and the appearance that they don't listen to or consider expert advice, draw most of their lessons from their own lived experience, think and act as if "they know it all," or "know better," and maybe even with a touch of grandiosity thrown in for good measure.

When this occurs the potential or actual mentor should realize that no matter how determined they are to make a positive impact in the career, life, and work of the mentee, how good or well packaged the advice that they give this individual is, nor how often it is transmitted, it will not make a difference.

In sum, one of the important issues tied to mentorship is receptivity. Some individuals don't really make good mentees. They do not listen, insist on doing things their own way, and unnecessarily sabotage their attempts to achieve their academic, career, or professional goals, however modest they may appear to be. Conflating the mentor–mentee relationship can lead to unnecessary abuse, confusion, and exploitation, all situations which are best to be avoided. On the other hand, there are lots of people who need and want talented mentors and they might actually benefit from an experienced and caring professor's advice, expertise, and skills.

Pathways to mentoring in Convict Criminology

There are several ways that instructors, professors, correctional workers, and graduate students become involved in the mentoring process and provide mentorship for convicts and ex-convicts wanting assistance from people in the CC network (e.g., Darke et al., 2018). And there is no shortage of individuals both part of and connected to CC who are willing to assist those in need. But how does the process typically work?

Usually someone who is incarcerated reaches out to one or more of the individuals who have authored articles, chapters, or books on CC. Alternatively, if a CC member has appeared on a podcast or a news segment, or has been quoted by the news media, then there is a higher likelihood of them being contacted. Sometimes friends and/or relatives of individuals behind bars (or recently released) may reach out to one or more members of the CC network as well. Alternatively, chairs and deans may receive letters from men and women while incarcerated, and they may pass this information on to individuals affiliated with the CC approach. Sometimes colleagues at other universities reach out to CC members to ask for assistance with one or more of their students who has a prior conviction or is incarcerated. These outside professors contact CC members via snail or electronic mail and sometimes through an intermediary, and occasionally at public forums like academic conferences, to inform us that they heard about CC in one shape or form.

Depending on the specifics, the CC member usually writes back and attempts to establish a dialogue and rapport. Over one or more interactions or conversations, CC members usually try to determine these potential mentee's educational levels, their aptitude for learning, and when and if they will be released. Most of all, individuals who are part of the CC network try to discuss the potential mentee's options.

Alternatively, someone who is FI, or justice-contacted, involved, or impacted, may show up at a conference, attend one or more CC panels, and engage with us before, during or after a session. Sometimes these are graduate students, soon-to-become graduate students, instructors, or professors. They may ask a question or offer their opinion at some point in time which opens the door for future exploration.

For example, a couple of years ago, I received an email from an individual who had heard me speak some time back at a federal penitentiary, and had since been released. This person wished to pursue his studies further and complete a bachelor's degree. He wanted to know if I knew of any financial aid opportunities. Shortly thereafter I had a colleague who told me that he was developing a university-level course for ex-convicts and wanted to know if I knew anyone who might be interested, so I provided the introduction between them. Students like these are often very smart and motivated (Mohammed, 2023), but they frequently need specialized mentoring that the instructors at their host institutions cannot adequately offer, but in this case it appears that a great match was made.

What duties are beyond the scope of mentoring incarcerated and formerly incarcerated individuals?

Both incarcerated and FI people have many needs, and there is no shortage of well-intentioned individuals (both academic and nonacademics) who would like to help. But sometimes the assistance become problematic. Quite often inmates, FI individuals, academic mentors, and casual observers do not understand or fail to respect the concept and practice of boundaries. In particular, several students, instructors, and outside observers are unsure about the sorts of assistance academic mentors can or should provide.

The kinds of things that a potential mentor may be asked to offer to FI people include, but are not limited to:

- assisting people to post bail if they are arrested or rearrested;
- acting as a dog or cat sitter (or walker), or providing childcare;

- acting as a drinking or drug-using partner, drug or alcohol counselor, friend, landlord, romantic or sexual partner, or lay therapist;
- sharing a room at a conference;
- loaning money, paying fines, medical bills, child support, application fees, tuition, books, rent, food, etc.;
- assisting with family-related issues (e.g., disputes, finances, etc.); and,
- within reason, writing letters on their behalf to judges, parole boards, parole officers, and lawyers in connection with their criminal charge/s or case.

In principle, although providing these kinds of things may be appropriate for a loved one or a friend, they are not really acceptable in a mentor–mentee relationship. It is essential for mentors to set professional boundaries with respect to what they will and will not do. This is often conveyed through a series of communications and interactions that develop over time.

What duties are appropriately performed by academic mentors of incarcerated or formerly incarcerated individuals?

Conversely there are numerous things that academic mentors can and should provide to convicts or FI individuals whom they have decided to assist. Ideally, this individual is an instructor or a professor in the department and university in which the FI person will enroll, or has enrolled, to pursue their graduate school studies, and this particular situation will form the basis of the balance of this discussion.

In order to minimize potential confusion, mentors should perform the following tasks including, but not limited to:

- recommending scholarly material to read;
- within reason, sending reading items to individuals who are behind bars;
- helping them with the selection of a promising topic to research, identifying important scholarly questions to investigate, research, etc.;
- helping students to clarify both term paper and dissertation questions and topics;
- providing feedback on writing and revising scholarly papers;
- advising them about which university-level courses they think will best suit their mentees;
- writing letters of recommendation in support of their applications to grants, fellowships, graduate programs, and jobs;
- co-authoring scholarly papers with graduate students;
- assisting graduate students in choosing non-required classes;
- assisting students choose suitable people to be on their dissertation committee and negotiating the informal dynamics of committee processes;
- assisting them in securing funding (including identifying appropriate funding sources and assisting with the application process);

- helping them navigate the Institutional Review Board process;
- co-presenting papers at scholarly conferences;
- guiding them through the publishing process;
- helping graduate students find gainful employment in academia and sometimes outside of the field;
- improving presentation skills;
- advising them on future job opportunities (including appearance-related items) (Alarid, 2016);
- assisting them in negotiating relationships with other students, professors, staff, and university administration at the institutions where they attend classes, consider attending, and/or may choose to work; and
- helping them adjust to working with academic departments, etc. (e.g., Ross et al., 2011a; Tietjen & Kavish, 2021; Tietjen et al., 2021).

Keep in mind that some mentors are better than others. Instructors, professors, and scholars are not taught how to mentor, so they often learn how to do this via experience or talking to other instructors. Several have unrealistic expectations related to their role or that of the mentee, or they are missing in action at critical times. They lack experience in how to be effective, but over time, they may improve at performing the tasks of being an academic mentor.

Searching for a suitable graduate mentor

Several prospective or current graduate students know or learn that their careers as graduate students and life beyond as instructors or professors would benefit from the identification and assistance of one or more appropriate graduate school mentors. Often the search for an suitable graduate school mentor starts, and is easier, before these students enter a program of study. Sometimes this is a relatively easy process, but most of the time it is a labor-intensive and frustrating experience.

Some academics find prospective and enrolled graduate students, regardless of the stage of their academic careers, to be an unnecessary nuisance that just waste their time. Thus, a handful of professors do not answer emails or phone calls from prospective or actual graduate students, or do this in a timely and helpful manner.

If, on the other hand, FI people manage to make contact with a professor that works in a subject area that appeals to them, and a potential mentor who is interested in considering them as their mentee, the next step is to attempt to build a helpful relationship. It is often a complex interaction, where adept parties pay close attention to subtle cues concerning authenticity, depth of commitment, interest, etc. In order to demonstrate interest it is crucial for prospective mentees to read almost everything their potential mentors have written, in particular the more recent things, attend talks they give, ask for feedback on papers or paper talks, and then ask to work with them in some meaningful capacity on their research. One of the difficult choices for graduate students is should FI individuals pursue a mentor who is well respected in their field, but relatively unhelpful, or a scholar who FI people have a good bond with who may be more junior or not that knowledgeable about their specific subject area?

Alternatively, graduate programs may automatically assign students an advisor, with the hope that this relationship may evolve into a mentor–mentee relationship. Many times these arrangements are very fruitful. The advisor knows all (or most) of the department, graduate school, and university policies, and all or most of the important players and assists FI men and women to navigate the complex rules, regulations, and norms of the organization and the profession.

Conversely many of the advisor–graduate student relationships are like marriages of convenience. They may last one or two semesters, but it is clear that there is a mismatch between them, and both parties go their separate ways. Plus, over time, the graduate student is no longer a rookie, and they may have a better idea about their preferred subject area of focus, ideal methodology, and maybe even a specific subject for their thesis or dissertation. Thus an internal shopping trip begins with the student looking for an appropriate in-house professor in their department.

Here the size of department, in terms of number of faculty members, is an essential factor. In principle, the bigger the academic department, the greater the diversity of specialization, and the smaller the department, the lower the chance a graduate student is going to find somebody who shares the specific interests of the mentee. Predictably, just because FI people find a professor in their department who has the same interests, it does not mean that there will be the necessary chemistry for FI individuals to succeed.

Finally, some departments have graduate student mentoring programs that are reasonably well designed and implemented. The professors meet with the students on a regular basis (e.g., once a week) and socialize them into the norms of a graduate career and the academic profession. In this context, mentoring graduate students is a part of the professor's job and students shouldn't feel unnecessarily intimidated or nervous. Many graduate students, whether they are FI or not, however, feel awkward and insecure in these exchanges because they suffer from imposter syndrome. But if experienced mentors acknowledge how the students are just starting out, and try to reassure the student, this can work wonders (see Exhibit Box 5.1).

Helping formerly incarcerated people get accepted into respectable graduate programs in Criminology/Criminal Justice

Earning a bachelor's degree from a respected institution of higher education, regardless of incarceration status, is no small feat. This is especially true for individuals who are, for example, the first in their family to go to college, a single

Exhibit Box 5.1: Benefits of having formerly incarcerated students in university classrooms

If the class size and instructional modality permits, FI students can bring numerous immediate benefits to undergraduate and graduate courses. To begin, FI students, depending on how open they are about their prior conviction, their comfort level, and knowledge, and the knowledge, skills, experience/effectiveness of the instructor, may serve to question the veracity of the content that is delivered by traditional Criminology, Criminal Justice, and Corrections courses and materials. They may be able to confront not only popular conceptions of crime, criminals, and convicts, but some unrealistic academic scholarship too (e.g., Frana et al., 2012). Given correctional facilities' historic and instrumental utility to colonialism and racial capitalism, and the role of prisons, FI prisoners can help to decolonialize the curriculum and university. FI individuals may be in a perfect position to serve as a foil to dominant narratives about prisons, the prison experience, and what life is like on the outside (e.g., Halkovic & Greene, 2015; Binnall et al., 2021; Harm & Bell, 2021).

mother, a foster child, someone with low literacy skills, limited financial means, FI people, or those with one or more criminal convictions.

Even greater challenges develop when individuals with criminal records want to enter a graduate program to pursue a master's or a Ph.D. in Criminology or Criminal Justice (or a similar field) (Swanson et al., 2010). Graduate school can be a great experience for FI students. It may also be a pathway that opens up more doors in terms of jobs and a career. This will increase the possibility that the person can financially support themselves and their loved ones, refrain from criminal activity, and perhaps create opportunities to engage in prosocial change.

Most people in this position, however, are poorly equipped to make this kind of leap. Many of these FI individuals have unrealistic expectations about the experience, including the challenges and the benefits that may accrue to them once they earn an advanced degree, and they are often poorly prepared for what awaits them. The bureaucracy of a university may seem very foreign and insurmountable to them. They may also have more complicated lives than traditional graduate students, including having additional financial and emotional challenges, a partner, the need to financially support a family, children to raise, and additional demands of negotiating parole requirements.

Many members of the CC network, including those who are part of the American Society of Criminology's DCC, are frequently approached both by instructors who reach out to us on behalf of their FI students and by students themselves, requesting our assistance regarding getting into an appropriate graduate school and identifying whom among our colleagues might be good mentors. Our response is that individuals who are affiliated with the CC approach are here to help.

One of the first questions CC members ask FI students interested in pursuing graduate school is why they want to make this kind of investment of resources? Many people, regardless of their backgrounds, have unrealistic ideas about the costs and benefits of a graduate school education. Individuals who are part of the CC network also ask why they do not wish to return to the university where they had earned their undergraduate degree. For some, they want or need to spread their wings; the possibility also exists that the program from which they graduated/are graduating from may no longer serve them well, while others have alienated key people at their former home institutions.

In many respects, providing advice to FI students about how to prepare for a graduate program, which ones to choose from, and which professor/s to work with (and whom they might want to avoid) is no different than what individuals who are affiliated with the CC approach would advise our typical students at the places individuals who are part of the CC network teach. However, the path for FI students wishing to pursue a master's or a doctorate in Criminology/Criminal Justice is a little more complicated. FI students encounter more challenges, including selecting a graduate program that is ex-convict friendly and finding suitable mentors in that program. Mentors may need to check up on the mentees more often (or on a more regular basis) least they fall off the radar due to the various challenges they confront. This approach is often referred to as meeting the person where they are. Mentors are resources to assist graduate students navigate the rough waters. They may be called upon to provide emotional support (as in telling the mentee that what they are experiencing is typical, or that they are doing a good job). As previously mentioned, some mentors are better than others at accomplishing these sorts of tasks.

Another important consideration for prospective mentees involves the challenge of "coming out." One of the questions formerly incarcerated people inevitably ask is how open they should be about their criminal past, both in their letter of application and in conversations with a graduate director or committee. If so, when should they disclose this information, to whom should they reveal it, and how should they disclose it? Sometimes this decision is presented to them in the application process, if they are asked whether they have any prior criminal convictions.

Just because some colleges, universities, or university systems no longer require prospective students to check a box on an application form indicating that they were arrested for a crime, convicted of a crime, convicted of a felony, or FI (part of the Ban the Box movement) does not mean a particular university is a good place to start and complete a post-baccalaureate degree. Similarly, even though an academic department mentions on its website that it is inclusionary, promotes social justice, and has professors who specialize in areas of study that align with a student's major interests, it may not necessarily be a good place for a FI person to get a suitable graduate education (see Exhibit Box 5.2).

Exhibit Box 5.2: Ban the Box

Beginning in the 1990s, a number of FI individuals, concerned citizens, political activists, and organizations started campaigning to have employers remove questions from job applications that asked individuals if they had ever been arrested, charged, convicted of a crime, and/or incarcerated. The activists believed that this step in the application process prevented people who were re-entering society from getting stable and respectable employment. As a consequence of this pressure, numerous states passed legislation in support of Ban the Box initiatives and expanded the process beyond incarceration to initiatives that were designed to curtail the requirement that job applicants needed to self-disclose if they were ever (variously) arrested, charged, or convicted of a misdemeanor or felony. The Ban the Box initiative was expanded beyond being hired for a job, to applications to educational institutions as a student. Some critics of the initiatives argued that just because a Ban the Box effort was implemented in work and educational venues did not prevent individuals from being subjected to a criminal background check at a later stage in the employment hiring or acceptance to college or university process. In other words, there are other ways to control people who the institution does not want to have as a student.

Moreover, although it may be relatively easy to gain admission to a respectable university and graduate program, be relatively frictionless to receive instruction and access, and be affordable, the educational institution may not be ideal for FI individuals as a place to study and earn one's master's or doctoral degree.

There are countless other issues to be aware of. For example, some FI individuals apply to graduate school some years after they earned their bachelor's degree. Thus, they may not know any of the professors in the program from which they graduated. Alternatively, the instructors they once had contact with may have retired, passed away, or be unwilling to write one or more letters of recommendation. It may also be the case that the FI person did not make any meaningful connections with the professors in their former university. Thus, they may need to seek advice and letters of support from professors whom they may not have any experience with.

Alternatively, sometimes an FI's degree may not be in the fields of Criminology or Criminal Justice, since they might possess a professional degree (e.g., law). Thus, the academic subject areas of Criminology and Criminal Justice might seem attractive, but untested, for them. Therefore, they may be tentative about this approach and in this situation we recommend that they start with a master's degree only before they move on to a riskier choice of doing a doctorate.

Many people in the CC network know which universities, programs, and scholars are best suited for prospective FI graduate students. Not only do several individuals who are affiliated with the CC approach try to make suggestions, but individuals who are part of the CC network often reach out to individuals who are part of (or allied with) the CC network and sometimes make personal introductions.

The CC network and the DCC believe in the power of mentorship. Thus, many individuals who are affiliated with the CC approach help to put FI students in touch with supportive individuals in our network. Members of the CC network frequently and freely give their opinion(s) on respective programs, whom to work with, whom to avoid, and how to improve the students' chances of getting selected into a program, including whom to ask for letters of recommendation and what those types of communication should emphasize.

Challenges with Convict Criminology mentoring

There are numerous challenges that crop up when faculty mentor FI graduate students. These include, but are not limited to:

- Some FI individuals might be afraid to be "open" prior to being on the job market. Predictably some prospective and actual graduate students may dislike the risk of being labeled a "convict criminologist." This question was present in the creation of the official American Society of Criminology DCC (e.g., Ross & Tietjen, 2022).
- Alternatively, FI graduate students might have well-intentioned mentors in the departments in which they are enrolled, that urge them to shy away from adopting a CC approach.
- Due to one or more bad experiences with people affiliated with the CC approach, a lack of a pipeline like Project Rebound, or Inside-Out, or more likely a poor understanding of CC, many prospective and actual graduate students, and professors, may view CC unfavorably.
- There is potential value in scholars with criminal records using their FI experience as a status symbol when on the job market, but otherwise they may pay lip-service to the approach.
- The "White male" stigma of CC occasionally persists or is misunderstood, thus making some African-American or female graduate students, instructors, and professors hesitant to reach out to members of the CC network, or become more involved with them. Elements of this sentiment were evidenced over a handful of years when some people affiliated with the CC presented papers that effectively echoed Belknap (2015) without noting or understanding the real challenges and changes that had occurred in the organization of CC (see Exhibit Box 5.3).

How to best address the challenges of Convict Criminology graduate school mentoring?

In a best case scenario, prospective graduate students should begin searching for a mentor before they apply to a particular department/school and university. Sometimes this can be an intimidating, overwhelming, and thus frustrating experience.

Exhibit Box 5.3: Project Rebound

Along with the Rising Scholars and Underground Scholars programs, Project Rebound is designed to assist FI individuals complete a university education in the State of California. Rebound was started in 1967, by John Irwin, when he was a tenure-track assistant professor of Sociology at San Francisco State University. As of 2023 the program is now available at 14 out of 23 campuses of California State Universities (CSU). In order to manage the offerings, a CSU Project Rebound Consortium was established and is supported by state funding and private donations. According to Murillo (2021), students who graduate from CSU programs that are managed by Project Rebound have a 0 percent recidivism rate, and 87 percent of the students have full-time jobs or enter a graduate degree program after their bachelor's degree (Project Rebound, 2021).

In order to maximize prospective FI graduate students' chances of finding a suitable academic mentor, it's important to avoid showing up (or dropping in) at the prospective faculty member's office unannounced, knowing very little about the scholarship that they do, and proclaim that they are looking for a mentor, or even prematurely ask "Will you be my mentor?"

Instead, in order for prospective FI graduate students to search for a suitable match they need to do their due diligence. This includes:

- Speaking with current and former graduate students and asking them if they can recommend particular faculty members and which ones to avoid. (But, just like Yelp reviews, don't take other students' word as gospel about the reputation of a professor.)
- Reading as much as possible the scholarship produced by the prospective mentor, especially what they have done in recent years.
- Attending one or more academic meetings or conferences and observing their potential mentor in action.
- Determining if their potential mentor has other students.

If everything checks out, then it is time to get in touch via email, phone, and/or, if it makes sense, arrange a face-to-face meeting.

In the context of the conversation better determine:

- The types of research projects the professor is currently doing and hopes to do over the next five years.
- What kinds of mentorship they have done with their previous graduate students, including finding out where they are now. (Are they still in the program? Did they enter academia? Or are they in the private sector? And what institutions or organizations do they work at?).
- Would they mind if you reached out and spoke with them?

If FI people are lucky enough to find a good graduate school mentor there is a strong possibility that this relationship will extend past this stage of their career and they may become part of their academic network. This relationship can help both parties achieve their mutual goals in the profession. On the other hand, sometimes it is not possible to find a suitable mentor in their own department or university. This complicates things, but it is also a situation that, with some skill, can be navigated. Many of the strategies that were outlined here can also be applied to this slightly different challenge.

Other problems with mentorship

In a perfect world prospective and actual graduate students have done their due diligence, located an appropriate graduate mentor (been accepted into a respectable program where the mentor teaches), and, for the time being, their graduate school experience exceeds their expectations.

On the other hand, for one reason or another, after entering a graduate program, and getting the lay of the land, they discover, much to their chagrin, that it is incredibly difficult to find and retain a suitable mentor.

This could be the result of a number of factors. These include, but are not limited to:

- No one in the department is really interested in the subject that the FI person is interested in/passionate about.
- Over time prospective FI graduate students interests change and the question that they wanted to answer is not covered by anyone in their department.
- FI people have difficulties working with the person who is the recognized expert in their program.
- Or the FI persons is or may be perceived to be a difficult individual to work with, and all the professors seem to want to limit their interactions with that student.

Alternatively, FI students may find themselves in a situation where their mentor:

- Goes on sabbatical and becomes incommunicado potentially because of the nature of their research (e.g., studying remote villagers in the Kalahari Desert).
- They have health issues that force them to cut back on graduate student supervision responsibilities.
- They develop psychological issues (i.e., suffer a mental breakdown).
- They move to a different university, or the private sector, and are unwilling or unable to properly supervise the mentee.
- Or, in the worst case situation, they die.

Keep in mind that the situation of FI graduate students is not uncommon, and each of these scenarios presents different challenges and alternative implications for graduate students.

But sooner or later graduate students will probably start asking themselves a bunch of questions:

- Should I switch topics or take a break from graduate studies?
- Do I remain in this department?
- Can I switch to a different department at the same university?
- Should I quit my current university and go somewhere else to pursue my graduate studies?
- Do I abandon my graduate studies?

These questions are not easily answered. Some of these difficulties and the decision/s FI individuals ultimately make will be bounded by how advanced they are in their program and how much resources they have at their disposal. But before FI individuals talk to their departmental director of graduate studies, they might wish to reach out to their network within or beyond their academic department, whose good counsel they trust.

Conclusion

This chapter provided a brief introduction to the role of mentoring in the CC approach. It is important to acknowledge that potential mentors are not under any obligation to take FI individuals on as students, and thus FI people have to do a good job convincing them that they are the perfect student to devote resources to training. It is also necessary to realize that mentees, as much as mentors, need to share the responsibility of maintaining the relationship so that it is mutually beneficial to both parties. In short, graduate student mentees need to take an active role in their education, training, and career, and do this in a professional manner. The fact that graduate school mentors don't know all the intricate organizational policies and practices is not the standard by which to evaluate them. Follow-through, sound advice, good communication skills, and the identification or creation of opportunities, are the criteria with which to best judge them. Conversely prospective and actual graduate students need to learn how to best approach their role. In order to get a deeper sense of how this is done, the following two chapters examine the process of integrating convicts and ex-convicts into scholarly research and how ex-convicts are assisted in applying to graduate school, surviving those years, and subsequently seeking academic jobs.

6

How Has Convict Criminology Engaged in Mentoring? Collaboration with Convicts and Formerly Incarcerated People on Scholarly Research

Introduction

Periodically, criminologists (or similar social scientists), convicts, and formerly incarcerated individuals team up to produce scholarly work (e.g., Toch, 1967; Carceral, 2003; 2005). This chapter includes the various reasons why this occurs, the challenges that these people experience, and suggestions on how this kind of activity can be facilitated (e.g., Ross et al., 2015b).[1] In order to gain a more comprehensive understanding of this process, this chapter:

- examines how these relationships develop;
- reviews the challenges and opportunities related to the scholarly research being pursued by convicts and convict/scholar teams behind bars;
- specifies the means of overcoming these obstacles;
- argues why a team research approach to enable collaborations between convicts/ex-convicts and scholars is helpful; and
- reviews the emergence of the scholarly journal *Journal of Prisoners on Prison* (Gaucher, 1988).

For one reason or another, various educated and intelligent convicts are interested in publishing in peer-reviewed scholarly journals. Many of them may be overly ambitious and lack the necessary resources (including training, dedication, etc.) to be able to successfully achieve such a goal. But for others with the requisite knowledge, skills, motivation, and tenacity, the potential benefits may be great.

Therefore, it is crucial that their enthusiasm is encouraged and not dampened. Regardless, most incarcerated individuals trying to do serious academic work will face some important obstacles that they must carefully negotiate. Likewise, many scholars (particularly those in the academic fields of Criminology/Criminal Justice) are interested in not only conducting research in corrections-related settings, but also enlisting the assistance of capable men and women behind bars. This situation provides numerous challenges to both groups.

Literature review

Throughout history, convicts have written articles and books not only about the crimes they once committed, but about their experiences of incarceration (e.g., Franklin, 1982; 1988). This material may also include poetry (e.g., Huckelbury, 2008; 2012), jailhouse journalism (Morris, 1998), autobiographical treatments (e.g., Abbot, 1981), and scholarly work. Some of this writing has been reflexive in nature, and a smaller subset of this body of literature would nominally qualify as being autoethnographic. The quality and impact of this writing varies, with some pieces being outstanding, while others are of lower-quality writing, research, and analysis.

Convicts submit their work to a variety of outlets, either on their own, or with the assistance of outsiders such as relatives, friends, prison activists, instructors, or professors. Publications interested in this content may include prison magazines and newspapers (e.g., *The Angolite*), mainstream newspapers and magazines, blogs, etc. In fact, over the past few decades, a small cadre of convicts has managed to publish not just articles for popular consumption, but material mainly targeted to scholarly audiences.

For example, Victor Hassine, now deceased, published *Life Without Parole* (1996/2011) (currently in its fifth edition) while he was incarcerated. And PEN Award-winning convict author Jon Marc Taylor, also deceased, in addition to publishing many articles, penned *Prisoners' Guerrilla Handbook to Correspondence Programs in the United States and Canada* (2002). While incarcerated, K.C. Carceral published two well-cited books with scholarly presses (2003, 2005), and upon release, one co-authored book, published with a university press, *The Cage of Days: Time and Temporal Experience in Prison* (Flaherty & Carceral, 2022). Nonetheless, this approach as solitary authors connected with the traditional publishing world is the exception rather than the rule (see Exhibit Boxes 6.1 and 6.2).

Others, such as Charles Lanier, who earned his Ph.D. after release and was one of the contributors to *Convict Criminology* (Ross & Richards, 2003), conducted research during the final months of his prison sentence. This work was later integrated into his scholarship. Alternatively, Richard McCleary, who also earned a doctorate, wrote *Dangerous Men* (1992 [1978]), a classic book on parole, after he was released from prison on parole. Some, like Seth Ferranti (2004) (a formerly incarcerated inmate and author of *Prison Stories*, who earned his

Exhibit Box 6.1: Victor Hassine

Victor Hassine (1955–2008) was born in Egypt and as a child immigrated with his parents to the United States. Shortly after earning a law degree, in 1981 he was convicted of murder and in 1983 sentenced "to life imprisonment for the murder … plus consecutive prison terms of ten to twenty years for the conspiracy conviction and two to five years for criminal attempt" (https://www.paed.uscourts.gov/documents/opinions/97D1201P.pdf, accessed October 12, 2023). Despite appealing his conviction, Hassine spent close to three decades behind bars in Pennsylvania prisons. In addition to submitting articles to external venues, while incarcerated, Hassine published *Life Without Parole: Living and Dying in Prison Today*, a book that is not only in its fifth edition, but is used in many relevant college and university courses. Over the time, that the book has been in print, it has had different foreword writers, including American University (Washington, DC) professor, Dr. Robert Johnson. In 2008, Hassine was found dead in his cell from an apparent hanging. Questions about the cause of his death exist. A memorial annual scholarship in Hassine's name was established at American University. The award "is given annually to one or more American University students or alumni who use creative work – literary and visual art, or some combination thereof – to educate the public on the pressing issues affecting the criminal justice system and the greater society" (https://www.american.edu/learning communities/honors/success/hassinescholarship2010.cfm, accessed October 12, 2023).

(Also consult case https://caselaw.findlaw.com/us-3rd-circuit/1021984.html and petition for habeus corpus https://www.paed.uscourts.gov/documents/opinions/97D1201P.pdf)

Exhibit Box 6.2: Jon Marc Taylor

At the age of 19, Jon Marc Taylor, Ph.D. (1959–2015) and his father were convicted of a brutal violent sexual assault and entered the Missouri Prison System. Over time, Taylor "earned his high school diploma, bachelor's of science and master's of arts through Ball State University, and finally his Doctorate in Public Administration from Kennedy Western University" (Zoukis, 2016). Throughout his two decades behind bars Taylor "published articles in over 50 different magazines, peer-reviewed journals, and newspapers, to include the *New York Times*, the *Journal of Correctional Education*, and the *Journal of Prisoners on Prisoners*" (Zoukis, 2016). One of his most well-known publications is the *Guerrilla Handbook to Correspondence Programs in the U.S. and Canada* (Taylor & Schwartzkopf, 2009), which was revised three times. Taylor's writing earned him "the prestigious Robert F. Kennedy Journalism Award for his writings on the need for Pell grants for prisoners" (Zoukis, 2016). In addition to focusing on prisoner education, Taylor was a tireless advocate for restoring Pell Grants for incarcerated people. Despite these accomplishments, and four attempts to gain parole, he failed to be released from prison. In February 2014 Taylor suffered a stroke, and eventually died of a second one in December 2015. His work has served as an inspiration to numerous convicts and ex-convicts.

master's while incarcerated, and owns and operates Gorilla Convict Publications), have transitioned into other forms of media.

Convict Criminology is at the forefront of encouraging convicts and ex-convicts, particularly those with Ph.Ds. or those about to complete a Ph.D., to conduct Corrections, Criminology, and Criminal Justice-relevant research. During the early days of Convict Criminology, these scholars envisioned a cadre of educated convicts at different stages of their sentences, conducting rigorous research behind bars. There was a general hope that more established formerly incarcerated scholars would mentor people behind bars, especially those who were about to be released, not to mention formerly incarcerated graduate students, to hone their scholarly abilities by assisting them to conduct academic research and prepare their writing for possible publication (Jones et al., 2009; Newbold et al., 2014). Despite this well-intentioned goal, a limited number of scholar–inmate research collaborations have occurred over the years (Newbold & Ross, 2012; Ross & Copes, 2022). It's unclear why there is a paucity of collaborative endeavors.

Challenges faced by investigators conducting research behind bars

Numerous scholars have reviewed the difficulty in obtaining access to correctional institutions as research settings (e.g., Marquart, 1986; Unnithan, 1986; Zwerman & Gardner, 1986; Farkas, 1992; Martin, 2000; Trulson et al., 2004; Wakai et al., 2009; Apa et al., 2012) and the challenges experienced in maintaining relationships with corrections staff and administrators and convicts (e.g., Patenaude, 2004). Some of this scholarship is presented in the form of rules or lessons learned (e.g.,Trulson et al., 2004; Fox et al., 2011). Other research has examined the complications related to applying specific research methods behind bars, especially participant observation (e.g., Jacobs, 1974; Marquart, 1986), interviewing (e.g., Schlosser, 2008), and ethnography (Jones, 1995; Liebling, 1999).

Although Jones (1995), who at the time was a short-timer convict (i.e., nearing the end of his prison sentence), was assisted by a professor on the outside who reviewed his research methods and co-authored several articles and a book with him upon release, only one set of scholars has explored specifically the pairing of a scholar with a convict in the production of academic research (Taylor & Tewksbury, 1995). These authors argued that this approach to scholarly research and writing had a number of advantages, including "providing a more balanced view of life; experience in the correctional milieu; allowing insights into previously restricted areas of the researcher's interests; uncovering more valid data: sidestepping procedural obstacles; overcoming … constraints of penological research" (Taylor & Tewksbury, 1995: 123). Taylor and Tewksbury also reviewed the drawbacks and logistical challenges to research conducted by a team of outside and inside researchers (1995: 127–129). Although unique and important in its contribution at the time, today the points made by these two scholars is somewhat outdated. Over the last three decades, not only have some aspects of correctional facilities and the incarceration experience changed, but their study was also published before the popularization of the Convict Criminology approach.

Finally, some may argue that individuals who are incarcerated or formerly incarcerated cannot conduct objective research, because of their bias, including the actual or potential cynicism they may have toward the corrections, criminal justice and legal systems (e.g., Mobley, 2003). This may be true, but this argument is akin to someone saying that women cannot be unbiased authors in the field of Feminist Studies, African-Americans cannot be objective in the subject areas of Race and Ethnic Studies, or former police officers cannot be objective when studying and teaching about law enforcement. Clearly being part of an entity (e.g., ethnicity, gender, organization, race, etc.) being studied does not inherently imply that bias is a natural and logical part of the approach to scholarship. Thus, the mere fact that someone has been incarcerated does not mean that a convict's views, experiences, and understandings are necessarily biased.

Why should educated convicts write for scholarly publications?

There are many reasons why convicts may choose to write for scholarly venues. First, an inmate may be considering pursuing a postgraduate degree (i.e., master's or Ph.D.). As with any prospective graduate student, having one or more sole or co-authored publications in peer-reviewed journals to one's credit should help such applicants gain entrance to respectable graduate programs. Additionally, earning a master's or professional degree (e.g., law) may enable a formerly incarcerated person to enter a teaching-related job in the field of academia once they are released from correctional custody. As most scholars know, publications are an essential currency on the job market (Applegate et al., 2009). Those lacking peer-reviewed articles typically find it much more difficult to secure academic positions. Hence, the challenges inherit to convicts' writing and publishing opportunities may (at least in part) explain the small number of such individuals being among university faculties. Needless to say, convicts who conduct academic research (whether by or among themselves or with the assistance of outside scholars) and who manage to get their work published accrue numerous benefits.

To begin with, these so-called convict scholars can provide an insider's perspective on "the pains of imprisonment" (Sykes, 1958). Rarely is the public given unfettered access to prison spaces, where most correctional activities take place. And even on the few occasions when access has been granted (to the news media, entertainment industry, or documentarians), or during educational tours, prison officials usually prevent visitors from seeing certain areas or speaking to a wide assortment of inmates (or they may place pressure on inmates to present the institution in the most favorable light possible) (Ross, 2008a: chapter 3;

Smith, 2013). Educated and published convicts, on the other hand, can expose the realities, including contradictions, inherent in the prison experience (Leyva & Bickel, 2010).

Additionally, convict scholars are in a unique position to advance practical solutions to some of the daily problems affecting corrections. Regardless, inmates are rarely consulted about how institutional rules and regulations do or will affect the prison population. New procedures are usually implemented from the top down, with little or no input from the convicts or line officers tasked with implementing and enforcing new policies and procedures. More often than not, this approach leads to many difficulties, which in turn breed a great deal of conflict between inmates and staff members. Through their scholarly writings, educated convicts can help to minimize these disruptions and provide workable solutions that promote not only the safety and orderly running of a correctional institution, but also the well-being of the inmate population (Richards & Ross, 2003a). Most contemporary theories of management (e.g., Total Quality Management) define as *best practices* the seeking of input from subordinates and consumers. Here, the eyes, ears, and educated understandings of convicts may offer opportunities for such input, but they are usually ignored or silenced.

Moreover, convict scholars are in an ideal position to expose the inconsistencies and injustices perpetuated by the criminal justice system. A good example of these harms is the legal havoc that United States Supreme Court cases such as Apprendi, Blakely, Booker, and Fanfan have wrecked on the federal courts system over the last 13 years (see, for example, Justice O'Conner's dissenting opinion in Blakely, 524 US at 324). These rulings not only effectively abolished the mandatory nature of the Federal Sentencing Guidelines, but they also eliminated the arbitrary manner in which prosecutors applied sentencing enhancements (Zaldivar, P., 2013).

Furthermore, by providing context, illustrations, and more nuanced understandings, convict scholars are in a unique position to counter the often misguided and ill-informed opinions of poorly informed ideologues, especially staunch conservatives, who for decades have created a potpourri of diverse ideas, often lacking empirical evidence, that have enabled policy makers to promote and/or pass an ever-increasing number of punitive laws (Clear, 1994: 86–88). Educated convicts can also help contextualize the writing of well-intentioned but misinformed liberal writers and activists. Here, again, insights and experiences with the "real" world of incarceration may assist in balancing overly ideological literature and scholarship on corrections.

Finally convict scholars can help dispel the negative perceptions and myths surrounding crime and corrections, many of which are exploited by the media and the entertainment industry (Ross, 2008a: 20–29; 2012c). The writings of educated convicts can provide an unadorned view of the men and women who are currently incarcerated in correctional institutions. If educated inmates were given more opportunities to disseminate their voices, especially through their writings, the public might discover that the image of the convict bogeyman (Irwin, 1985b;

2003) that has been sold to them is nothing more than a caricature of the people who are wasting away behind bars. While doing this kind of research and writing clearly presents benefits and epistemological advantages, it also produces numerous challenges. The following section reviews these difficulties.

Constraints to conducting scholarly research and publishing in scholarly venues while incarcerated

Numerous obstacles prevent outside and convict researchers from conducting scholarly research behind bars, and from writing up their findings and submitting them to peer-reviewed journals. These challenges are discussed in order from the least to the most perceived importance.

First of all, *many of the research methods available to investigators in the free world are not applicable behind bars*. Although most correctional systems do not explicitly forbid the conduct of research by inmates, other policies and practices (i.e., impediments) ensure that such work is rarely, if ever, completed. The Federal Bureau of Prisons, for example, does not have a specific policy that prohibits inmates from conducting research or writing for scholarly venues. However, the Federal Bureau of Prisons does have policies that ban convicts from circulating petitions and other "unauthorized" materials (PS 5270.08/336 Circulating A Petition). Similarly, there are policies that explicitly restrict communication with outside sources, such as the mass media and private organizations. Such policies result in limiting convicts' opportunities to expose staff corruption and/or human rights violations.[2] All in all, this means that conducting surveys is very difficult while incarcerated.

Second, if a convict researcher wants to conduct a survey that is going to survive external review and if he or she eventually wants the results to be published in a reputable, peer-reviewed journal, then the inmate needs to secure human subject approval from an Institutional Review Board (IRB). This is extremely difficult for convict researchers to obtain, because few correctional facilities have one of these bodies, and few senior-level prison administrators either know about this kind of hurdle or want to deal with this extra burden. For those convicts with an affiliation or status at an outside educational institution, an IRB may be available to them, but accessing it may be a challenge, particularly if an online submission is required. And in all likelihood, most such studies would require a letter of support from the correctional authorities. Although not impossible, this kind of approval is rarely given.

Third, conducting scholarly research and writing up one's findings requires resources and can be relatively costly. Convict researchers do not have appropriate access to the internet or other sources of information, such as research libraries. Gaining access to peer-reviewed articles as a means to develop better literature reviews is difficult. Whatever books and/or articles convicts cite in an academic piece must be obtained (typically through purchase) from the free world. Office supplies, stationary, and postage stamps must be bought from the commissary.

These expenses may seem trivial to those in academia, but for inmates earning anywhere from $0.10 to $1.50 per hour, they are significant. Convicts who want to write have to cover all of their expenses out of (usually empty) pockets, rather than having free access to them, as is usually the case for those working for a university or research institution.

Fourth, prisons are not conducive to research and writing. They are noisy and crowded, and inmates lack privacy. In addition to dealing with numerous distractions, finding a quiet place to work can be extremely vexing. Even prison libraries are often chaotic spaces that are not conducive to the writing process. In many instances, the best time to write is between the hours of midnight and five a.m., when the inmate population is asleep.

Fifth, regular access to typewriters and/or computers is difficult, if not impossible. If this word processing technology is even available to inmates, there are usually only a handful of these machines in poor working condition; the times at which they can be used are limited by institutional rules, and there is often intense competition for their use. For instance, during lockdowns, weekends, and holidays, an Education Department may be closed. Sending in a submission to a scholarly journal that requires accessing online submission systems, having up-to-date versions of word-processing programs, or even simply being able to send out a piece of mail containing all the sheets of paper encompassing an article are very basic obstacles convicts may encounter.

Sixth, prisoners wishing to conduct research and write for scholarly venues have a difficult time gaining access to outside assistance. Without support from the free world, even the simplest of tasks may become an overwhelming barrier. For example, carrying out revisions in a timely manner can be quite challenging for inmates who do not have email/web access to journals and editors. Convict authors must often rely on the kindness of family members and/or friends for everything from editing papers to maintaining communication with editors.

Seventh, sharing drafts, editing one another's work, and ensuring that all ideas, intentions, and interpretations are agreed upon is extremely time-consuming. The addition of go-betweens to facilitate communications and mundane tasks can be successfully negotiated, but this is always a source of stress and a not-infrequent cause of miscommunication, delay, and/or mistakes. The "convict" label is a major impediment for educated inmates trying to penetrate the annals of scholarly venues. For many in the free world, the convict label automatically conveys images of chicanery, capriciousness, and dishonesty, which may call into question the credibility of inmates trying to provide the public with an unadorned rendering of crime and corrections. Unfortunately, convicts themselves often contribute to these negative views (Zaldivar, M., 2013). Simply being a prisoner carries significant stigma and introduces prejudices and skepticism regarding how one's work is perceived, reviewed, and accepted (Tietjen & Kavish, 2021).

The shortage of fellow educated inmates complicates the research and writing process. However, even the most prolific of writers consult with trusted colleagues; rarely do convicts have this luxury. Unless they work with an outside team member and then contend with the challenges of delays and distance, convict authors must flesh out ideas on their own without the benefit of educated sounding boards. This is perhaps why a considerable amount of contemporary scholarship in the field of Criminal Justice and Criminology is co-authored, often with more than one co-author (Tewksbury & Mustaine, 2011; Gonzalez-Alcaide et al., 2013; Lemke, 2013).

Eighth, educated and motivated convict scholars suffer from a dearth of insightful feedback or collaborators. This situation not only frustrates the writing process, but also often leads to skewed arguments, as convict authors are at risk of access to or interpreting their surroundings through solely individualized experiences. With few exceptions, the more prestigious publishing venues generally reject this kind of writing.

Lastly, the lack of appropriate published research materials is a serious discouraging obstacle that educated inmates face when writing scholarly work. Without access to academic, peer-reviewed articles and books, it is impossible to develop substantive pieces capable of surviving the stringent review process of most scholarly journals. Prison libraries do not hold the kinds of materials found in the typical university library. Inter-library loan is not available, and due to costs, controls on internet access, or the complete absence of internet access, retrieving journal articles, reports, and other documents online from a correctional facility is next to impossible. Regrettably, this hurdle is not easy to remedy.

Strategies to overcome the constraints

Just because challenges to conducting research and writing behind bars exist does not mean that this activity should be abandoned. There are ways that convict researchers can deal with and overcome the obstacles that they face.

Develop a research to-do list

Although research ideas that originate while incarcerated may not be easily acted upon behind bars, this does not mean that they should be totally abandoned. If convicts are serious about applying for admission to a graduate program and/ or striving for a career as a researcher/scholar, then their ideas can eventually be researched at a rudimentary level and returned to later in their careers (i.e., after release), especially when they are enrolled in or have earned a masters or doctorate at a respected university. The ideas developed while in jail or prison should be filed away somewhere (perhaps sent to a friend or relative on the outside), and the convict can put them in his or her queue as possible projects to complete after being released from prison.

Serve as a reviewer for scholarly papers that are under review by academic journals

Convict scholars can write to selected editors of journals explaining their qualifications and offering to review papers in their specialization. The previously mentioned *Journal of Prisoners on Prison* is an example of a journal that utilizes this kind of practice. Inmates may also suggest to journal editors that they are in a perfect position to offer well-conceived critiques of correctional policies, practices, and research, and try to get these published. Convicts could also offer to write book reviews, a relatively thankless task that many professors are often requested to undertake, though few actually do. Convicts may also offer critiques of papers that scholars may be working on or have published.

Inmates can gather rudimentary data in a systematic fashion, keeping in mind that at the backbone of Convict Criminology is autoethnography (e.g., Pelias, 1994; Gatson, 2003; Ellis & Bochner, 2005) as the original preferred data collection method. Jones (1995), for example, championed the importance of journaling, field notes, and letters sent to outside researchers. This method can be supplemented through phone calls and face-to-face meetings. It is also crucial for the convict researcher to minimize perceptions among his or her fellow inmates, as well as the correctional officers and administrators, that he or she is somehow a spy or snitch for someone outside or elsewhere in the department of corrections. This can be done by informing jail or prison authorities about the purpose of note-taking. Educated convicts should speak with the most amenable staff around them about the work they are doing. In addition, before asking fellow inmates research questions, the convict scholar should take a few minutes to explain what he or she is doing. Thus, the researcher should not only keep staff informed, but also ease inmates' trepidations toward the research.

Scholarly research is not simply about collecting data in a systematic fashion and subjecting it to rigorous analysis. Several important analyses dealing with correctional themes have been conducted using secondary source material that may after some expenditure of energy become available to inmates.

Co-author with other educated inmates and outside scholars

In almost every correctional facility, one or more educated convicts can be sought out for guidance and mentorship. Approached the right way, these people may assist convicts in conducting their research. The *Journal of Prisoners on Prisons*, for example, facilitates this process by requiring all papers to be written either by a convict, or by a prisoner and a free-world scholar team. For various reasons, some college instructors and professors are willing to mentor and publish with convicts, especially if they show initiative and intelligence. In fact, some scholars have observed that many of these individuals exhibit more curiosity and enthusiasm for learning than their own bachelor's, master's, and Ph.D. free-world students and colleagues.

Given this state of affairs, the best that educated convicts can do while incarcerated is to use their time behind bars to become familiar with not only the intimate workings of their correctional institution, but with the classic works in Corrections, Criminology/Criminal Justice, and beyond. Reading important books, taking notes on them, and critically evaluating them is an crucial exercise. To further this process, some academics will send convicts reading lists and copies of articles to read. Proceeding in this fashion, aspiring convict scholars will be better prepared for scholarly pursuits once they are released from incarceration (see Exhibit Box 6.3).

Exhibit Box 6.3: Thomas J. Bernard

Thomas J. Bernard, Ph.D. (1945–2009), who earned his Ph.D. in 1981 at the State University of New York at Albany, was a professor of Sociology and Criminal Justice at Pennsylvania State University. In addition to publishing several scholarly articles, Bernard was instrumental in revising and co-authoring *Vold's Theoretical Criminology; Consensus Conflict Debate: Form and Content in Social Theories* (Bernard & Vold, 1986), and sole-authoring *The Cycle of Juvenile Justice* (1992). During his career he assisted numerous inmates or formerly incarcerated individuals with their education and in their publishing endeavors. One the earliest and most well-known convict authors that Bernard worked with was Victor Hassine, whom he assisted getting his book *Life without Parole* published (Johnson, 2012). Bernard served as editor or co-author of books written by convicts or ex-convicts such as *Behind a Convict's Eyes: Doing Time in a Modern Prison; Life for a Life: Life Imprisonment, America's Other Death Penalty; Prison, Inc.: A Convict Exposes Life Inside a Private Prison* (https://www.statecollege.com/obituaries/obituary-of-thomas-joseph-bernard-64/).

Conclusion

Authoring or co-authoring one or more scholarly publications may help a convict get into a bachelor's, master's, or Ph.D. program after being released. If a convict already has a Ph.D., then the publications may assist them in their search for a position as an adjunct or a full-time instructor or professor upon release. It is important that instructors, professors, and journal editors encourage and facilitate the ambition and enthusiasm of convicts who are interested, capable, and willing to conduct academic research and scholarly writing. This includes enabling them to contribute to peer-reviewed papers and books under development.

In order for these men and women to conduct research and publish in academic venues, they not only must surmount overwhelming obstacles, but they also need to be careful about the implications of their published work (especially if they expose abysmal jail or prison conditions and treatment they and others endure), in case it may somehow place their safety and well-being in jeopardy. In addition, convicts desiring to publish their research will find themselves relying frequently on the generosity and support of scholars outside of prison. In this manner one of the central tenets of Convict Criminology can be achieved (Ross & Richards, 2003). One last point is in order here: formerly incarcerated students and professors are best advised to develop a network of individuals whom they can trust to give them helpful advice and counsel. This is not an easy task, but one that will serve them well in their careers and the future.

Part III

Activism and Public Policy Work

7

What Is Prison Activism?

Introduction

The third major emphasis of Convict Criminology is jail or prison activism. This initiative can be seen under a larger goal of promoting carceral citizenship (Smith & Kunzel, 2020). In short, carceral citizenship is the recognition that having a criminal record, at least in the United States, strips an individual of numerous inalienable rights not just while a person is incarcerated, but after they are released.

Unfortunately many individuals, have very narrow ideas about what politics and political activity consist of. For them, the political process is limited to voting or attending a protest. And yet there are several types of actions in which the public can engage that can have a political and social impact, including signing petitions, letter-writing, posting and responding to posts on social media, and making donations to political campaigns. When it comes to prison reform, there are multiple ways that the public can participate.

In order to explore these paths, this chapter covers:

- The history and scope of prison activism and prisoner movements in the United States.
- Who are the prison activists and organizations?
- The history of prison reform.
- Prison abolition.
- The differences between prison reform and prison abolition.
- Sentencing reform.

The history and scope of prison activism and prisoner movements in the United States

Since the emergence of modern prisons in Europe and later in the United States, many outsiders (i.e., people, groups, organizations) have tried to either change correctional policies and practices and/or attempted to cast doubt on the legitimacy of incarceration and worked to close jails, prisons, and juvenile detention facilities.[1] In general, these efforts are part of a larger discussion of prison abolition, activism, reform, unions, and sentencing. To better understand these interrelated processes, they will be discussed here.

It is worth noting that

> while changes to the prison system throughout history are usually referred to as "reforms," the goals of early reforms were not necessarily aligned with the approach of prison activists of today. ... Rather, historical prison reformers ... were often just as concerned with improving the security or efficiency of prisons as they were with ameliorating conditions inside them. (Piper, 2005: 8)

In general, prison activism refers to "a broad-based social movement that addresses injustices in the criminal justice system" (Piper, 2005: 7). Although some constituencies want to reform the prison system, others want to abolish it. Also, it is difficult to date the origins of prison activism and to know exactly how many people and organizations are involved with behaviors that may fall under this rubric. Nevertheless, this review will attempt to touch on the more notable individuals and organizations.

Who are the prison activists and organizations?

With respect to the numbers of individuals participating in changing prisons, according to Piper (2005), "[t]housands of individuals and organizations are moved to action by the current U.S. prison crisis and are working to change or abolish the system. Their work takes different forms and has varying goals that are not always in accordance with each other" (Piper, 2005: 7–8).

A variety of people from different walks of life and professional backgrounds participate in prison activism and abolition. Front and center have been convicts, inmates, and prisoners (Ross, 2010), as their lives are the most directly impacted by the conditions of confinement and they have spent considerable effort to change their immediate living environment. Also essential are the many lawyers or men and women with legal backgrounds who have participated in calling attention to substandard prison conditions, policies, and practices. In the United States, these efforts can be traced back to prominent lawyers like Clarence Darrow (1857–1938), and they extend to well-known "radical" celebrity lawyers like William Kunstler (1919–1995) and Ron Kuby (1956–present). Furthermore, a handful of prisoners have succeeded in garnering public recognition for their work while behind bars to change prison policies and practices. For example, Caryl Chessman (1920–1961), while on death row at San Quentin Prison (California), managed to change prison policy in that state (Piper, 2005: 8; see Exhibit Box 7.1).

Exhibit Box 7.1: Prominent lawyers who have attempted to change prison conditions in the United States

Bryan Stevenson: Founder and executive director of the Equal Justice Initiative, Stevenson has fought against harsh sentencing, excessive punishment, and racial bias in the criminal justice system.

Soffiyah Elijah: Elijah is a respected attorney and advocate who has focused on criminal justice reform, particularly addressing issues such as the treatment of women in prison, juvenile justice, and re-entry programs for formerly incarcerated individuals.

Vanita Gupta: As the former head of the Civil Rights Division at the Department of Justice, Gupta advocated for criminal justice reform and challenging unconstitutional practices within prisons.

David Rudovsky: An experienced civil rights lawyer, Rudovsky has litigated cases addressing issues such as overcrowding, inadequate medical care, and abusive practices in prisons.

Jonathan Rapping: Rapping founded Gideon's Promise, an organization that trains public defenders to provide quality representation for indigent defendants and promote fair and just outcomes.

Elizabeth Alexander: The director of the American Civil Liberties Union's (ACLU) National Prison Project, Alexander has been instrumental in advocating for prisoners' rights, challenging inhumane conditions, and fighting against abuse within the correctional system.

Jenny-Brooke Condon: Condon is a renowned attorney and advocate who has championed prison reform and worked on landmark cases addressing issues such as solitary confinement and excessive use of force by prison staff.

Nicole Porter: As the director of advocacy at the Sentencing Project, Porter has been actively involved in efforts to reduce mass incarceration, eliminate racial disparities, and promote alternatives to prison.

Bryan Gowdy: An attorney based in Florida, Gowdy has litigated cases related to the treatment of prisoners, including issues like access to healthcare, mental health services, and the use of excessive force by prison staff.

Mary B. McCord: McCord is a former federal prosecutor and currently serves as the Legal Director for the Institute for Constitutional Advocacy and Protection at Georgetown Law. She has been involved in litigation challenging various aspects of the criminal justice system, including solitary confinement and excessive use of force in prisons.

David Fathi: Fathi is Director of the ACLU's National Prison Project and has been at the forefront of advocating for prisoner rights and challenging unconstitutional conditions of confinement. He has litigated cases related to overcrowding, inadequate healthcare, and discriminatory practices within prisons.

> Cecillia D. Wang: Wang is a civil rights attorney who has worked on cases related to prison conditions and criminal justice reform. She has been involved in litigation addressing issues such as the use of excessive force by prison staff, denial of adequate medical care, and unconstitutional treatment of prisoners.

Likewise, numerous organizations in the United States participate in prison activism (Sudbury, 2004). They vary in terms of their size, mission, and lifespan. Many of these groups have narrowly focused objectives (e.g., the Sentencing Project). Some have religious leanings (e.g., assisting prisoners with their spiritual needs), while others concentrate on political issues (e.g., expanding inmates' ability to vote). Others, like Mothers Against Mandatory Minimums, have focused heavily on sentencing reform, often forming alliances with like-minded organizations, such as the Sentencing Project. Some organizations specialize in the plight of juveniles who are incarcerated, while others concentrate on women who are behind bars (Katzenstein, 2005). Several prison activist organizations have a broader set of objectives in terms of corrections in the United States. They want to start or improve rehabilitation programs in correctional facilities, provide better medical, dental, and psychiatric care, and/or fight against censorship of materials coming into and out of jails and prisons.

On the other hand, there are many organizations whose primary concentration is correctional system reform, including the Prison Moratorium, Prison Activist Resource Center, and Citizens United for Rehabilitation of Errants (CURE) (see Exhibit Box 7.2). Some of them focus on one specific correctional facility or all institutions in a single state. For example, members of Schools not Jails (Acey, 2000) channeled their energies into reforming correctional facilities in California only.

Meanwhile, a number of organizations adopt, as part of their larger mission, a focus on prisoners and on conditions in correctional facilities. This includes international organizations like Amnesty International and Human Rights Watch. The former concentrates on the human right violations, and the application of the death penalty, while the latter is concerned with all manner of behaviors that encroach upon the rights of individuals who are unnecessarily detained or subjected to substandard conditions of confinement. U.S. organizations that serve a broad mission include the ACLU and the NLG. The ACLU, through its National Prison Project, monitors persistent legal violations perpetrated by jails and prisons, and the National Lawyers Guild has two committees that provide assistance to those behind bars. Meanwhile, the Sentencing Project works on numerous issues affecting the rights of people who are incarcerated and negatively affected by the criminal justice system. In this context, it promotes campaigns that raise awareness about certain prisoners or classes of prisoners. Some organizations, like the Soros Foundation, have been involved in prison

Exhibit Box 7.2: Citizens United for Rehabilitation of Errants

CURE is a nonprofit organization committed to advocating for criminal justice reform and rehabilitation of offenders. Founded in 1972 by Charlie and Pauline Sullivan in the belief that punitive measures alone are not effective in reducing crime rates and fostering a safer society, CURE strives to bring attention to the importance of rehabilitation and support for those who have been incarcerated. CURE's mission encompasses various objectives, including promoting restorative justice, providing education and job training for inmates, and advocating for fair and humane treatment within correctional facilities. The organization also seeks to reduce recidivism rates by addressing the root causes of criminal behavior and supporting successful reintegration into society post-incarceration. Through grassroots efforts, research, and policy initiatives, CURE works to influence lawmakers, criminal justice professionals, and the public to adopt evidence-based practices that prioritize rehabilitation and reduce the stigma associated with incarceration. By shedding light on the transformative power of rehabilitation, CURE continues to play a vital role in shaping the dialogue surrounding criminal justice reform.

activism by supporting individuals (i.e., scholars and journalists) who work on behalf of prison reform.

Almost every large city in the United States has a prison activist community that organizes and participates in demonstrations, letter-writing campaigns, etc. Many of the people who belong in these groups do not limit their activities to protesting the conditions of confinement in one correctional facility only, nor one political cause.

All in all, these organizations engage in several activities, including litigation,

> helping inmates with their individual legal battles, and in Congress lobbying for the protection of prisoners' rights and policy changes. Others run workshops in prisons. There are books-to-prisoner programs to supplement poorly stocked prison libraries. Post-release organizations work to fill the void left by the state by offering education, job training, and placement opportunities to recently released prisoners. Many groups work on public education, exposing myths about crime in the United States and the disproportionate impact of race, gender, and class in the criminal justice system. (Piper, 2005: 8)

This can take the form of organizing letter-writing campaigns, publishing, and legal activism, including filing lawsuits against a correctional facility or a correctional system (e.g., local, state, and federal).

History of prison reform

The dust had hardly settled on the construction of the first prisons when efforts to change and reform them started. For example, British social reformer Jeremy Bentham's (1748–1832) panopticon idea was one of the earliest and most publicized attempts to reform the layout of prisons. The Quakers, who proposed, constructed, and managed Philadelphia's Walnut Street Jail (1790–1838), were similarly minded. Some might even say that the history of corrections is the history of reform. This discussion also includes an expansion of prisoner rights.

During the 1960s, numerous activist groups, such as the Black Panther Party, had prison outreach programs. Also prominent were anti-war and civil rights movements that took an interest in prisoner rights and joined forces with prison activists. It was not until the 1970s, however, that there was increase in the amount of prison activism in the United States. In many respects, this development began with what are referred to as prisoner movements, in particular prisoner unions, which formed inside correctional facilities (Zonn, 1977). In general, "[t]he term 'prisoners unions' [was] used for a variety of movements which have developed in various states since 1970" (Huff, 1974: 10). The origins of prisoner unions can be traced back to the early 1970s at Folsom State Prison in California:

> A great deal of the impetus for other prisoner unions in the United States comes from this San Francisco based organization. … Prisoner union movements have arisen in many other states … they have proliferated (and deteriorated) so rapidly that it is nearly impossible at any given time to list them accordingly or to assess their current strengths and weaknesses. (Huff, 1974: 13)

Many of them found considerable opposition from correctional officers, workers, and administrators, partially because of the alliances they made with activists (e.g., Black Panther Party, various anarchist groups, etc.) on the outside.

It is understandable that the prisoner movements and unions started during this time period, right on the heels of the burgeoning civil rights movement and calls for greater racial and ethnic equality in the United States. In the post-Watergate era (1972), a considerable amount of attention was devoted to organizations that assisted with religious services in prisons, such as the work by Charles "Chuck" Colson, who was convicted of crimes during the Reagan administration and who, shortly after his release, founded Prison Fellowship, an evangelical organization that worked with prisoners.

During the 1970s, almost all of the public protests against correctional institutions and their policies and practices were in support of imprisoned men. This shortcoming was noticed during the 1980s and soon thereafter groups like Critical Resistance (Braz et al., 2000) and Women's Advocacy Ministry, as well as individuals like well-known political activists such as Angela Davis and Kathy Boudin, brought attention to the conditions in women's prisons and laid out a political agenda that was directed toward reforming or abolishing women's facilities (Piper, 2005: 9). Some of the core issues that were addressed dealt with incarcerated mothers, including women who were pregnant behind bars and formerly incarcerated women and their struggles with re-entry (Barry, 2000).

Prison abolition

Over the past four-and-a-half decades, one of the most radical positions advocated by some progressives has been the call for prison abolition. This movement seeks to either completely eliminate specific elements of the current punishment system, introduce alternatives, or bring about its complete dissolution (Greene, 2005: 2). In the forefront of this movement are "activists, ex-prisoners, academics, religious actors, politicians, inmates and their families" (Greene, 2005: 2). The modern origins of prison abolition started during the 1960s in Scandinavia and soon spread to other Western countries. In the United States, the prison abolition movement began in 1976 with the help of Quaker and prison minister Fay Honey Knopp, who established the Prison Research Education Project in Philadelphia and later authored the well-known book, *Instead of Prisons: A Handbook for Abolitionists* (1976). In 1981, the Canadian Quaker Committee for Jails and Justice started advocating for prison abolition, and two years later, the very first International Conference on Prison Abolition was held in Toronto (Ross, 1983). Since then, the organization has evolved, including a name change, substituting the words "circle" for "conference" and "prison" for "penal," so that the organization is now called the International Circle on Penal Abolition. Accompanying this movement is a considerable amount of scholarship exploring the different facets of abolition (Ruggiero, 2010; Brown & Schept, 2017).

Distinguishing between prison reform and prison abolition

In general, prison reformers have tried to force governments and departments of corrections to change jail and prison conditions and policies, including minimizing crowding/overcrowding, providing educational opportunities, reinstating Pell Grants, etc. Some of this work has been in the area of sentencing, particularly with efforts to prevent individuals from going to jail or prison in the first place.

> In addition to improving services within prison walls, reform groups often seek to reduce the number of people incarcerated. To that end, they support alternative punishments, including mandated drug treatment, community service, house arrest, and other intermediate sanctions. Prison reform organizations also try to improve current conditions within prisons by targeting such issues as prisoner rape, denial of civil rights, conditions in super maximum facilities, and poor health. (Piper, 2005: 9)

Advocates of prison abolition, on the other hand, believe that these reforms do not go far enough. They "argue that restructuring services within prisons and the criminal justice system serves only to retrench the inequalities that these institutions create" (Piper, 2005: 9). "Rather than finding a replacement for prison, they work to develop solutions outside the criminal justice system, focusing on justice rather than punishment" (Piper, 2005: 9). Piper cites the decriminalization of drugs and the interpretation of drug addiction as a medical challenge rather than a criminal justice problem as one of many solutions proposed by prison abolitionists.

Sentencing reform

Although numerous constituencies have been involved in prison activism and abolition, some have disproportionately focused their resources on changing particular types of prison sentences, which they argue do extreme harm to inmates. This includes efforts organized around abolishing mandatory minimums and the death penalty/capital punishment (e.g., Haines, 1996). First, starting in 1990, several prison activists have tried to call attention to and lobbied members of Congress to reduce the more severe sentencing for crack possession (a crime typically associated with young African-American males) versus the less punitive sentences linked to the possession of powder cocaine (a crime typically associated with White males).

Second, different constituencies have tried to either curtail or abolish the death penalty. Although not strictly a kind of prison reform, these efforts are related, since capital punishment currently exists in 31 states (Ross, 2016: chapter 11). As early as 1845, an organization called the American Society for the Abolition of Capital Punishment was formed. "Since then, work has occurred at both the state and national levels in faith-based, political, and legal organizations. These groups fight both for the abolition of the death penalty and for individuals facing execution" (Piper, 2005: 10).

Conclusion

This chapter reviewed the intertwined concepts and practices of prison abolition, activism, unions, and reform. The number of ways both prisoners and those on the outside are attempting to change correctional institutions and the way that jails and prisons supervise and detain inmates is limitless. Those committed to improving jail and prison conditions, or eliminating them all together, would be well-advised to review the lessons from the history of these movements as a means to improve their efforts for change and praxis.

It is also important to consider that because the conditions of confinement typically restrict the kinds of actions prisoners can engage in, a correctional facility may retaliate against inmate activists by restricting access to different forms of communication. That is why it is important to have activists and activist organizations on the outside of jails and prisons to advocate for reform and change in correctional policies and practices, and conditions of confinement.

8

How Has Convict Criminology Engaged in Activism?

Introduction

Most individuals believe that politics and political activity encompasses either voting or attending a protest (Ginsberg, 1981).[1] However, there are numerous behaviors that the public can engage in that can have a political and social impact, including, but not limited to, letter-writing, social media activities, and donations to political campaigns, candidates, and parties (Hirsch, 1993; Doherty et al., 2015; Rhodes et al., 2018). When ostensibly apolitical organizations, like those built around scholarship, formally and informally engage in political activities, things become complex. The demarcation between scholarship and activism in this context are often blurry. Moreover, a common misconception is to exclusively link activism with left-wing politics. Activism, however, transcends the ideological spectrum, and this phenomenon is observed across all academic disciplines

Now that this book has covered scholarly research and mentorship, it is wise to devote some attention to the activism that Convict Criminology (CC) has engaged in, is currently doing, and wants to do in the future. Although none of the previous critiques of CC (e.g., Larsen & Piché, 2012; Newbold & Ross, 2012; Belknap, 2015) have accused CC of being insufficiently engaged in activism, there has been some internal discussion about the need to do more in this area. Why? Part of the mission of CC is to engage with the public, politicians, and the news media and educate them about prisons, corrections, and the devastating effects of mass incarceration. Thus this section of the book examines the different political aspects of CC praxis (Aresti & Darke, 2016; Aresti et al., 2016; Cann & DeMeulenaere, 2020; Smith & Kinzel, 2021; Smith, 2021).

Some of the work of CC encompasses what some scholars (e.g., Loader & Sparks, 2010; Uggen & Inderbitzin, 2010) call Public Criminology. This involves attempts to bring the findings of criminological research to audiences beyond academic criminologists, and is motivated by the perception that scholars are often "preaching to the choir," as in individuals who do not need to be won over. Much political activism extends beyond the classrooms and conferences, and incorporates engagement with a variety of media by serving as sources for articles or broadcasts that reporters are writing/producing, consenting to be interviewed, and writing op-eds.

This chapter reflects upon the role of activism in the CC context. To begin with, many people affiliated with the CC perspective have, in one way or another, long participated in progressive-leaning political activity in support of CC. It is important to critically examine this work to understand what CC members and supporters have done, where they have made contributions, and the specific ways that this activity can be improved. In sum, this chapter explores, but is not limited to, the differing political aspects of CC praxis (Aresti & Darke, 2016; Aresti et al., 2016; Cann & DeMeulenaere, 2020; Smith, 2020; Smith & Kinzel, 2021). It mainly reviews and contextualizes U.S.-based CC activist initiatives.

What is activism? Why is it essential for Convict Criminology?

Several college-level instructors, professors, academic administrators, and poorly informed constituencies consider activism by scholars, professors, and university-level instructors to be controversial, and they may even frown upon this activity. Why? Academia lacks clear-cut guidelines about the role that activism can or should play in professors' work. Also, some instructors, professors, and administrators believe that scholars should devote more time to research, teaching, and university service rather than to political activities. They do not want the proverbial boat to be rocked or to potentially draw negative attention to universities and their subunits. There is also considerable confusion surrounding the notion of free speech and how and where it is best exercised. Participating in activism is risky for many instructors, particularly those who occupy precarious positions of employment. Most importantly, system-impacted scholars may find themselves more susceptible to status fragility when they engage in activism (Tietjen & Kavish, 2021). Moreover, some professors argue that their scholarship and teaching is a form of activism and/or praxis (i.e., turning theory into action). As they sometimes argue, clear-cut lines between what is and what is not activism do not exist.

To start with, a handful of scholars (e.g., Maruna, 2001; LeBel, 2007; 2008; 2009; Ross, 2018) have noted that many formerly incarcerated people engage in activism. This behavior is often a way to deal with the stigma of a criminal conviction and to participate in an activity that is therapeutic, if not transformational.

On the one hand, the activism aspect of CC is not very well developed, frequently functioning as the most nebulous and neglected element of the organization (e.g., Smith, 2020; Smith & Kinzel, 2021). Conversely, settling on a widely agreed-upon definition of activism in CC may not be possible. Why?

Considerable diversity exists across the spectrum of the group's membership and supporters. Furthermore, the original formation of CC, members' engagement in universities (including bringing CC ideas to classrooms and faculty committees), and advocacy for system-impacted students can be offered as alternative evidence of activism.

Thus, the definition of activism within CC may depend on which convict criminologist individuals speak to or observe. And as understood, there are a variety of different types of members, ranging from students to college-level instructors, to professors, to formerly incarcerated individuals and justice-contacted, involved or impacted men and women, to those who self-identify as activists and allies of CC.

To begin with, some people may consider the creation of CC in 1997 and the establishment of the Division of Convict Criminology (DCC) in 2020 as acts of activism in and of themselves. More specifically, the founding of CC was propelled by, among other reasons, a desire to confront the bias that formerly incarcerated scholars commonly experienced and to elevate the system-impacted voice in post-secondary education and scholarship circles (King, 2018).

As Richards (2013) explains, "Convict Criminology was born of the frustration ex-convict graduate students and ex-convict professors felt reading the academic literature on prisons. In our view, most academic textbooks and journal articles reflected the ideas of prison administrators, while largely ignoring what convicts knew about the day-to-day realities of imprisonment" (2013: 377). Thus, if someone identifies with CC and engages in scholarship from a CC perspective, this could also potentially be regarded as activism (see Exhibit Box 8.1).

Exhibit Box 8.1: Examples of activities considered to be political activism

- celebrity endorsements
- civil disobedience
- direct action
- educational campaigns
- forming coalitions and alliances
- news media outreach
- rallies and protests
- petitions
- social media campaigns
- lobbying
- boycotts
- letter-writing and email campaigns
- grassroots organizing
- online fundraising

A brief history of activism in Convict Criminology

Before the creation of the DCC within the American Society of Criminology (ASC), the CC organization functioned as an informal network of scholars, students, academics, and activists with varying levels of engagement with CC advocacy. As new people joined the group and others left, the type and amount of activism changed. For example, in the early years, few of the members were interested in prison abolition, but now several members of the CC network are. Similarly, the new, diverse, and expanded membership of CC (Ross et al., 2016) is engaging more with underrepresented and marginalized populations (i.e., African-American, feminists, LGTBQIA+, etc.) and the issues that directly impact these constituencies (e.g., Woodall & Boeri, 2014; Malkin & DeJong, 2019). In addition, CC activist work continues to broaden its focus to further include international academics (from Argentina, Australia, Brazil, Germany, Italy, and the United Kingdom), whose scholarship and other activities are aligned with the CC mission (Ross & Darke, 2018; Ross & Vianello, 2021; Veigh Weis, 2021).

It may be helpful to identify the range of activism that CC members and the group in general engage in. Three specific categories of activism can be seen in the CC space: activist scholarship, mentorship as activism, and direct activism.

Activist scholarship

The most common form of activism performed within CC might be called activist scholarship. CC's research functions as a form of scholarly activism that sheds light on the experiences of directly impacted individuals, who are often disregarded or unseen in conventional criminological research (Smith & Kinzel, 2021; Tietjen, forthcoming). Due to the direct criminal justice contact of many CC scholars, they possess a unique potential to illuminate the value of lived experiences within the discipline of criminological research, which can lean heavily toward soulless quantitative research. As Aresti et al. (2016) explain:

> Through its combining of insider and critical research action perspectives on penalty, it is our contention that Convict Criminology is well equipped to challenge public misconceptions on prisons and prisoners. Further, by insisting on the need to privilege the knowledge and standpoint of those with firsthand experience of prison, convict criminologists find themselves in a strong position to resist institutional pressure to produce quantitative, hypothesis-testing (voodoo, positivistic) research. (Aresti et al., 2016: 6)

Although it might be easy for some critics of CC to argue that lived-experience scholarship is too biased and, thus, does not have any "activist" value within criminology, Newbold et al. (2014) point out that as long as the lived-experience perspective does not excessively influence a researcher's objectivity, it can have a valuable place within a criminological study. These researchers, referencing Jewkes (2012), emphasize that the insider's views can add "color, context, and contour" (Newbold et al., 2014: 6) to scholarly findings.

That being said, in order for academic research and writing to have an activist component, it is necessary for CC scholarship to not only get into the hands of the individuals who can best use it (i.e., relevant prison activists or policy makers and practitioners), but for these people to read this material and attempt to alter correctional-relevant policies and practices based on this information. Also keep in mind that scholarship is not limited to researching, writing, reviewing, and publishing, since it can also involve the transmission of knowledge at conferences, where attendees, such as formerly incarcerated and justice-contacted, involved, and impacted individuals, attend and discuss CC ideas.

In short, the type of work that CC does can be considered "scholarvism" (Green, 2018). It is a collaborative-activist type of scholarship that involves credentialed experts whose activist work is based on rigorous, refereed research and scholarship. This would include, for example, Francesca Vianello's research team's work and her role in establishing and directing the M.A. in Critical Criminology program at the University of Padua. In the spirit of CC, her involvement in these activities has created opportunities for system-impacted scholars to earn graduate degrees and contribute research to the field of Criminology/Criminal Justice.

Mentorship as activism

Since its formation, CC has actively attempted to mentor individuals who are interested in this perspective. This includes people who are incarcerated (Ross et al., 2011a; 2015b; Darke & Aresti, 2016; Ross, 2019; Tewksbury & Ross, 2019) and those who are formerly incarcerated. Some of these men and women enroll in and complete bachelor's, master's, and doctoral degrees, while others already hold academic positions. As previously mentioned, this mentorship includes conducting research together, collaboratively presenting findings on academic panels, co-authoring/co-editing papers for publication, offering advisement on the academic job market, including writing letters of recommendation and providing feedback on departmental/college/university politics. CC has performed many of the typical tasks typically pursued by undergraduate and graduate advisors. As testimony to this perspective, Tietjen et al. (2021) outlined how formerly incarcerated research participants described the mentorship they received from CC mentors, who have provided them with the tools and knowledge to "harness the value of his own lived experiences through higher education" (Tietjen et al., 2021: 7).

Direct activism

Introduction

The last type of activism involves the jail and prison impacted scholars, students, and allies who not only created CC, but who through the reclaiming of the word *convict* (Ortiz et al., 2022) took a stand against mainstream criminologists and some prison activists (whom some CC scholars saw as having been co-opted by the criminal justice system) and the criminal justice system itself (Ross & Richards, 2003; Richards, 2009). More than just bringing the voices of those convicted of crimes to the criminological discipline, CC expanded the utility of the lived-experience autoethnography as a means to both augment and challenge the managerial scholarship of conventional criminology.

Direct activism also includes more concrete and less symbolic kinds of behavior. CC members have participated in this kind of activity by writing news articles or op-eds (e.g., Kalica, 2021); functioning as credible sources for reporters who are writing stories about corrections- and CC-related research (e.g., Tietjen, 2017); participating on Institutional Review Boards (IRBs); delivering public lectures and periodic public statements from the ASC DCC executive; and participating in protest activism, supporting Black Lives Matter, critical resistance, etc.

Convict Criminology engaging in news-making criminology

Over the past three decades, motivated in part by Barak's (1988) classic article on news-making criminology, CC scholars have written op-eds about correctional issues and have been used as subject matter expert sources for the news media. They have made connections with reporters and editors of news organizations, and with the increasing proliferation of blogs, podcasts, and YouTube, they have disseminated information about the challenges of the criminal justice system in general and corrections in particular.

Participating as prisoner representatives on Institutional Review Boards or panels examining corrections

Some CC members have served on important committees that are relevant to the subject area of corrections. For example, in the 1990s, Greg Newbold acted as a consultant prior to the introduction of private prisons to New Zealand (Newbold & Smith, 1996). In 2008 and 2009, Jeffrey Ian Ross and Daniel Murphy served on the prisoner liaison committee for the National Institute of Health/National Institute of Medicine task force, when these institutes revised their protocols on drug and medical testing practices involving prisoners (Ross & Hornblum, 2009). Miguel Zaldivar, a formerly incarcerated individual, who completed an undergraduate degree behind bars and has been periodically associated with CC, served as a prisoner representative on an IRB with the University of Miami. From

2011 to 2013, Grant Tietjen served as an IRB representative for correctional research at the University of Nebraska-Lincoln. Also, Francesca Vianello has served on numerous commissions charged with making recommendations for the reform of the Italian penitentiary system. Moreover, Daniel Kavish and Adrian Heurta serve as board members for the Carceral Studies Consortium (https://architecture.ou.edu/csc/), Kavish as a core affiliate board member, and Huerta as an affiliate board member. Although having formerly incarcerated individuals on IRBs may appear to be lip-service or tokenism, in most cases CC members are able to assist these bodies to do a better (more thoughtful) job.

Serving on editorial boards/reviewing papers for academic journals

Some CC scholars serve on the editorial boards of Criminology/Criminal Justice journals and/or actively participate in the peer-review process. This work can assist these publications when other editorial board members or reviewers of papers are unfamiliar or poorly informed about CC, its history, and CC's body of scholarship. This kind of service also extends to reviewing papers for academic journals.

The American Society of Criminology Division of Convict Criminology's periodic public statements

Shortly after CC became an official division of the ASC, the executive of the DCC released a number of statements via Twitter and Facebook. The first was in reaction to the death of George Floyd, the 41-year-old African-American man who was killed by a White Minneapolis police officer in May 2020. This was followed a month later by a statement regarding the presence of COVID-19 in our country's correctional facilities and the failure of state, local, and federal governments to properly respond. In January 2021, the DCC executive launched its third public statement condemning the insurrection at the United States Capitol. Later in January 2021, the DCC also released a statement addressing Ban the Box.

Participating in contemporary progressive activist movements

Many members of CC are passionate about allied progressive activist causes. They frequently see connections between what CC stands for and these larger contemporary movements. Thus some CC members have participated in activism surrounding Black Lives Matter, LGBTQIA+ rights, the rights of incarcerated and formerly incarcerated people, and the prison abolition movement, all of which inform the formal and informal discussions and actions that CC members engage in. These issues are discussed during scholarly panels and at social events. Other work includes organizing and attending rallies and public meetings, and participating in diversity committees at various universities. On a related note, other engagement includes actively lobbying against the building of correctional facilities.

More concretely, CC has been identified as a good organization to serve as a "Haven for Radical Racial Exploration" (Williams, 2021). Although "carcerality" is a central theme in CC, this topic is not solely limited to incarceration experiences. Rather, as Williams (2021: 13) argued, it is crucial to incorporate an intersectional lens when examining carceral experiences to account for the "carcerality of Blackness" in the United States, institutions of higher education, and the criminal legal system.

Even though these examples are important, they must also be placed in context. Just because a scholar is sympathetic to the CC perspective and sits on a relevant academic board or committee does not necessarily mean that they are engaging in activism. Instead, their work may more accurately be called service. The degree of meaningful participation is what is crucial here. Either way, CC members or individuals sympathetic to the CC mission have the potential of engaging in activism, especially drawing attention to the convict voice, advocating for the rights of prisoners and ex-prisoners, and minimizing the default to mass incarceration.

Challenges for instructors and professors who engage in activism

Balancing competing demands

University instructors and professors, especially those who are formerly incarcerated, face many challenges, including balancing the role of researcher or activist. They may interpret their need, desire or obligation to engage in scholarly research and participate in activism as competing for their attention. Like a zero-sum game, some individuals believe that the more resources (especially time) they spend on one activity, the less resources they can or need to spend on the other. Alternatively instructors or professors may embrace or master only one of the two roles (i.e., activist versus scholar or vice versa) or interests.

How might this happen? Formerly incarcerated individuals may enjoy or identify more with one role/interest over the other, depending on the degree to which formerly incarcerated individuals agree with the activists and scholars formerly incarcerated individuals encounter, the messages they advance, how much fun or aggravation the individuals experience with each respective crowd, and the time CC individuals spend working together in pursuit of the same shared goal. Thus, CC persons may be subject to a push–pull dynamic where formerly incarcerated individuals deepen prospective formerly incarcerated graduate students' commitment to one network of individuals over the other.

Conversely, some instructors and professors may view their aspiration to be both a scholar and an activist as mutually reinforcing. Although much harder to successfully accomplish, these individuals are able to maintain a healthy balance between their scholarship and activism. Although some may question whether writing the occasional op-ed counts as activism, many professors contend that their professional work is mutually beneficial, since their scholarship and their teaching are their own forms of activism. For example, working with a group that deals with food insecurity may generate research ideas for a new scholarly paper that a professor might start. Or fighting for racial justice may expose an instructor to legal cases that they never considered and are worth writing about in an academic context. Some professors may even be able to get their scholarly research into the hands of policy makers or leaders of organizations who can affect legislative change.

Another dilemma exists in regards to spending too much time on traditional kinds of activism, which may ultimately reduce the amount of time one can devote to scholarship. How might formerly incarcerated individuals' activism negatively affect them? Engaging in activism has distracted many students, instructors and professors, not just in the liberal arts, but in programs in medicine, law, and technology as well. Yes, they may win approval for their activism from some fellow activists, the students they teach, and even fellow instructors, professors, and administrators in their program or universities, but they still have to adequately juggle the numerous deadlines bearing down on them (e.g., papers and exams to grade, papers to write, etc.). If formerly incarcerated individuals are adjunct instructors vying for a position in an academic department (that values scholarly research) but have not done a sufficient amount of this type of work, no amount of activism will typically help them in the hiring process. Lastly, if formerly incarcerated individuals are also tenure-track professors, no matter how much their colleagues agree with their activism, they will usually not cut them any slack in the promotion process by giving formerly incarcerated individuals a pass if they failed to meet various organizational mandated standards of research productivity.

Granted, as prospective formerly incarcerated individuals' careers progress and they move up through the ranks (from graduate student, to untenured assistant professors, to securing tenure), they may believe that they will have more time and freedom to engage in activism, but there may also be new things that formerly incarcerated people will be forced to consider. These may include different and additional pressures on their time (e.g., building a family), mentoring and supervising students, and fulfilling university service requirements. If these individuals' activism negatively affects their ability to perform their job and results in a possible job loss or even incarceration, this can have very real negative effects. Thus, activism may end up taking a back seat for a given time. In short, it is important to do a good job estimating the costs and benefits (both pecuniary and emotional), and to carefully engage where formerly incarcerated individuals believe that their efforts can make the most difference.

To put things in context, the activist side to the CC movement has gone through some growing pains over the years as CC members, many struggling with the stresses of incarceration and difficult pasts, try to work through their trauma and the injustices they endured while learning to be more effective activists. It can be a long road for several men and women affiliated with the CC approach as they to learn how to be activist scholars.

Conclusion

Summing up, CC incorporates activist scholarship, activism through mentorship, and direct activism. Nevertheless, activism in CC has varied over time, and individuals have struggled with how, when, and why they should engage in this activity. Why is this so? Formerly incarcerated CC members (not to mention those who may be justice-contacted, involved, or impacted) may have difficulty with personal traumas and stresses from their incarcerations and difficult pasts (Kirk & Wakefield, 2018), while learning to be more effective activists. Alternatively, they may be using activism in an attempt to "take ownership" of their trauma and stress (and thereby overcome it). On the other hand, members who are not formerly incarcerated or justice-contacted, involved or impacted may be unaware of the most effective ways to engage in activism with this group.

Both types of individuals may have competing obligations. They may want to be good scholars, instructors, and citizens in their universities and communities, but they may also have parental or caregiver obligations. In addition, many individuals who have aligned themselves with CC are trying to complete a doctorate or earn tenure. In this case, the focus of their efforts is often on publishing a considerable amount of scholarship, securing favorable teaching evaluations, engaging in departmental, college, and university service, and not protesting in the streets and joining or manning the barricades in public demonstrations. With this in mind, the more established members of CC or other individuals and organizations may be in a better position to engage in the activism that individuals in the CC network do. Conversely the newer and younger members of the CC group frequently find their way to the CC organization through their involvement in activism. In sum, it is a long and sometimes difficult journey for many CC members and those aligned with the mission to learn to effectively balance the two roles of activist and scholar.

Regardless, CC needs to continue to engage with its respective audiences (i.e., fellow criminologists, students, community groups they are part of or interact with, and the news media). It is essential to understand and reach out to the people new to the CC organization who may be interested in the broad span of ideas relevant to corrections, re-entry in general and CC in particular.

9

What Does the Future of Convict Criminology Look Like?

Introduction

Convict Criminology (CC) is over a quarter of a century old.[1] During those years, this approach has produced scholarly literature and mentored actual and aspiring doctoral students who have been incarcerated and released from correctional custody, assisting them in their careers and engaging in corrections-related policy debates and activism. As the academic fields and real-world practice of Corrections and Critical Criminology have changed, and the people who have been involved in CC have come and gone, CC has evolved. This chapter briefly reviews the aims and history of CC, then applies a strength, weaknesses, opportunities, and threats (SWOT) analysis to CC with the goal of suggesting ways that the leadership, members, and allies of the CC approach might best further its mission.

The CC idea started out as a series of conversations between Stephen C. Richards and Jeffrey Ian Ross, then morphed through a number of panels held at academic conferences, the production of scholarly studies, and the development into a worldwide global approach, collective, field, framework, group, movement, network, organization, perspective, school, and theory.[2]

Given a suitable quantity and quality of resources (including interest), the implications of each of these different labels, the relative suitability of them, and their advantages and disadvantages could be traced. Researchers might even be able to set up a rough heuristic by which to judge how relevant each of these terms might be and under what circumstances they apply or have manifested themselves, but that exercise would probably not be much more than a temporary distraction. In reality, CC is a little of each of these things. In other words, it fits into each one of these categories just a bit, and that is why CC is somewhat difficult to categorize and, for those not familiar with it, to understand.

Undoubtedly, whichever label is applied to CC will inevitably beg a number of questions. Most importantly, what are the implications of using one label over another, and how should individuals in the CC network measure the success or failure of this entity? Again, this effort might likely turn into a rabbit hole, with minimal gains to be achieved. That being said, it is probably a good idea to clarify the original aims of CC. When the initial ideas were articulated in the mid-1990s, its founders shared a general belief that the convict/ex-convict voice was ignored, if not at least marginalized, in the academic fields of Criminology, Criminal Justice, and Corrections, in addition to policy-making contexts (Ross & Richards, 2003). CC also sought to help people who had been incarcerated, as well as those who had been released from jails or prisons who were interested in pursuing graduate degrees and perhaps careers in academia.

CC also attempted to engage in jail, prison, and criminal justice/legal activism and policy work, as a means to reform and transform corrections and the criminal justice system. Originally this kind of activity was difficult to do as older, former, or original members of CC were preoccupied and focused on organizational maintenance and development (Ross & Tietjen, 2023). Many individuals currently associated with CC feel that correctional reform is a treadmill and a futile endeavor; they want to do more than transform corrections, but want to change not just how the criminal justice/legal system operates, but also modify its goals, including a focus on de-carceration/prison abolition (Kalica, 2018) and a greater commitment to social justice. This focus may reflect the kinds of literature, instruction, and mentoring that the newer generation of CC members have been exposed to versus the older ones, which includes, but is not limited to, concentrations on popular Black feminist research, and sluggish criminal justice and correctional reforms.[3] It may also be a reflection of exposure to current social and cultural movements like Black Lives Matter and #MeToo. These subtle changes in CC's overall direction may also be the result of an increased awareness of these issues.

Meanwhile, CC was and still remains global in scope (e.g., Ross & Vianello, 2021), and this approach has developed due to the constant production of CC scholarship, the world wide web, increased social media attention, and an influx of new and more diverse members. In other words, the CC approach could be applied to any country that locks up a disproportionate number of its citizens, and not simply the locations where CC emerged.

Another thing to keep in mind is that CC was not established exclusively for convicts and ex-convicts, but also for individuals who were justice-contacted, justice-involved, and justice-impacted, and individuals who might be considered or self-identify as prison activists (Tietjen, 2019). Why? There are a significant number of men and women who, because of prior suspected or actual criminal activity committed by themselves or by a loved one, had close contact with the criminal justice system but were never charged, convicted, or incarcerated. This experience had a long lasting and deep effect on many of our colleagues, thus they support the overall CC mission and share its goals and vision.

Regardless, both the objectives of CC and most of the individuals who have been drawn to the network were and remain relatively heterogeneous but committed to the basic goals of the approach. The growth of CC, much like negotiating traffic whether as a pedestrian, bicyclist, or motorist, has been at times exciting, frustrating, and fun. On the plus side, CC has granted those affiliated with the group the opportunity to play a small part in advising (and in some cases mentoring) those released from correctional custody through their bachelor's and graduate degrees and into professional jobs. On the other hand, it can often be challenging to encounter individuals whose sole purpose seems to be to disrupt rather than to build consensus.

Why is it important to have a sense of where Convict Criminology is now and the future of the network?

Although one might wish to distinguish between the CC network and the official American Society of Criminology (ASC) Division of Convict Criminology (DCC), in reality, members of these two approaches to CC are comingled. In principle, this exercise can assist us with the strategic planning process. CC has limited resources (e.g., time, social capital, etc.), so it is wise to consider carefully their appropriate application and choose approaches that will minimize wastefulness. This strategic planning will also assist CC in adapting to current circumstances and enabling the network to achieve its stated goals.

How might the future of Convict Criminology be determined?

It is difficult to predict the future. This notion is even more salient when the world experiences black-swan events, such as the global COVID-19 pandemic. Nevertheless, experts have developed numerous qualitative and quantitative methods to assist them in trying to determine what the future might look like for a variety of situations and organizations. Choosing a suitable strategy among these options depends upon a number of factors, including the quality of the data and the resources that are available to perform the analysis.[4]

Written statements

Before trying to forecast the future of CC, select publicly available information may prove helpful to shaping our analysis. This includes the conclusions of major books on CC and published critiques of CC.

Conclusions of major books on Convict Criminology

Perhaps there is some merit in consulting the relatively short conclusions of the major CC texts (i.e., Ross & Richards, 2003; Earle, 2016, Ross & Vianello, 2021). Although the last chapters of the monographs predictably review or summarize the contents of the studies, only the two edited books by Ross and Richards, and Ross and Vianello, make suggestions for the future.

Moreover, although Richards and Ross (2003b) outline what they believe needs to be done to improve or reform the field of corrections, they do not make specific predictions or recommendations about what is in store for CC.[5]

Vianello and Ross, on the other hand, basically argue that the network should continue to do what it is doing, and they outline five "practical suggestions" (2021: 214–216). They are:

- "CC panels must be organized to accommodate the growing interest in the group" (p. 215);
- "strengthen our active involvement in prisoner education" (p. 215);
- develop and increase "contacts within the nonprofit sector (e.g., Foundations) and among prisoner support groups which advocate for prisoner rights and criminal reform and carry out awareness-raising campaigns" (p. 215);
- "take seriously the challenges of internationalization" (p. 216); and,
- "develop new opportunities inside the university environment (visiting professorships and exchanges for Ph.D. students) dedicated to former prisoners (which also means finding the funding for this purpose" (p. 216).

These recommendations were published in 2021. Although it might be useful determining where CC is with each of these suggestions, this strategy might be a little premature to engage in right now.

Critiques of Convict Criminology

Meanwhile, and as previously mentioned, a handful of critiques of CC have been published (e.g., Larsen & Piché, 2012; Newbold & Ross, 2012; Belknap, 2015). In sum, these evaluations point to three primary shortcomings within the CC framework: the CC methodology is not sufficiently rigorous; CC seems to be unnecessarily exclusive; and CC needs to do more to include women, ethnic minorities, and members of the LGBTQIA+ community.

Some of these criticisms are legitimate, whereas others are unfounded or based on a poor understanding of CC (Ross et al., 2016).[6] Currently, the most helpful approach to move CC forward is probably to perform a SWOT analysis.

Strengths, weaknesses, opportunities, and threats analysis

One of the prominent ways to determine the status of an organization and where it is going is the SWOT analysis method. Although many strategic planners and keen observers are aware of the flaws of this technique and, thus, disinclined to utilize this analytical approach, the SWOT method is relatively easy to perform, and thus an appropriate place to start this examination. In short, if it stimulates some productive conversations, then it will have served its purpose.

In my SWOT analysis, I focus primarily on the CC network, though I also comingle my review with the the DCC, and the field of corrections. In outlining what I believe are CC's current strengths, weaknesses, opportunities, and threats, issues might spill over from one category to another.

Strengths

Compared to other recent approaches to understanding and reforming corrections, CC remains a realistic policy-oriented approach to understanding and improving the lives of the many men and women who are incarcerated or released from correctional custody.

CC has close to three decades of scholarship, mentorship, activism, and experience to draw on, which includes providing a realistic picture of life behind bars, the experience of re-entry, and the fight to end mass incarceration, both in the United States and elsewhere. CC has assisted several formerly incarcerated men and women through their bachelor's, master's, and doctoral degrees. CC has also connected with a relatively large number of individuals who are interested in the subject and network. These men and women are not simply scholars, but are also students (at different levels of their formal education), people who are or were incarcerated, and supportive individuals who have not had direct contact with the criminal justice system.

In terms of scholarship, one of the more exciting developments has been the translation of Ross and Vianello's *Convict Criminology for the Future* into Portuguese and its publication as *A Criminologia dos Condenados e o Futuro*, by Brazilian publisher Tirant Lo Branch. Now that the book has been translated, it will be most useful to Portuguese-speaking students and scholars of Criminology/Criminal Justice and Corrections, journalists, prison activists, and relevant policy makers, legislators, and practitioners (i.e., especially individuals who work in correctional institutions) or those who are incarcerated. Among the ten countries where Portuguese is the principal language, the book may find its greatest utility in Brazil and Portugal, countries that have some of the highest numbers of people who are incarcerated.

Over the past decade, various Brazilian criminologists and lawyers have been introduced to CC scholarship and pedagogy. Hopefully, *A Criminologia dos Condenados e o Futuro* will be useful for them. The translation of the book into Portuguese should also increase discussions regarding not just the role of convicts and ex-convicts in the scholarly study of criminology/criminal justice, including much-needed reforms, but it will serve as a catalyst to greater cross-national co-operation in addressing the challenges faced by incarcerated individuals who are pursuing postgraduate studies while behind bars and upon release.

As previously mentioned, CC is now an official division of the ASC. The DCC also has a significant number of members. By latest counts, the division has 80 members in good standing (i.e., people who are officially registered and have paid their dues). Panels are well attended, as are the social functions that the division sponsors.

Why is this a good number? The division was granted official status during the COVID-19 pandemic, and the DCC now has more members than many other divisions of the ASC that were also recently started (https://asc41.com/divisions/division-account-balances-membership-figures/, accessed October 18, 2023). The DCC also has excellent relationships with other ASC divisions, including the divisions of Critical Criminology & Social Justice, People of Color & Crime, Queer Criminology, Victimology, and the Division of Feminist Criminology.

In 2023, the eight-member executive board of the DCC is diverse in terms of ethnicity, gender, and race, and at least half of this leadership body are women. A similar pattern exists in terms of the committees that report directly to the board. In short, CC has social capital. In a broader sense, no country has yet to abolish its correctional facilities nor is this going to happen any time soon. Furthermore, at least in the United States, the number of individuals who are being sent to jails and prisons is decreasing (Gramlich, 2021), while due to COVID-19 a greater number appear to have been released. Several of these men and women wish to complete not just bachelor's degrees, but advanced degrees as well. In the United States and Canada, at least, academia represents a real option for those men and women who will re-enter society. In other words, they may not be able to get a job in a trade, especially one that requires state licensing, but they may be able to secure a job and excel at teaching in a community college or university (see Exhibit Box 9.1).

Weaknesses

With respect to weaknesses, there continues to be a number of individuals who make and hold unfounded assumptions about CC. These beliefs are often based on rumors, incomplete information, or a poor understanding about the aims of CC, what CC does, and what it has accomplished. Why is this the case? It may have something to do with:

- the so-called death of expertise (e.g., Nichols, 2018);
- the exponential increase in the presence of and reliance on social media;
- confusion and poor understanding surrounding the role of lived experiences, and some people's and organizations' commitment to reifying the "lived experience"; and
- a disinclination, not just by the general public, but by many of our Criminology colleagues, to avoid reading peer-reviewed research and properly understanding it.

Why is this bad? CC constantly wages a battle against misinformation, and this becomes exhausting and frustrating. Several CC members appear to be burned out from continually having to explain CC concepts, ideas, and the purpose of this approach to critics who have read very little or no CC scholarship/literature at all. Since members of the network often juggle competing teaching, scholarship, service, and family demands, this becomes an additional burden.

Exhibit Box 9.1: Jennifer Marie Ortiz

Jennifer Marie Ortiz, Ph.D. (1986–) grew up in Brooklyn, New York City. At 15 years old she joined a street gang and at 19 years old, she was wrongfully arrested, which led to a lengthy legal battle. This experience inspired her to work for criminal justice reform. After enrolling at John Jay College of Criminal Justice, Ortiz moved away from gang life and began her work in Critical Criminology. She earned both a bachelor's and master's degree by the age of 23. She then enrolled in the doctoral program at the CUNY Graduate Center in New York City. Her dissertation advisor was the critical gang researcher, David Brotherton, who she originally met while still an active gang member. During her time in the doctoral program, Ortiz worked with the New York State Permanent Commission on Sentencing to reform the New York State penal code. Upon completing her doctoral degree, she began working as an assistant professor at Indiana University Southeast. During this time, her research focus shifted to prisoner re-entry, which was inspired by her marriage to a formerly incarcerated man. Ortiz launched a multi-year study on re-entry experiences in the Southern Indiana and Kentucky regions. Results from this study have been published in multiple journals and book chapters. Her personal experience and familial experience inspired her to work within CC to advocate for reform within the prison system. Ortiz served as an Executive Counselor on the inaugural board of the DCC. In this position, she developed a travel scholarship for system-impacted scholars. In 2022, Ortiz was elected to serve as the Chair of the DCC and has subsequently outlined her vision for the future of CC (2023a; 2023b). Ortiz is the author and co-author of numerous articles and chapters in scholarly books. She is the editor of *Critical and Intersectional Gang Studies* (Ortiz, 2023c).

Closely connected to this last point is the fact that several formerly incarcerated individuals seem to disengage with the CC network once they get out of prison or reach one or more educational milestones (i.e., bachelor's, master's, or doctoral degrees) (Ross & Tietjen, 2022).

Opportunities

The creation of the DCC represents a true opportunity. When the founders and their allies got together during the 1990s, they had very modest goals, which clarified ever so slightly over time. One of them was to not become a division of the ASC. In fact, there was quite a bit of resistance to this specific development, but over time, opposition to this idea softened.

On a related note, and as alluded to earlier, at no point in time has CC had as diverse a leadership group as it currently does. CC has also managed to attract a large number of curious and energetic graduate students.

Furthermore, CC possesses a very strong intellectual scholarly base (of peer-reviewed articles, chapters, and books) to draw on (Ross & Copes, 2022; Ross & Tietjen, 2022). One aspect of this effort has been a strong attachment to the

Journal of Prisoners on Prisons, which specializes in publishing convict authors in a peer-reviewed academic journal.

Threats

All organizations, learned or otherwise, will encounter obstacles both internally and externally, and CC is no different. CC will have to face a number of challenges in both the near and long term. (These cluster around the field, the division, universities, and society in general.) To begin with, there is often a tendency for individuals connected to this approach to get sidelined and go down rabbit holes. One of these tangents is the perennial discussion regarding changing the network's name, as well as that of the ASC division. In response, this issue was addressed in a joint article (Ortiz et al., 2022) that critically analyzed the ownership of the term *convict*. In general, six prominent considerations need to be addressed.

The academic subject area of Criminology/Criminal Justice has a tendency to begin new branches. Every few years, it seems that a new iteration of Criminology emerges (e.g., Cultural, Environmental, Ghost, Green, Rural, etc.). This creates distracting and competing pressure for our limited resources, especially in this attention-strapped economy.

Meanwhile, both correctional institutions and public universities continue to cut back on the funds they spend on academic activities. In the field of education this results in less money being made available to faculty and students to attend conferences, conduct research, graduate student stipends, etc.

The CC network has always had difficulty organizing people (not just those who are incarcerated) who share the CC mission, but are diverse and geographically spread out. This is especially true in terms of recently released individuals, who for valid reasons often prefer to fly below the radar. Also, they may or may not have access to financial resources to enroll in schools or attend conferences, plus, like all of us, they have competing demands.

The CC network also frequently struggles with individuals interested in CC not wanting to attend academic events. Formerly incarcerated members are often reluctant to tell individuals that they were formerly incarcerated, particularly in public settings, and CC never compels anyone to reveal their prior criminal or incarceration history. This is a totally personal decision. Having a criminal record, however, prevents the formerly incarcerated from doing numerous things. This is all part of the collateral consequences of incarceration. Most men and women closely affiliated with CC understand this dilemma, which affects the degree and quality of participation among individuals who are on the margins of CC.

As mentioned earlier, from the beginning, a considerable amount of misinformation or misperceptions about CC proliferated, including what CC is and what its goals are.[7] In order to address this issue both the network and organization has tried to minimize the negative reactions through the creation of a website, the launching of an official ASC division, the effective use of social media, the publishing of high quality, peer-reviewed research, and regular participation at academic Criminology/Criminal Justice conferences.

Finally, CC and the DCC periodically have to deal with a handful of so-called bad actors, bad ambassadors, bomb throwers, and contrarians. Some individuals attend DCC meetings, but due to a variety of dynamics, their primary goal often seems to be to disrupt, seek attention, or engage in intellectual one-upmanship. The actions of these people can have a debilitating effect on recruitment and retention, thus becoming a resource consuming distraction (Ross & Tietjen, 2022).

Suggestions for the future of Convict Criminology

There is no shortage of ideas to further the agenda and mission of Convict Criminology; members of the network talk about these possible initiatives on a regular basis. Moving forward involves being aware of the weaknesses and threats confronting CC, addressing them in a realistic and expeditious manner, and successfully marshalling the organization's strengths to make optimal use of its opportunities. The following are ten major suggestions for the future of CC that are reviewed from least to most important. However, before considering them, I wish to mention one direction that I do not think would be immediately useful.

Convict Criminology's presence in other learned organizations

Many of the large scholarly Criminology organizations have divisions on Corrections but lack Convict Criminology sections. For example, similar to what happened with the ASC Division of Critical Criminology & Social Justice, CC might consider starting a division of Convict Criminology with the Academy of Criminal Justice Sciences. Although this could be helpful, it is not pressing, since it may drain resources that could be best spent assisting the newly formed DCC. More useful are the following approaches and initiatives.

Better tracking of Convict Criminology accomplishments

Many CC members engage in considerable scholarship, mentoring, and activism, but this is rarely tracked or communicated to others. This critical step is often ignored because it is boring, time-consuming, distracting, or perceived as pretentious. By the same token, this kind of effort is necessary for members of the group to learn how to improve what they do and to demonstrate to external audiences our productivity and the breadth of our engagement. The Division of Convict Criminology official newsletter, "Criminology with Conviction," may be a suitable communication vehicle to capture this activity.

Continuously engage in self-reflection

If the CC network is going to grow and flourish, both the members and leadership must engage in self-reflection, carefully listen to its membership, and actively seek out the membership's desires, wants, and needs. It should also remain attuned to the fact that the person shouting the loudest may not necessarily reflect the best direction that the organization should take or be attuned to what is going on at a deeper level.

Regularly release Convict Criminology-relevant communications

To fulfill the activism mission of CC, the executive needs to release regular statements about issues that currently or will affect its membership and constituency. In support of this initiative, the DCC produced its very first newsletter in the fall of 2021, followed by another one in the fall of 2023. This is a resource-intensive exercise, but the DCC should now strive to release newsletters more frequently.

Periodically hold conferences separate from the American Society of Criminology

It is crucial for members of the CC network to meet on a regular basis to exchange scholarly communications, mentor junior colleagues, and develop a sense of community. This is why the annual conferences of the ASC are so essential to the maintenance of the CC approach. Also helpful are periodic meetings for people who are interested in CC but who may not live in the United States, where the majority of the ASC meetings take place. Examples of this kind of engagement were the Tampere, Finland (2010), Padua, Italy (2019), and London, England (2023) conferences. The CC network should re-examine the possibility of holding a CC conference in South America (Ross & Darke, 2018; Vegh Weis, 2021), for which Rio de Janeiro or São Paulo, Brazil, might be good locations. Why? Darke and Aresti have developed strong connections to a number of Brazilian criminologists and doctoral students there, and *Convict Criminology for the Future* (Ross & Vianello, 2021) was recently translated into Portuguese.

One of the issues that the CC network has also discussed is the failure of CC to take on much presence in other European countries. In 2023, a special issue of *Kriminologie*, a German scholarly journal (Graebsch & Knop, 2023), and a follow-up article (Graebsch & Ross, 2023) discuss why "Convict Criminology" has not received much traction in Germany and some of the other European countries. In short, the adoption of CC has a lot to do with how the academic study of Criminology/Criminal Justice is organized/taught in those locations, including dominant theoretical critiques that exist there. In many European countries, for example, Criminology/Criminal Justice is taught in law schools, but takes a back seat to understanding jurisprudence, etc. In Germany, in particular, there is a heavy emphasis on learning theory as a proxy for Critical Criminology and most other subdisciplines of this branch of Criminology appear to be missing.

Reconsider the necessity of separate national Convict Criminology groups

When CC originated, there was a belief that because the practice of corrections is slightly different in each country (Aresti & Darke, 2016; Earle, 2018) and because formerly incarcerated individuals often experience international travel restrictions, it might be wise to create separate CC organizations in places like the United Kingdom, Australia, and New Zealand (Carey et al., 2022). Over time, however, because of the ebb and flow of people who have come in and out of the network, and improvements in web-based electronic communications (e.g., Facetime, Skype, Zoom, etc.), the need and desire to form country-specific divisions or chapters seems less important now than it once did (e.g., Aresti et al., 2023).

Adopt new communication technologies

Closely connected to the previous point, conferences are expensive to attend, frequently requiring flights and hotel stays, as well as conference fees. They are also very time-consuming. One way to counter these costs is to increase the use of online conferences. In order to do that, individuals in the CC network need to master communication strategies like Zoom or other web-based conference applications. For example, one of the first times this method was successfully utilized was during the (2021) ASC annual conference that was held in Chicago. At this venue, the DCC customized a system using personal Zoom presentations that were then streamed to individual computers.

Organize special issues of relevant academic journals

Over the history of CC, the *Journal of Prisoners on Prisons* has published three special issues devoted to the network. The very first was edited by Stephen Richards and Mike Lenza, and the second by Aresti and Darke, while the third was managed by Grant Tietjen, Alison Cox, and J. Renee Trombley (2021–2023). Each team has brought with it a set of unique knowledge and skills, attracting and mentoring new people to CC through their respective networks.[8]

Battle misinformation

It is important to quickly identify specious arguments advanced about Corrections in general and CC in particular by individuals who have minimal contact and understanding of these fields, or have overly ideological viewpoints. Often these men and women show up at CC panels and meetings, and make broad overgeneralizations about jails, prisons, convicts, and unfounded claims about CC. If CC representatives are amenable, they should spend the necessary resources trying to educate these individuals. This requires sending these people articles and chapters to read, as well as challenging their misinformed and poorly conceived arguments in a systematic but nonthreatening manner.

Boost ongoing mentoring efforts

Finally, and most importantly, there is a continuous need to recruit the next generation of capable individuals into the CC field. This involves being sensitive to the issues of gender, ethnicity, race and socioeconomic class, and requires proper mentoring (Tietjen et al., 2021). In the past, various members of CC have tried to launch an essay-writing program, but the responses were lackluster. Part of the reason for this failure was that many CC members are graduate students who have numerous obligations and limited resources (e.g., free time). Also, some people do not know the potential of the organization. Thus, CC needs dedicated and rational leaders that will step up to meet that challenge by continuing to disseminate the framework's ideas and mentoring a younger generation. This could be done in the context of conferences, papers, and publications (Ross et al., 2015b).

Conclusion

Although CC has contributed to the scholarly literature in Criminology and Criminal Justice in general, and Corrections and Critical Criminology in particular (Ross & Copes, 2022), mentored numerous individuals from incarceration through release (and throughout the completion of undergraduate, master's, and doctoral degrees), and advocated for prison reform, the way forward for CC is anything but clear.

Understandably, a considerable amount of interesting scholarship, mentorship, and activism is being accomplished by newer members of the ASC DCC and beyond. And the increasing diversity of the CC group bodes well for the network's attempts to expand its base and outreach. Ultimately, the future of CC depends on the commitment of its members, and the skills and personalities of its leaders. The future will also be shaped, to some extent, by the organization's relationship to the ASC, and changes taking place in the wider fields of Critical Criminology and Corrections.

However, if CC and the DCC can be strategic about the environment in which they operate, the individuals who are interested in the CC approach, and their goals, they will enhance their ability to make a positive contribution to the academic fields of Critical Criminology, Criminology, Criminal Justice, and Corrections by assisting people who are incarcerated and recently released to earn bachelor's, master's, and doctoral degrees, and to take their place in academia, or wherever their knowledge and skills can be best used.

Because it deserves repeating, an individual does not need to be formerly incarcerated to identify with the CC perspective nor must one be a member of the ASC DCC to be considered a convict criminologist (Ross et al., 2016).

CC would like others to participate in its journey, to be part of its story, and to ultimately improve the lives of men and women who are or were once incarcerated, as well as the lives of their loved ones who have been justice-contacted, involved, or impacted. The hope is to assist formerly incarcerated people to successfully re-enter society, earn degrees, and make valuable contributions to their communities. This is why CC should not be seen as a destination or an end in itself, but a work in progress.

Part of CC's success will be tied to its ability to achieve its modest goals. CC, more specifically the DCC, has a diverse, energetic, experienced, knowledgeable, and thoughtful leadership that is committed to the success of the organization. However, CC will also need to create meaningful feedback loops with its membership and audience, while remaining committed to deliberately pursuing goals in a more strategic way. CC also needs to do a better job encouraging individuals to read the scholarship on CC, and to not simply jump to conclusions about what they think they know about the field. Other things CC should do in the future are to be mindful of inclusion and to prevent the naysayers and bomb throwers from distracting it from achieving its mission (Ross, 2020). Lastly, CC may want to tease out a theory that is meaningful to constituencies who want this sort of thing.

In principle, CC will still be around as long as the voices of prisoners are ignored, and system-contacted, system-involved, and system-impacted people continue to be marginalized, want to bond with each other, and correctional facilities exist. The DCC expects to be active for many years to come. CC sincerely believes in the power of transformation. Together the CC network can further strive to change policy, practices, and laws dealing with incarceration.

Over time, the number of individuals interested in the CC approach has increased. Today the network includes several ex-convict professors, Ph.D. students, and prison activist scholars that conduct research and write together. Members of the group actively participate in mentoring initiatives and, time permitting, various types of activism. The organization impacts both the academic study of jails, prisons, and policy makers who are in positions to initiate changes in correctional facilities.

Most of these people demonstrate a passion for the study of contemporary correctional facilities and the lived experience of men and women who do or have done time there. Their knowledge is not simply derived from reading scholarly and popular texts, watching documentaries and television reality shows, and occasional visits to correctional institutions.

Unlike other ex-convicts who reoffend, and are sent back to prison, or are content to live their lives working in marginal jobs, keeping quiet and out of sight, not rocking the boat, most convict criminologists put their experience to good use through scholarship, teaching, activism, and news media outreach. This does not mean that they always agree on controversial issues. Sometimes the CC network have heated and exhausting debates about the subject matter they research and the appropriate way to get an idea across. Fortunately, individuals committed to the CC approach see this dialectic as a strength rather than a shortcoming of our relationships and intellectual collaboration.

CC is a work in progress, and is subject to debate, but not unless those coming to the table are well informed and well intentioned. It is hoped that this book, in some small way, has contributed to the foundational knowledge of this approach. Thanks to all who have made CC a reality.

APPENDIX

Chronology of the History
of Convict Criminology

1938	Ex-convict and Columbia University professor Frank Tannenbaum (1893–1969) publishes *Crime and Community*, based on his experiences of being incarcerated, a scholar, and a prison reformer.
1970	Ex-convict and San Francisco State University professor John Irwin (1929–2010) publishes *The Felon*, based on his lived experience as a prisoner and as an academic researcher.
1983	First Prison Abolition Conference held in Toronto, Canada.
1988	Canadian scholars Howard Davidson, Liz Elliott, and Robert Gaucher establish *Journal of Prisoners on Prisons*, the first scholarly journal devoted to publishing peer-reviewed research by convicts and ex-convicts.
1992	Jeffrey Ian Ross and Stephen C. Richards are introduced to each other, and discuss multiple issues connected to crime, criminal justice, and corrections.
1997	First panel of ex-convicts who had earned a Ph.D. or were in the process of completing one is held at the American Society of Criminology's (ASC) annual meeting in San Diego.
1998	Ross and Richards coin the term Convict Criminology (CC) and decide to co-edit a scholarly book on the subject.

INTRODUCTION TO CONVICT CRIMINOLOGY

2003	Ross and Richards' co-edited *Convict Criminology* is published.
2004–2015	Richards and Chris Rose lead the "Inviting Convicts to College" Program in two Wisconsin state prisons and use *Convict Criminology* as the core text.
2007	Ikponwosa "Silver" Ekunwe and Richard L. Jones hold the "Global Perspectives on Re-Entry" conference in Tampere, Finland. At least half of the paper presenters were members of the CC network.
2011	Ekunwe and Jones' co-edited *Global Perspectives on Re-Entry*, which includes the papers presented at the conference, is published.
2011	Sacha Darke, Andy Aresti, and Rod Earle hold panel on CC, at the annual meeting of the British Society of Criminology, in Newcastle, England.
2012	Richards and Mike Lenza co-edit special issue of *Journal of Prisoners on Prison* on CC.
2012	Darke, Aresti, and Earle establish British Convict Criminology group.
2016	Formerly incarcerated professor, Earle, at the Open University, publishes *Convict Criminology: Inside and Out*, the first sole-authored book on Convict Criminology, that primarily examines the prehistory of CC.
2016–2019	Darke and Aresti organize and participate in a series of workshops on CC in Brazil.
2018	Darke and Aresti co-edit a special issue of *Journal of Prisoners on Prison* on CC.
2018	American CC group adopts their first constitution at the ASC meetings in Philadelphia. Grant Tietjen and Denise Woodall elected as co-chairs.
2019	Francesca Vianello and Ross hold the conference "Convict Criminology for the Future" at the University of Padua. Attended by several CC members.

APPENDIX

2020	Executive of the ASC approve creation of a formal Division of Convict Criminology.
2020	Ross and Vianello's co-edited *Convict Criminology for the Future* is published.
2021	ASC Division of Convict Criminology celebrates its first year in operation. Organization establishes several awards in research and mentoring.
2022	*Convict Criminology for the Future* is translated into Portuguese, by Maria Lucia Karam, and published as *A Criminologia dos Condenados e o Futuro*, by the Brazilian publisher Tirant Lo Blanch.
2022	Jennifer Ortiz is elected as chair of the Division of Convict Criminology.
2023	Grant Tietjen, Alison Cox, and J. Renee Trombley edit the special issue, "25 Years of Convict Criminology," for the *Journal of Prisoners of Prison*.
2023	Convict Criminology in Italy organization established.
2023	Under the leadership of professors Breanna (Bree) Bopree and Alison Cox, the ASC Division of Convict Criminology sponsors its first formal mentoring program.
2023	Darke and Aresti (under the auspices of the Convict Criminology at University of Westminster program) organize a four-day symposium, "Inside Prison Perspectives in Europe & the Americas." Panels are held at HMP Coldingley, HMP Pentonville, HMP Gendron, and the University of Westminster.

Note

Special thanks to Andy Aresti, Sacha Darke, Daniel Ryan Kavish, and Grant Tietjen for comments on an earlier version of this appendix.

Keywords

Activism

A variety of activities (including but not limited to signing a petition, engaging in a protest, etc.) that individuals may engage in to further a political or social cause.

Activist

A person who engages in behaviors associated with activism. These actions include, but are not limited to, organizing or joining protests, participating in boycotts, engaging in letter-writing campaigns, etc.

Activist scholarship

Academic research and inquiry that is driven by a commitment to social and political activism. It emphasizes scholarly methods and expertise to address and challenge systems of oppression, inequality, and injustice.

Approach

A method used to address a challenge, problem, tackle a task, achieve a goal, or understand a situation. It provides a structured framework or set of guiding principles that enable decision-making and actions.

Authenticity politics

The recognition, struggle, promotion, and efforts engaged in by people, their collectives, and supporters who have direct experience with an issue, or are part of a specific organization from which they derive their identity, to be the primary voice of that group or collectivity.

Autobiography

A narrative of a person's life written by the person whose life is discussed. Unlike a memoir, an autobiography attempts to cover the individual's entire life.

Autoethnography	A qualitative research method using first-person accounts and experiences, that are collected and analyzed in a systematic fashion.
Bad ambassadors	Current or former members of a group, or those who claim to be, that have negative interactions with outsiders, including people who may be interested in the activities of the organizations and/or joining in its collective mission, but end up alienating these individuals, including dissuading them from learning more about the organization, and possibly assisting or joining the collective.
Ban the Box	Efforts by activists, including prison reformers, to remove questions about criminal history from job and educational applications. Critics argued that workplace and educational institutions can still conduct criminal background checks later, maintaining control over student acceptance and continued employment.
Biography	A written account of an individual's life story not written by the person whose life is discussed. It typically includes information about the person's background, experiences, achievements, and significant events, providing insights into their personal, professional, or historical significance.
Carceral	Of, relating, or pertaining to a system where individuals are locked up and their basic rights are taken away. Similar to a total institution (Goffman, 1961). Places where this occurs include, but are not limited to: civil commitment centers, correctional boot camps, jails, prisons, juvenile justice facilities, halfway houses, immigration detention centers, immigration removal centers, mental hospitals, military detention centers, secure treatment facilities, and secure residential treatment centers.
Carceral citizenship	The reduced rights (e.g., voting, participating in juries, etc.) that people who have been

convicted of a crime and released from correctional facilities are relegated to. This may lead to efforts by formerly incarcerated individuals to expand these rights and protect themselves and others from discrimination once released (i.e., the collateral consequences of incarceration).

Civil commitment

A process where an individual is legally detained by the government. Places where a person can be detained can include a mental hospital, juvenile institution, or correctional facility (e.g., jail or prison).

Community corrections

Refers to a set of sanctions, such as probation and parole, applied to individuals convicted of a crime, allowing them to serve their sentence within the community rather than in a correctional facility.

Community service

A type or part of a criminal sentence, that an individual convicted of a crime may be ordered by a judge to perform. It typically involves some sort of work that will benefit the neighborhood, town, or city where the crime was committed.

Convict

An individual who has not simply been convicted of a crime, but who has spent a reasonable period of time (not a weekend) incarcerated in a jail or prison at the local, state, or federal level (the term is typically used as a synonym for prisoner or inmate).

Convict Criminology

A group, field, framework, movement, perspective, movement, network, organization, theory, or more appropriately an approach that recognizes that the prisoner voice has typically been ignored in scholarship on corrections, and in policy debates. It also confronts knowledge about jails, prisons, and re-entry that is based on untested assumptions or poor research. Convict Criminology rests on three pillars: scholarship, mentoring, and policy and activism. It also

	encourages the scholarship of individuals who have experience of incarceration, but also have earned a Ph.D. in Criminology/Criminal Justice or a related field.
Correctional facility/institution	A secure setting that includes, but is not limited to, correctional boot camps, jails, prisons, juvenile justice facilities, and halfway houses.
Correctional officer (CO)	Individual who is responsible for maintaining custody of prisoners and order in the cellblocks, tiers, and wings of a correctional facility.
Correctional worker	This includes not simply correctional officers, but also social workers, psychologists, and other front-line staff who work in a correctional facility.
Corrections	Broad encompassing term that covers the institutions/facilities, policies, procedures, programs, and services that we associate with jails, prisons, inmates, COs, and administrators and other correctional workers.
Criminal justice	The study of law enforcement (i.e., policing), corrections (including probation and parole), courts, and juvenile justice.
Criminal justice industrial complex	The set of linkages among both the public and private sector which support criminal justice sanctions and institutions as the major solutions for dealing with crime and deviance in society and profit from this relationship.
Criminal justice system	A set of government institutions (i.e., police, courts, corrections, and juvenile justice) that are responsible for arresting, convicting, and punishing individuals who break the criminal law.
Criminal justice system-contacted (or system-contacted for short)	Refers to individuals who have had direct contact with law enforcement or the criminal justice system either as victims, witnesses, or suspects, but their involvement might

	be incidental or peripheral to the main case or investigation.
Criminal justice system–involved (or system–involved for short)	Refers to people who are actively participating or engaged in the criminal justice system. It includes men and women who have been accused, arrested, charged, or convicted of a crime and are going through various stages of the legal process, such as investigation, trial, or serving a sentence.
Criminal justice system–impacted (or system–impacted for short)	Refers to someone who experiences the effects of the system without necessarily being a direct participant in criminal activities or legal proceedings. This category can include families of victims, communities affected by crime, and individuals who may face collateral consequences from the criminal justice process.
Criminology	The academic study of the causes and effects of crime.
Critical Criminology	A perspective that emphasizes "[q]uestioning, challenging and examining all sides of various [crime and criminal justice] problems and issues … delves under the surface … it dispels many myths and misconceptions … it demystifies the objectives, processes and outcomes … and offers alternative interpretations and solutions" (Welch, 1996: 6).
Deterrence	Method/s preventing individuals from committing crime.
Discretion	A decision made by criminal justice practitioners to invoke the law/criminal sanction. In the case of police, it includes the decision to stop, question, search, ticket, warn, arrest, and to use deadly force against a suspect.
Doing time	Refers to the period an individual spends incarcerated or serving a prison sentence. It implies enduring the confinement, restrictions, and challenges associated with imprisonment,

	including the loss of personal freedom, separation from society, and the passage of time within a correctional facility.
Ethnography	Qualitative research method that involves systematic observation and interaction (i.e., talking/listening) with research subjects and behavior under investigation.
Faith-based programming	Using the skills and resources of religious communities, especially evangelical Christian, to help in the reform of people who are incarcerated.
Fake allies	Individuals or groups who claim to support marginalized communities, including social justice or diversity initiatives, but engage in performative actions without genuine commitment or substantive change. These entities may publicly espouse progressive values but fail to take meaningful steps to address systemic issues or actively perpetuate oppressive dynamics in the spaces they live and work.
Feminist Convict Criminology	The application of feminist ideas to those advanced by Convict Criminology.
Fine	Financial payment made to the courts and/or judge as a sanction in criminal matter.
Formerly incarcerated	Term used to describe a person who spent time behind bars but has since been released.
General Education Development (GED)	A high-school equivalency program and credential in the United States. It provides individuals who did not complete traditional high-school education with an opportunity to demonstrate their knowledge and skills in subjects such as math, science, social studies, and language arts through a series of exams. Upon passing the GED tests, individuals receive a credential equivalent to a high school diploma.
Gender	A person's classification into male or female. Also involves societies' social construction of

	male and female roles in relation to society or a culture.
Imposter syndrome	A situation in which a person occasionally or persistently doubts their own abilities and fears being exposed as a fraud, despite evidence of their competence. These individuals regularly feel inadequate, and think that their achievements are the result of luck or deception rather than genuine skill or merit.
Imprisonment	The act of confining someone in a correctional facility as a punishment for committing a crime. It typically involves longer-term confinement, where individuals are sentenced by a court of law after being found guilty of a crime.
Incarceration	Term that generally refers to the act of confining someone in a jail, prison, or detention facility as a form of punishment or while awaiting trial. It is a broad term that encompasses various forms of confinement, including both imprisonment and other methods of restricting a person's freedom, such as house arrest or detention centers for immigration purposes.
Inmate	Popularly used as a synonym for prisoner or convict. Perceived by some people to be a pejorative term used against individuals who are incarcerated.
"Inside-Out Prison Exchange" Program	Started in 1997, by Lori Pompa, as a pilot program, at Temple University, this initiative brings undergraduate students into the local prisons where they, along with inmates, both receive instruction for credit, in university classes.
Institutional Review Board (IRB)	An administrative body typically established in a research institution or university, that ensures the ethical and regulatory compliance of research involving human and animal subjects. The IRB reviews, approves, and monitors

research protocols to protect the rights, welfare, and privacy of research participants/subjects and attempts to protect the institution from liability claims.

Intersectionality

The acknowledgement that people may share multiple backgrounds built upon ethnicity, race, class, gender, and sexuality. Convict Criminology has attempted to incorporate diverse voices from these groups and backgrounds to accommodate how they influence the experiences and perspectives of individuals within the criminal justice system.

Jail

Term used in some Anglo-American democracies, to refer to state-run correctional institutions where inmates either await trial or are sentenced for up to one year.

Jailhouse lawyer

Inmate, sometimes with formal legal training, who assists other prisoners in the preparation of legal documents and advises them about the criminal legal processes.

Law

The system of rules that a particular jurisdiction establishes to regulate the actions of its members and may enforce by the imposition of penalties.

Learned society

An academic organization that specializes in a particular field of study or discipline. It typically fosters the exchange of knowledge, research, and expertise among its members through conferences, publications, and other related activities. It may also serve as a platform for networking and information about available jobs and grants.

Life without parole

Sentence given to a person convicted of a serious felony. Convicts given this kind of sanction are required to spend the balance of their life locked up in a correctional facility. In the United States, in general, this sanction is no longer applicable to juveniles who have committed felonies.

Lived experience	The knowledge, skills, and understandings acquired by an individual (usually a convict or ex-convict) who has had significant contact with the criminal justice system, specifically through incarceration or prior incarceration.
Mass imprisonment	A situation where a jurisdiction incarcerates almost everyone who is convicted of a crime no matter how minor it is.
Mass media	A collection of media technologies that reach a large audience via mass communication. Includes a variety of mechanisms such as movies, newspapers, social media, etc.
Media	Tools used to store and deliver information or data.
Memoir	A story written by a person that recounts a narrow (and significant) portion of that person's life.
Mentoring	The provision of meaningful and helpful assistance to individuals who are trying to achieve an important goal. In academic contexts, mentoring goes beyond instructing and basic activities like writing letters of recommendation, to typically include the provision of career advice and guidance.
Mutual help	A situation when individuals who share similar backgrounds provide assistance to each other to improve the collective resources of one another.
Net widening	The recognition that over time, instead of closing jails and prisons, the criminal justice systems develops new ways to monitor and sanction people who break the law. Also includes the expansion of probation and parole to include things like urine tests, home detention, etc. Perceived to be a negative trend.
Network	In the context of academia, this is a system connecting scholars, researchers, and

	institutions in the academic community. It promotes collaboration, knowledge sharing, and idea exchange through partnerships, conferences, and online platforms, facilitating research and education across disciplines and locations.
News media	Elements of the mass media that focus on delivering news to the general public or a target audience (i.e., via print media, broadcast news, internet, etc.).
Newsmaking Criminology	An approach within the academic fields of Criminology/Criminal Justice that examines the role of news media in shaping public perceptions and understandings of crime and criminal behavior. It explores how media representations and coverage influence public opinion, policy making, and the criminal justice system's response to crime-related issues.
No Frill Prisons Act	Passed in 2001, this legislation bars such amenities as televisions and coffee pots in Federal Bureau of Prisons cells.
Observation	Qualitative study that only involves observation of subjects or their behavior in particular settings or situations.
Parole	When an inmate is released from a correctional facility back into the community in advance of the expiration of their sentence. They are subjected to numerous sanctions that they must abide by.
Participant observation	When the researcher partakes in the behavior under investigation to better understand the thoughts and motivations of individuals who engage in a particular kind of behavior under investigation.
Peacemaking Criminology	A branch of Critical Criminology proposed by Pepinsky and Quinney (1991), that argues the dominant way that crime and criminal justice

in the United States is handled is similar to a war and this approach produces more harm than good. They argue instead that there must be peace among perpetrators, victims of crime, criminal justice practitioners, and the wider community.

Peer-review research

Research that is submitted to a respectable and/or recognized peer-reviewed scholarly journal or book publisher. If the paper/draft book manuscript holds merit, the editor then sends it out to three or more subject matter expert reviewers/referees. The writer's identity is concealed, as is the identity of the reviewers/referees. This process of quality control, called "blind review," is meant to guard against bias. Reviewers try to determine the merit of the research. Referees generally make one of three recommendations: accept, reject, or revise and resubmit. Peer-reviewed research is more credible than non-peer-reviewed research.

Pell Grant

Named after Senator Claiborne Pell, this federal government financial aid program is designed to help eligible undergraduate students with limited financial resources to achieve their higher education. Pell Grants are awarded based on financial need, taking into account factors such as family income, assets, and the cost of attendance. The grant does not need to be repaid, making it a valuable resource for students seeking to cover tuition fees, books, and other educational expenses

Policy

A written or verbal understanding and/or guideline on how to approach a particular situation.

Praxis

Refers to the process of applying theoretical knowledge or beliefs into practical action. In this context scholarly ideas are tested and transformed through real-world engagement, aiming to create meaningful and transformative change.

Prison	A physical institution where individuals who are convicted of a crime are incarcerated. Typically the person has committed a felony and the duration of the sentence is more than a year.
Prison abolition	The goal of a social movement dedicated to eradicating parts and/or the entire current institutional criminal punishment system (i.e., jails, prisons and other correctional facilities) in the United States and elsewhere.
Prison industrial complex	"[A] set of bureaucratic, political, and economic interests that encourage increased spending on imprisonment, regardless of the actual need" (Schlosser, 1998: 54).
Prisoner re-entry	The practice of releasing prisoners from jail and prison through mandatory release and/or parole back into society.
Prisoner union	An organized group of incarcerated individuals who join together to collectively advocate for their rights, improve living conditions, and address issues such as healthcare, education, visitation rights, and fair treatment within correctional facilities.
Prisonization	When a prisoner accommodates to the norms and routines of the correctional facility.
Probation	A person convicted of a crime is given a jail or prison sentence, but it is suspended if they comply with certain conditions (e.g., seek employment, or work a job, attend an educational institution, etc.) while out in the community.
Project Rebound	An educational initiative that provides support and resources to formerly incarcerated individuals seeking university education in publicly funded California State universities. It aims to increase access to education, reduce recidivism rates, and promote successful reintegration into society by offering academic advising,

counseling, mentorship, and other services to help individuals navigate the educational system.

Public Criminology

Attempts to bring the findings of criminological research to audiences beyond academic criminologists. This includes engagement with a variety of media by serving as sources for articles that reporters are writing, consenting to be interviewed, and writing op-eds.

Qualitative research

Research that depends upon the collection and analysis of non-numerical data, including words, images, and observations of the investigator.

Quantitative research

Research that primarily involves the collection and analysis of statistics or numerical data.

Recidivism

A measure that can include one of the following alternative kinds of interrelated actions/behaviors: ex-convicts committing another crime; ex-convicts being arrested; ex-convicts charged with a crime; and ex-convicts returning to jail or prison.

Rehabilitation

Programs and practices (typically educational, skills training, and counselling) used in correctional facilities to assist convicts so that upon release they will be better able to function in society and give up a life of crime.

Restitution

Court-ordered sanction imposed on a person convicted of a crime, requiring them to pay compensation for injuries sustained or loss of wages or goods, or a requirement that a convicted individual provides a service directly to a victim, the victim's family, or an organization (e.g., business).

Retribution

Harsh response by victim, their family, friends, and/or the community to a person who is suspected of, or has been convicted of a crime.

Scholarship

Research that goes beyond acquiring facts. Mainly uses rigorous scientific methods and critical analysis. The research is usually published in a respected academic venue, attempts to push disciplinary boundaries, and develop new insights. Scholars contribute to their disciplines/fields with new ideas and discoveries.

Scientific research A way of testing theories and hypotheses by applying certain rules or methods of analysis to observations and interpretation of reality under strictly delineated circumstances.

Second Chance Act Federal legislation, passed in 2008, which provides additional resources to states and private entities to help prisoners make the transition back to the community.

Security level Classification used in correctional settings based on the dangerousness of inmates. Includes Supermax, maximum, medium, and minimum security correctional facilities. As the conditions move from Supermax to minimum they are more relaxed at less secure facilities.

Social media Computer-mediated technologies that allow communicators to view, create, and share a variety of different types of information to virtual communities and networks.

Social movement A collection of like-minded individuals organized to bring about social or political change. It involves a sustained campaign, often involving protests, activism, and advocacy, with the aim of challenging existing power structures, addressing specific grievances, and promoting societal transformation.

Special interest group An organization, typically composed of dues-paying members, that work on behalf of the collective membership to achieve an objective. This includes unions, associations, and political organizations other than political parties.

Status fragility Refers to the vulnerability or instability of one's social or hierarchical position within a given context. It describes a condition in which an individual's status or social standing is susceptible to disruption, challenges, or loss due to external factors, changes in circumstances, or power dynamics within a social system.

Theory

A comprehensive explanation of a phenomenon that occurs in the natural world. Typically includes a set of principles, laws, and hypotheses that are supported by extensive empirical evidence and have withstood rigorous testing and scrutiny. They are also used to explain and predict phenomena, providing a coherent and logical explanation of how and why certain events occur.

Total Quality Management

Management philosophy and approach (including a system of techniques) that are designed to continuously improve products produced or services delivered, customer satisfaction, and the involvement of all employees in an organization. It emphasizes the importance of quality in all aspects of operations, processes, products, and services to achieve organizational excellence and long-term success.

Victim–offender mediation

A formal method that brings victims of crimes and the individual who perpetrated those crimes together, to discuss how the incident negatively affected the victim's life, and perhaps understand why the perpetrator engaged in that behavior. The hope is that it will enable the perpetrator to take responsibility for their actions, perhaps feel and express remorse, and possibly lead to some sort of resolution for both parties.

Virtue signaling

Expressing a moral value, belief, or position in a public forum (e.g., via speech, social media post, etc.) mainly to seek the approval from a social group aligned with that position, without actually having to engage in any meaningful actions in support of that belief.

Notes

Preface: Getting Started with Convict Criminology

[1] Unless otherwise specified, all future references to prisons should also assume that the author is also talking about jails.

[2] The concept of lived experience will be discussed in greater detail later in this book.

[3] These terms are explained in greater detail in the book and in the Keywords section.

[4] Unfortunately, when examples of CC activity in foreign countries are provided, they may be similar in some respects to CC activity, but do not conform to the CC approach (see especially discussion in Chapter 1).

[5] Crim 343 "Convict Criminology," St. John Fisher College; Crim 311 "Convict Criminology," University of Southern Indiana; and CJ 353 "Convict Criminology," University of Wisconsin–Oshkosh.

[6] 01:202:303 "Prison and Prisoners," Rutgers University; CRJ 420/520 "Seminar in Correctional Criminology," Delta State University.

Chapter 1

[1] Numerous relatively brief overviews of the history of Convict Criminology have been published (e.g., Richards & Ross, 2005; Ross & Richards, 2005; Richards et al., 2007; 2009; Jones et al., 2009; Mobley, 2010; Newbold et al., 2010; Ross et al., 2011b; Earle, 2016; Newbold, 2017; Ross, 2021b).

[2] Although this perception has not been empirically tested, one might legitimately ask why does it exist? One widely held belief is that many of the individuals who were understood to be experts in corrections at that time demonstrated elitist and protectionist attitudes and behaviors. Thus, they became gatekeepers and wanted to control the narrative about who has the credentials to speak with authority about jails, prisons, etc., what subject matters are most important, which research methods are best used to understand what goes on behind bars, and thus who is the real expert? This explanation may find its roots in the work of Bachrach and Baratz (1962), who advanced the concept of mobilization of bias.

[3] In some respects this perspective shares some intellectual space with Scott's (1991) writing on "The evidence of experience" and feminist standpoint theory (e.g., Harding, 2004), but also differs in several important respects.

[4] Two issues are important here. First, these categories can overlap, and individuals may transition from one category to another over the course of a criminal case. Second, the criminal justice system is complex, involving various stakeholders such as law enforcement, prosecutors, defense attorneys, judges, and corrections personnel, all of whom can be considered "system-involved" in their respective roles. Great examples of scholarship discussing these categories include, but are not limited to, Cox (2021) and Disha et al. (2021).

[5] See, for example, Fisher-Giorlando (2003).

INTRODUCTION TO CONVICT CRIMINOLOGY

[6] In recent years, this criterion has been called into question. Why? Increasingly a handful of formerly incarcerated individuals, who have earned a master's degree, but fallen short of earning a doctorate, are publishing about CC content in scholarly journals.

[7] In many respects CC is similar to the wounded healer concept and the third mile resistance approach.

[8] This section builds upon Ross (2021d).

[9] See, for example, scholarship in the field of "Mad Studies" (e.g., Beresford & Russo, 2021).

[10] Also, the discussion here is not about cultural appropriation or situations such as the ones involving former George Washington University professor, Dr. Jessica Krug, or former Spokane National Association for the Advancement of Colored People (NAACP) chapter president, Rachel Dolezal, both of whom were from White families, but tried to pass as African-Americans. Nor does it refer to University of California Riverside Professor Andrea Smith, also from a White family who has claimed to be Native American but appears to lack any documentary evidence to support this claim (Viren, 2021).

[11] Earle, a convict criminologist, said it best when he stated, "To be clear, though, I do not argue that lived experience provides necessarily or intrinsically 'better' forms of understanding, or that 'lived experience' exists in any unitary, essential form of knowledge about prison" (2020: 81).

[12] For a discussion of different levels of understanding of what occurs in correctional facilities, see for example Ross (2021c).

[13] We could probably add the myth of assuming that Convict Criminology is an ideology, but this claim probably stems from a poor understanding of what an ideology is.

[14] Earle, without pointing to specific scholarship or public statements, argues, "The very idea of convict criminology seems to condense these differences into a single unitary perspective, almost a master-narrative. I struggle with that reduction" (2020: 82).

[15] For an argument how a prison sentence is like receiving the death penalty consult Ross (2012b).

[16] Thanks to Daniel Kavish for this insight.

[17] Irwin also notes that "Convict Criminology tends to exist in tension with administrative criminology, an approach where academics are hired by the state which is likely to control everything the researcher will ultimately write and discover. The theoretical grounding of this is that administrative criminology assumes that the criminal justice system works and that all you need to do is to make it run better" (2020: 142).

[18] Nellis (2013), in a review of *Convict Criminology* (Ross & Richards, 2003), argues that Cultural and Convict Criminology are "seen as related developments with convict criminology very much the subsidiary" (Nellis, 2013: 237). Critical Criminology has also been in the forefront of critiquing the net-widening phenomenon of the criminal justice system.

[19] It is essential to note that over the past five decades numerous subdisciplines of Critical Criminology have evolved, including: Cultural Criminology, Green Criminology, Peacemaking Criminology, Realist Criminology, Southern Criminology, etc.

[20] Additional scholarship includes Presser and Sandberg (2015). For a critique of Narrative Criminology see, for example, Maruna and Liem (2021).

[21] For a recent critique of scholarly studies on gangs, see, for example, Ortiz (2023c).

[22] Undoubtedly this begs the question of what qualifies as a significant period of time. There are no hard and fast rules establishing a criteria. Although some have suggested that in order to fully identify as a convict criminologist one needs to go to prison as opposed to jail, after careful reflection this distinction is probably insufficient to understand the carceral experience.

Chapter 2

[1] See, for example, the chronology included as the appendix in Ross and Vianello (2021).

[2] Other so-called tertiary developments could include Reflexive Criminology (e.g., Lumdsen & Winter, 2014), Narrative Criminology (e.g., Presser & Sandberg, 2015), and Intersectionality (e.g., Crenshaw, 2017).

NOTES

3   Tietjen and Kavish (2021) point out that CC's body of research and criminal justice worldview was premised in the tough-on-crime era of the 1990s. Framing criminology from this perspective may not appropriately capture the current 21st-century societal stances toward criminal justice. Thus, a shift toward focusing research to reflect on the current criminal justice era is suggested.

4   Possessing a criminal record is not a requirement for membership in CC. The CC organization is comprised of individuals with no criminal justice system contact and those with criminal justice system contact of many types.

5   Alternatively, some have argued that the academic Criminological and Criminal Justice fields should change and become less oppressive.

6   Thanks to Lukas Carey (telephone conversation, July 12, 2023) and to Suzanne Reich (e-mail conversation, December 17, 2023) for clarifications on the state of CC in Australia.

7   These statistics are derived from https://www.prisonstudies.org/highest-to-lowest/prison-pop ulation-total?field_region_taxonomy_tid=All (accessed October 20, 2023).

8   Although the negative commentary is published in scholarly sources, they may not be peer-reviewed or the peer-review process is weak or nonexistent. For example, in the case of Belknap (2015), presidential speeches that are later published in *Criminology* are not peer-reviewed. Had the speech/paper been peer-reviewed, by knowledgeable people, then some of the issues that Dr. Belknap raises might not have taken on the salience that they did.

9   Occasionally criticisms of CC have argued that it has an unnecessary focus on activities that have taken place in the United States or that there has been a privileging of American CC. This position is typically poorly argued and fails to take into account and really understand what is happening in CC circles in international contexts.

10   This includes, but is not limited to, Archambeault (2003), Owen (2003), Bozkurt et al. (2021), and Bozkurt (2022).

11   See discussion of lived experience and CC by Warr (2021).

Chapter 3

1   This section and the following builds upon the ideas expressed by Manheim and Rich (1986) and Maxfield and Babbie (2014).

2   Although one of the first scholarly articles that mentions CC is Arrigo (2000), it is primarily a passing reference to the forthcoming book *Convict Criminology* (Ross & Richards, 2003). Also, to be included in the content analysis, the article or chapter needed to be at a minimum listed in Google Scholar (e.g., publicly available), but not necessarily assigned to a specific issue.

3   All books that were not edited collections were excluded. Thus Earle (2016) was not subject to content analysis.

Chapter 4

1   An earlier version of the first half of this chapter was presented as Ross (2022).

2   Most prison educational programs are limited to the Adult Basic Education (ABE) certificate, which is generally understood to be an eighth-grade education, and the General Education Development (GED) certificate, basically a high-school diploma.

3   The staff is concerned about drugs (e.g., sheets of LSD, heroin, or cocaine), weapons (e.g., razors or hacksaw blades), or money being hidden in a cloth, cardboard, or paper cover.

4   In most correctional facilities, inmates are not allowed internet access, however they may be able to access www.corrlinks.com, which they can use for email. Alternatively, sometimes a link to a particular online educational interface can be arranged on an individual basis.

5   Personal correspondence with Lori Pompa, August 3, 2007.

6   Personal correspondence with Lori Pompa, August 3, 2007.

7   Downloaded December 3, 2015.

8   Personal correspondence with Stephen C. Richards, Ph.D., July 16, 2007.

INTRODUCTION TO CONVICT CRIMINOLOGY

[9] Email conversation with Christopher Rose, Ph.D., September 1, 2015.

[10] The reader is advised that this section is meant to be illustrative and not comprehensive.

[11] Though similar in mission, the Prisoners' Education Trust is separate from the Prisoner Reform Trust.

[12] Prior to the Fishmongers incident there were close to 34 educational programs operating across prisons in England and Wales. One of the initiatives, under the Learning Together program, was run by Bill Davies, Ph.D. a formerly incarcerated professor, who identifies with the CC approach, and Alexandria Bradley, both from Leeds Beckett University "at HMP Full Sutton, a Category A prison outside York. In excess of 40 prisoners have gained university level academic credits as a result of this program" (https://www.leedsbeckett.ac.uk/staff/dr-bill-davies/). The program teaches Level 6 university content, provides the learners inside and out 20 credits toward HE qualifications, and is paid for by the prison.

[13] Personal correspondence with David Honeywell, Ph.D., February 7, 2023.

[14] Personal correspondence with Bill Davies, Ph.D., February 6, 2023.

[15] See also Bint Faisel et al. (2018) for a student-centered description of this process.

[16] Special thanks to Jose Aguiar for sharing his insight about this challenge (telephone conversation, July 26, 2023).

[17] Vianello (2021: 105–109) also makes a handful of recommendations to improve the delivery of prison education in Italy.

Chapter 5

[1] Parts of this chapter build upon Ross (2021a).

[2] Alternative models similar to Timor et al. (2023) include motivated students going into correctional facilities and working with inmates on a one-to-one basis to assist them with their academic work.

[3] This section builds upon Ross (2021d).

Chapter 6

[1] This chapter builds upon Ross et al. (2015b).

[2] For example, 327 Unauthorized contact with the public, p. 199, Conduct which disrupts or interferes with the security or the orderly running of an institution or the BOP; 305 Possession of anything not authorized for retention or receipt by the inmate, and not issued to him through regular channels; and 315 Participating in an unauthorized meeting or gathering).

Chapter 7

[1] This section builds upon Ross (2018).

Chapter 8

[1] This section builds upon Ross and Tietjen (2022).

Chapter 9

[1] This chapter builds upon Ross (2023).

[2] There are also arguments for calling CC a theory (Richards, 2013), and an interesting debate surrounds this issue, but it is not essential to the points that I am reviewing in this chapter.

[3] Ross and Tietjen (2022) expand on the differences between the older generation of convict criminologists and the newer ones.

[4] Surveys of the membership might be an option. However, there are numerous individuals who for one reason or another are not "members in good standing" (i.e., they have not paid

NOTES

their annual dues) to the official division, and these individuals may have useful opinions, thus circumscribing the sample to membership only might produce skewed results.

[5] A multi-authored chapter, "Convict criminology: Prisoner re-entry policy recommendations" (Richards et al., 2011) makes some policy recommendations, but they are not specifically directed toward the field of CC.

[6] I do not believe that it is necessary to go into a detailed analysis of why most of these criticisms are unfounded here. Readers interested in exploring this argument can consult, for example, Ross et al. (2016).

[7] For example, a phantom CC website now exists.

[8] On a related note, in 2012, Richards edited a special issue of *Euro Vista: Probation and Community Justice*. Most of the contributors were ex-convicts.

References

Abbot, J.H. (1981). *In the belly of the beast: Letters from prison*. New York, NY: Random House.

Acey, C.E.S.A. (2000). This is an illogical statement: Dangerous trends in anti-prison activism. *Social Justice*, 27(3), 206–211.

Adams, T.E., Holman Jones, S., & Ellis, C. (Eds.) (2022). *Handbook of autoethnography* (2nd Edn). New York, NY: Routledge.

Ahmed, R., Johnson, M., Caudill, C., Diedrich, N., Mains, D., & Key, A. (2019). Cons and pros: Education through the eyes of the prison educated. *Review of Communication*, 19(1), 69–76.

Aitken, J. (2014). *Meaningful mentoring*. London: Centre for Social Justice.

Alarid, L.F. (2016). How to secure your first academic job out of graduate school. *Journal of Criminal Justice Education*, 27(2), 160–174.

Anderson, L. (2015). In memory of Dr. Liz Elliott: Founding director of the Centre for Restorative Justice at SFU. https://www.sfu.ca/crj/about/liz-elliott.html (accessed February 3, 2022).

Apa, Z.L., Bai, R., Mukherejee, D.V., Herzig, C.T., Koenigsmann, C., Lowy, F.D., & Larson, E.L. (2012). Challenges and strategies for research in prisons. *Public Health Nursing*, 29(5), 467–472.

Applegate, B.K., Cable, C.R., & Sitren, A.H. (2009). Academia's most wanted: The characteristics of desirable academic job candidates in criminology and criminal justice. *Journal of Criminal Justice Education*, 20(1), 20–39.

Archambeault, W.G. (2003). Soar like an eagle, dive like a loon: Human diversity and social justice in the Native American prison experience, in Ross, J.I. & Richards, S.C. (Eds.) *Convict criminology* (pp. 287–308). Belmont, CA: Wadsworth Publishing.

Aresti, A. (2012). Developing a convict criminology group in the UK. *Journal of Prisoners on Prison*, 21(1/2), 148–165.

Aresti, A. & Darke, S. (2016). Practicing convict criminology: Lessons learned from British academic activism. *Critical Criminology: An International Journal*, 24(4), 533–547.

Aresti, A., Darke, S., & Manlow, D. (2016). Bridging the gap: Giving public voice to prisoners and former prisoners through research activism. *Prison Service Journal*, 224, 3–13.

Aresti, A., Darke, S., & Ross, J.I. (2023). Against bifurcation: Why it is in the best interests of convict criminology to be international in scope & not a collection of individual country level organizations. *Justice, Power and Resistance*, 6(2), 246–261.

Armstrong, R. & Ludlow, A. (2016). Educational partnerships between universities and prisons: How learning together can be individually, socially and institutionally transformative. *Prison Service Journal*, 225, 9–17.

Arrigo, B.A. (2000). Law and social inquiry: Commentary on a psychoanalytic semiotics of law. *International Journal for the Semiotics of Law*, 13(1), 127–132.

Arrigo, B.A. (2003). Convict criminology and the mentally ill offender: Prisoners of confinement, in Ross, J.I. & Richards, S.C. (Eds.) *Convict criminology* (pp. 267–286). Belmont, CA: Wadsworth Publishing.

Austin, J. (2003). The use of science to justify the imprisonment binge, in Ross, J.I. & Richards, S.C. (Eds.) *Convict criminology* (pp. 17–36). Belmont, CA: Wadsworth Publishing.

Austin, J. & Irwin, J. (2012). *It is about time: America's imprisonment binge* (3rd Edn). Belmont, CA: Wadsworth.

Bachrach, P. & Baratz, M.S. (1962). Two faces of power. *American Political Science Review*, 5(4), 947–952.

Barak, G. (1988). Newsmaking criminology: Reflections of the media, intellectuals, and crime. *Justice Quarterly*, 5(4), 565–587.

Barry, E.M. (2000). Women prisoners on the cutting edge: Development of the activist women's prisoners' rights movement. *Social Justice*, 27(3), 168–175.

Bartley, L. (2021). I am not your inmate. *The Marshall Project*. https://www.themarshallproject.org/2021/04/12/i-am-not-your-inmate (accessed July 27, 2023).

Becker, H.S. (1978). The relevance of life histories, in Denzin, N.K. (Ed.) *Sociological methods* (pp. 289–295). New York, NY: McGraw Hill.

Belknap, J. (2015). Activist criminology: Criminologists' responsibility to advocate for social and legal justice. The 2014 American Society of Criminology presidential address. *Criminology*, 53(1), 1–22.

Beresford, P. & Russo, J. (Eds.). (2021). *The Routledge international handbook of mad studies*. New York, NY: Routledge.

Bernard, T. (1992). *The cycle of juvenile justice*. New York, NY: Oxford University Press.

Bernard, T. & Vold, G.B. (1986). *Vold's theoretical criminology. Consensus conflict debate: Form and content in social theories* (3rd Edn). New York, NY: Oxford University Press.

Bernasco, W. (2020). *Offenders on offending: Learning about crime from criminals*. Cullompton: Willan Publishing.

Betts, R.D. (2018). Incarcerated language. *The Yale Review*, 106(4), 30–36.

Binnall, J.M. (2021). *Twenty million angry men: The case for including convicted felons in our jury system*. Los Angeles, CA: University of California Press.

REFERENCES

Binnall, J.M., Scott-Hayward, C., Petersen, S., & Gonzalez, R.M. (2021). Taking roll: College students' views of their formerly incarcerated classmates. *Journal of Criminal Justice Education*, 33(3), 347–367.

Bint Faisal, A., Dean, M., Demirtas, M., Dharmarajah, S., Hinde, D., Mathias, M., & Taylor, G. (2018). Insider perspectives in higher education within the British prison system. *Journal of Prisoners on Prisons*, 27(2), 75–90.

Bloom, T. & Bradshaw, G.A. (2022). Inside of a prison: How a culture of punishment prevents rehabilitation. *Peace and Conflict: Journal of Peace Psychology*, 28(1), 140–143.

Borghini, A. (2018). Il Progetto Dei Poli Uniersitari Penitenziari Tra Filantropia e Istituzi-onalizzazione. Alcune Riflessioni Sociologiche [The project of the penitentiary university poles between philanthropy and institutionalization: Some sociological reflections]. *The Lab's Quarterly*, 20(3), 37–52

Borghini, A. & Pastore, G. (2021). University education in prison and convict criminology: Reflections from a field research study, in Ross, J.I. & Vianello, F. (Eds.) *Convict criminology for the future* (pp. 127–141). New York, NY: Routledge.

Bozkurt, S. (2022). *Behind bars: Exploring the prison and post release experiences of minoritised mothers*. Doctoral dissertation, University of Westminster.

Bozkurt, S., Merico, M., Aresti, A., & Darke, S. (2021). Crossing borders, pushing boundaries and privileging "marginalized" voices: Surviving motherhood and prison, in Ross, J.I. & Vianello, F. (Eds.) *Convict criminology for the future* (pp. 21–34). New York, NY: Routledge.

Bradley, A. & Davies, B. (2021). Devastation and innovation: Examining prison education during a national pandemic. *Journal of Criminal Psychology*, 11(3), 173–187.

Braz, R., Brown, B., Gilmore, C., Gilmore, R., Hunter, D., Parenti, C, Rodriguez, D., Shaylor, C., Stoller, N, & Sudbury, J. (2000). The history of critical resistance. *Social Justice*, 27(3), 6–10.

Brown, M. & Schept, J. (2017). New abolition, criminology and a critical carceral studies. *Punishment & Society*, 19(4), 440–462.

Burnett, J.L. & Williams, D.J. (2012). Convict criminology and community collaboration: Developing a unique program to empower vulnerable youth in Idaho. *Journal of Prisoners on Prison*, 21(1 & 2), 48–58.

Cann, C. & DeMeulenaere, E. (2020). *The activist academic: Engaged scholarship for resistance, hope and social change*. Gorham, ME: Myers Education Press.

Carceral, K.C. (2003). *Behind a convict's eyes: Doing time in a modern prison*. Belmont, CA: Wadsworth Publishing.

Carceral, K.C. (2005). *Prison, Inc.: A convict exposes life inside a private prison*. New York, NY: New York University Press.

Carey, L., Aresti, A., & Darke, S. (2022). What are the barriers to the development of convict criminology in Australia? *Journal of Prisoners on Prison*, 30(1), 77–96.

Carrier, N. & Piché, J. (2015). Blind spots of abolitionist thought in academia: On longstanding and emerging challenges. *Champ Penal/Penal Field*, 12. https://journals.openedition.org/champpenal/9162 (accessed May 17, 2018).

Chevaliar, J.M. & Buckles, D.J. (2019). *Participatory action research: Theory and methods for engaged inquiry* (2nd Edn). New York, NY: Routledge Publishers.

Chiola, G. (2021). Italian penitentiary university centers: Promoting the inclusion of prisoners through university education. *Journal of Learning and Educational Policy*, 1(2), 1–6.

Clark, R. (2016). How education transforms: Evidence from the experience of Prisoners' Education Trust on how education supports prisoner journeys. *Prison Service Journal*, 225, 3–8.

Clear, T.R. (1994). *Harm in American penology*. Albany, NY: State University of New York Press.

Clear, T.R. (2009). *Imprisoning communities: How mass incarceration makes disadvantaged neighborhoods worse*. New York, NY: Oxford University Press.

Clemmer, D. (1940). *The prison community*. Boston, MA: Christopher Publishing House.

Coates, S. (2016). *Unlocking potential: A review of education in prison*. https://assets. publishing.service.gov.uk/government/uploads/system/uploads/attachment_d ata/file/524013/education-review-report.pdf (accessed July 31, 2023).

Condliffe Lagemann, E. (2011). What can college mean? Lessons from the Bard Prison Initiative. *Change: The Magazine of Higher Learning*, 43(6), 14–19.

Copes, H. & Pogrebin, M. (Eds.) (2012). *Voices from criminal justice: Thinking and reflecting on the system*. New York, NY: Routledge.

Cox, A. (2020). The language of incarceration. *Incarceration*, 1(1), 1–13.

Cox, A. (2021). A convict criminology approach to prisoner families, in Ross, J.I. & Vianello, F. (Eds.) *Convict criminology for the future* (pp. 82–97). New York, NY: Routledge.

Cox, A. & Malkin, M.L. (2023). Feminist convict criminology for the future. *Critical Criminology: An International Journal*, 1–21.

Crenshaw, K.W. (2017). *On intersectionality: Essential writings*. New York, NY: The New Press.

Cressey, D. (1965). Social psychological foundations for using criminals in the rehabilitation of criminals. *Journal of Research in Crime and Delinquency*, 2(1), 49–59.

Curtis, C.A., Evans, D., & Pelletier, E. (2021). Developing social capital through postsecondary correctional education. *Journal of Offender Rehabilitation*, 60(4), 270–290.

Curtis, R.L. Jr. & Zurcher, L. (1974). Social movements: An analytical exploration of organizational forms. *Social Problems*, 21(2), 356–370.

Custer, B.D., Malkin, M.L., & Castillo, G. (2020). Criminal justice system-impacted faculty: Motivations, barriers, and successes on the academic job market. *Journal of Education Human Resources*, 38(3), 336–364.

Darke, S. (2018). *Conviviality and survival: Co-producing Brazilian prison order*. Basingstoke: Palgrave Macmillan.

Darke, S. & Aresti, A. (2016). Connecting prisons and universities through higher education. *Prison Service Journal*, 225, 26–32.

Darke, S., Aresti, A., Bint Faisel, A., & Ellis, N. (2020). Prisoner university partnerships at Westminster, in Shecaira, S.S. et al. (Eds.) *Criminologoa: Estudos em Homenagem ao Alvino Augusto de Sá* (pp. 475–498). Belo Horizonte: D'Placido.

Darke, S., Aresti, A., & Earle, R. (2012). British convict criminology: Developing critical insider perspectives. *Inside Times*, August. https://insidetime.org/brit ish-convict-criminologydeveloping-critical-insider-perspectives-on-prison/ (accessed October 20, 2023).

Darke, S., Aresti, A., & Ellis-Rexhi, N. (2018). Supporting prisoners into academia, in Frisco, V. & Decembrotto, L. (Eds.) *Universita a carcere: Ill diritto alllo studio tra vincoli e progettulia* (pp. 217–237). Milan: Edizioni Guerini Scientifica.

Davies, W. & Nichols, H. (Eds.) (2016). PRisoN: Unlocking prison research (special edition). *Prison Service Journal*, 223.

Davis, L.M., Bozick, R., Steele, J.L., Saunders, J., & Miles, J.N.V. (2013). *Evaluating the effectiveness of correctional education: A meta-analysis of programs that provide education to incarcerated adults*. Santa Monica, CA: Rand Corporation.

Degenhardt, T. & Vianello, F. (2010). Convict criminology: Provocazioni da Oltreoceano La ricera ethnographia in carcere [Provocations from overseas ethnographic research in prison]. *Studi sulla questione criminal*, 5(1), 9–23.

DeKeseredy, W.S. & Dragiewicz, M. (Eds.) (2018). *Routledge handbook of critical criminology* (2nd Edn). New York, NY: Routledge.

Dennison, C.R. (2019). The crime-reducing benefits of a college degree: Evidence from a nationally representative US sample. *Criminal Justice Studies*, 32(4), 297–316.

Denver, M., Pickett, J., & Bushway, J. (2021). The language of stigmatization and the mark of violence: Experimental evidence on the social construction and use of criminal record stigma. *Criminology*, 55(3), 664–690.

Dirga, L. (2017). Convict criminology: nový směr vězeňského výzkumu? [A new direction in prison research?]. *Česká kriminologie*, 2(1), 1–10.

Disha, I., Eren, C., & Leyro, S. (2021). People you care about in and out of the system: The impact of arrest on CJ major choice and career motivations. *Journal of Criminal Justice Education*, 31(1), 60–89.

Doherty, C., Kiley, J., Tyson, A., & Jameson, B. (2015). Beyond distrust: How Americans view their government. Pew Research Center. https://www.pewr esearch.org/politics/2015/11/23/beyond-distrust-how-americans-view-their-government/ (accessed December 27, 2021).

Donnermeyer, J. (2012). Rural crime and critical criminology, in DeKeseredy, W.S. & Dragiewicz, M. (Eds.) *Routledge handbook of critical criminology* (pp. 289–301). New York, NY: Routledge.

Doyle, C., Gardner, K., & Wells, K. (2021). The importance of incorporating lived experience in efforts to reduce Australian reincarceration rates. *International Journal for Crime, Justice and Social Democracy*, 10(2), 83–98.

Drake, D.H., Earle, R., & Sloan, J. (Eds.) (2015). *The Palgrave handbook of prison ethnography*. London: Palgrave Macmillan.

Dupont, I. (2008). Beyond doing no harm: A call for participatory action research with marginalized populations in criminological research. *Critical Criminology: An International Journal*, 16(3), 197–207.

Earle, R. (2016). *Convict criminology: Inside and out*. Bristol: Policy Press.

Earle, R. (2018). Convict criminology in England: Developments and dilemmas. *British Journal of Criminology*, 58(6), 1499–1516.

Earle, R. (2019). Narrative convictions, conviction narratives: The prospects of convict criminology, in Fleetwood, J., Presser, L., Sandberg, S., & Ugelvik, T. (Eds.) *The Emerald handbook of narrative criminology* (pp. 63–83). Bingley: Emerald Publishing Limited.

Earle, R. (2020). Exploring narrative, convictions and autoethnography as a convict criminologist. *Tijdschrift over Cultuur & Criminaliteit [Journal of Culture and Crime]*, 3, 80–96.

Earle, R. (2021). Doing time for convict criminology, in Ross, J.I. & Vianello, F. (Eds.) *Convict criminology for the future* (pp. 35–49). New York, NY: Routledge.

Earle, R., Darley, D., Davies, B., Honeywell, D., & Schreeche-Powell, E. (2023). Convict criminology without guarantees: Proposing hard labour for an unfinished criminology, in Liebling, A., Maruna, S., & McAra, L. (Eds.) *Oxford handbook of criminology* (7th Edn, pp. 911–932). Oxford: Oxford University Press.

Earle, R. & Mehigan, J. (Eds.) (2020). *Degrees of freedom: Prison education at The Open University*. Bristol: Policy Press.

Eglash, A. (1958). Adults anonymous: A mutual help program for inmates and ex-inmates. *Journal of Criminal Law and Criminology*, 49(1), 237–245.

Eglash, A. (1977). Beyond restitution: Creative restitution, in Hudson, J. & Galaway, B. (Eds.) *Restitution in criminal justice* (pp. 91–129). Lexington, MA: D.C. Heath.

Ekunwe, I. (2007). *Gentle justice: Analysis of open prison systems in Finland. A way to the future?* Doctoral dissertation, University of Tampere.

Ekunwe, I.O. & Jones, R.S. (Eds.) (2011). *Global perspectives on re-entry*. Tampere: Tampere University Press.

Ellis, A. & Marques, O. (2022). The advancement of thug criminology: Towards the decolonization of "street/gang." *Research and Pedagogy, Decolonization of Criminology and Justice*, 4(2), 35–58.

Ellis, C.S., Adams, T.E., & Bochner, A.P. (2011). Autoethnography: An overview. *Historical social research/Historische sozialforschung*, 12(4), 273–290.

Ellis, C.S. & Bochner, A.P. (2005). Autoethnography, narrative, reflexivity, in Denzin, N.K. & Lincoln, Y.S. (Eds.) *Handbook of qualitative research* (2nd Edn) (pp. 733–768). Thousand Oaks, CA: SAGE.

Ellis, C.S. & Bochner, A.P. (2006). Analyzing analytic autoethnography: An autopsy. *Journal of Contemporary Ethnography*, 35(4), 429–449.

Fagen, K. (2010). Criminal turned criminologist John Irwin dies. *San Francisco Chronicle*, January 7. https://www.sfgate.com/bayarea/article/Criminal-turned-criminologist-John-Irwin-dies-3205069.php (accessed October 20, 2023).

Farkas, M. (1992). The impact of the correctional field setting on the research experience: A research chronicle. *Journal of Crime and Justice*, 15(2), 177–184.

Ferranti, S. (2004). *Prison stories*. Gorilla Convict Publications.

Ferrell, J. (2018). Criminological ethnography: Living and knowing, in Rice, S.K. & Maltz, M.D. (Eds.) *Doing ethnography in criminology* (pp. 147–161). New York, NY: Springer.

Fine, M., Torre, M.E., Boudin, K., Bowen, I., Clark, J., Hylton, D., Martinez, M., "Missy," Rivera, M., Roberts, R.A., Smart, P., & Upegui, D. (2003). Participatory action research: Within and beyond bars, in Camic, P., Rhodes, J.E., & Yardley, L. (Eds.) *Qualitative research in psychology: Expanding perspectives in methodology and design* (pp. 173–198). Washington, DC: American Psychological Association.

Fisher-Giorlando, M. (2003). Why I study prisons: My twenty-year personal and professional odyssey and understanding of southern prisons, in Ross, J.I. & Richards, S.C. (Eds.) *Convict criminology* (pp. 59–76). Belmont, CA: Wadsworth Publishing.

Flaherty, M.G. & Carceral, K.C. (2022). *The cage of days: Time and temporal experience in prison*. New York, NY: Columbia University Press.

Flynn, N. & Higdon, R. (2022). Prison education: Beyond review and evaluation. *The Prison Journal*, 102(2), 196–216.

Forster, W. (1996). England and Wales: The state of prison education. *Journal of Correctional Education*, 47(2), 101–105.

Fox, K., Zambrana, K., & Lane, J. (2011). Getting in (and staying in) when everyone else wants to get out: 10 lessons learned from conducting research with inmates. *Journal of Criminal Justice Education*, 22(2), 304–327.

Frana, J.F., Lenza, M., & Schroeder, R.D. (2012). Convict criminologists in the classroom. *Journal of Prisoners on Prison*, 21(1 & 2), 35–47.

Franklin, H.B. (1982). *Prison literature in America: The victim as criminal and artist*. Westport, CT: Lawrence Hill and Company.

Franklin, H.B. (Ed.) (1988). *Prison writing in twentieth-century America*. New York, NY: Penguin.

Gacek, J. & Ricciardelli, R. (2021). Rethinking punishment: Prison research and the (un)intended challenges of institutional research ethics review, in Ross, J.I. & Vianello, F. (Eds.) *Convict criminology for the future* (pp. 197–210). New York, NY: Routledge.

Gatson, S. (2003). On being amorphous: Autoethnography, genealogy, and multiracial identity. *Qualitative Inquiry*, 9(1), 28–48.

Gaucher, R. (1988). The prisoner as ethnographer. *Journal of Prisoners on Prisons*, 1(1), 1–6.

Gauke, D. (2018). From the wings to the workplace: The route to reducing reoffending. Original script of Secretary of State for Justice's speech at the Education and Employment Strategy Launch at HMP Isis. May 24. https:// www.gov.uk/ government/speeches/from-the-wings-to-the-workplace-the- route-to-reducing-reoffending (accessed October 20, 2023).

Gillis, A.R., Silverman, B., Avison, W.R., Cousineau, D., Hagan, J., Hirschi, T., & Ross, C. (2008). Obituary: Gwynn Nettler, 1913–2007. *Footnotes, American Sociological Association*, 36(1), 15. https://www.asanet.org/wp-content/uploads/fn_2008_01.pdf (accessed August 6, 2023).

Ginsberg, B. (1981). *The consequences of consent: Elections, citizen control, and popular acquiescence*. Reading, MA: Addison Wesley Publishing.

Goffman, E. (1961). *Asylums: Essays on the social situation of mental patients and other inmates*. New York, NY: Anchor Books.

Gonzalez-Alcaide, G., Melero-Fuentes, D., Aleixandre-Benavent, R., & Valderrama-Zuria'n, J .C. (2013). Productive and collaboration in scientific publications in criminology. *Journal of Criminal Justice Education*, 24(1), 15–37.

Graebsch, C. & Knop, J. (2023). Über oder mit "Verurteilten" sprechen? Möglichkeiten und Grenzen einer "Convict Criminology" in Deutschland [Talk about or with "convicts"? Possibilities and limits of a "Convict Criminology" in Germany]. *Kriminologisches Journal*, 55(2), 158–166.

Graebsch, C. & Ross, J.I. (2023). Im Gespräch: Convict criminology (interview of Jeffrey Ian Ross by Christine Graebsch). *Kriminologisches Journal*, 55(2), 167–174.

Gramlich, J. (2021). America's incarceration rate falls to lowest level since 1995. Pew Research Center. https://www.pewresearch.org/fact-tank/2021/08/16/americas-incarceration-rate-lowest-since-1995/ (accessed November 1, 2022).

Green, C.M. (2018). *Against criminalization and pathology: The making of a black achievement praxis*. Doctoral dissertation, CUNY Graduate Center. https://academicworks.cuny.edu/cgi/viewcontent.cgi?article=3981&context=gc_etds (accessed July 23, 2023).

Greene, D. (2005). Abolition, in Bosworth, M. (Ed.) *Encyclopedia of prisons & correctional facilities* (pp. 2–5). Thousand Oaks, CA: SAGE.

Haines, H.H. (1996). *Against capital punishment: The anti-death penalty movement in America, 1972–1994*. New York, NY: Oxford University Press.

Halkovic, A. & Greene, A.C. (2015). Bearing stigma, carrying gifts: What colleges can learn from students with incarceration experience. *The Urban Review*, 47(4), 759–782.

Harding, S.G. (1991). *Whose science? Whose knowledge? Thinking from women's lives*. Ithaca, NY: Cornell University Press.

Harding, S.G. (Ed.) (2004). *The feminist standpoint theory reader: Intellectual and political controversies*. New York, NY: Psychology Press.

Harm, A.L. & Bell, C. (2021). Teaching beyond the textbook: Integrating formerly incarcerated individuals into criminal justice learning environments. *Journal of Criminal Justice Education*, 32(1), 126–142.

Hassine, V. (1996 [2011]). *Life without parole: Living in prison today* (5th Edn). New York, NY: Oxford University Press.

Haverkate, D.L., Meyers, T.J., Telepa, C.W., & Wright, K.A. (2020). On PAR with the yard: Participatory action research to advance knowledge in corrections. *Corrections*, 5(1), 28–43.

REFERENCES

Hirsch, D.J. (1993). Politics through action: Student service and activism in the 90s. *Change: The Magazine of Higher Learning*, 25(5), 32–36.

Honeywell, D. (2015). Doing time with lifers: A reflective study of life sentence prisoners. *British Journal of Community Justice*, 13(1), 93–104.

Honeywell, D. (2021). *The ambiguities of desistance.* Bingley: Emerald Publishing.

Huckelbury, C. (2008). *Tales from the purple penguin.* New York, NY: BleakHouse Publishing.

Huckelbury, C. (2012). *Distant thunder.* New York, NY: BleakHouse Publishing.

Huff, C.R. (1974). Unionization behind the walls. *Criminology*, 12(2), 175–194.

Irwin, J. (1970). *The felon.* Englewood Cliffs, NJ: Prentice Hall.

Irwin, J. (1980). *Prisons in turmoil.* Boston: Little, Brown and Company.

Irwin, J. (1985a). *The jail.* Berkeley, CA: University of California Press.

Irwin, J. (1985b). *The return of the bogeyman.* San Diego, CA: Keynote Address at American Society of Criminology.

Irwin, J. (1987). Reflections on ethnography. *Journal of Contemporary Ethnography*, 16(1), 41–48.

Irwin, J. (2003). Preface, in Ross, J.I. & Richards, S.C. (Eds.) *Convict criminology* (pp. xvii–xxii). Belmont, CA: Wadsworth Publishers.

Irwin, J. (2005). *The warehouse prison.* Los Angeles, CA: Roxbury Press.

Irwin, J. (2009). *Lifers: Seeking redemption in prison.* London: Routledge.

Irwin, J. & Austin, J. (1994). *It is about time: Imprisonment binge.* Belmont, CA: Wadsworth.

Irwin, M. (2020). From Open University in prison to convict criminology upon release, in Earle, R. & Mehigan, J. (Eds.) *Degrees of freedom: Prison education at the Open University* (pp. 139–159). Bristol: Policy Press.

Jackson, A., Kania, J., & Montgomery, T. (2020). Effective change requires proximate leaders. *Stanford Social Innovation Review*, October 2. https://ssir.org/articles/entry/effective_change_requires_proximate_leaders (accessed October 20, 2023).

Jacobs, J.B. (1974). Participant observation in prison. *Urban Life and Culture*, 3, 221–240.

Jewkes, Y. (2012). Autoethnography and emotion as intellectual resources: Doing prison research differently. *Qualitative Inquiry*, 18(1), 63–75.

Johnson, R. (2012). Reflections on convict criminologists in the classroom, *Journal of Prisoners on Prison*, 21(1 & 2), 195–198.

Jones, R.S. (1995). Uncovering the hidden social world: Insider research in prison. *Journal of Contemporary Criminal Justice*, 11(2), 106–118.

Jones, R.S. (2003). Excon: Managing a spoiled identity, in Ross, J.I. & Richards, S.C. (Eds.) *Convict criminology* (pp. 191–208). Belmont, CA: Wadsworth Publishing.

Jones, R.S., Ross, J.I., Richards, S.C., & Murphy, D.S. (2009). The first dime: A decade of convict criminology. *The Prison Journal*, 89(2), 151–171.

Kalica, E. (2018). Convict criminology and abolitionism: Looking towards a horizon without prisons. *Journal of Prisoners on Prisons*, 27(2), 91–107.

Kalica, E. (2021). A convict-counter information to contest crime-press disinformation, in Ross, J.I. & Vianello, F. (Eds.) *Convict criminology for the future* (pp. 50–65). New York, NY: Routledge.

Kalica, E. & Santorosa, S. (2018). *Farsi la galera. Spazi e culture del penitenziario* [Go to jail: Penitentiary spaces and cultures]. Milan: Editore Ombre Corte.

Karpowitz, D. (2017). *College in prison: Reading in an age of mass incarceration.* New Brunswick, NJ: Rutgers University Press.

Katzenstein, M.F. (2005). Rights without citizenship: Activist politics and prison reform in the United States, in Meyer, D.S., Jenness, V., & Ingram, H.M. (Eds.) *Routing the opposition: Social movements, public policy, and democracy* (pp. 236–258). Minneapolis, MN: University of Minnesota Press.

Kim, R.H. & Clark, D. (2013). The effect of prison-based college education programs on recidivism: Propensity score matching approach. *Journal of Criminal Justice,* 41(3), 196–204.

King, A. (2018). Just mercy through cultural and convict criminology. *Journal of Criminal Psychology,* 8(1), 80–95.

Kirk, D.S. & Wakefield, S. (2018). Collateral consequences of punishment: A critical review and path forward. *Annual Review of Criminology,* 1, 171–194.

Knopp, F.H. (1976). *Instead of prisons: A handbook for abolitionists.* Syracuse, NY: Prison Education Action Research Project.

Krippendorff, K. (2018 [1980]). *Content analysis: An introduction to its methodology.* Newbury Park, CA: SAGE.

Lanier, C.S., Philliber, S., & Philliber, W.W. (1994). Prisoners with a profession: Earning graduate degrees behind bars. *Journal of Criminal Justice Education,* 5(1), 15–29.

Larsen, M. & Piché, J. (2012). A challenge from and challenge to convict criminology. *Journal of Prisoners on Prison,* 21(1 & 2), 199–202.

LeBel, T.P. (2007). An examination of the impact of formerly incarcerated persons helping others. *Journal of Offender Rehabilitation,* 46(1/2), 1–24.

LeBel, T.P. (2008). Perceptions of and responses to stigma. *Sociology Compass,* 2(2), 409–432.

LeBel, T.P. (2009). Formerly incarcerated persons use of advocacy/activism as a coping orientation in the reintegration process, in Veysey, B., Christian, J., & Martinez, D.J. (Eds.), *How offenders transform their lives* (pp. 165–187). Cullompton: Willan.

Lemke, R. (2013). Perceptions on the trend of multi-authored collaboration: Results from a national survey of criminal justice and criminology faculty. *Journal of Criminal Justice Education,* 24(3), 316–338.

Leyva, M. & Bickel, C. (2010). From corrections to college: The value of a convict voice. *Western Criminology Review,* 11(1), 50–60.

Liebling, A. (1999). Doing research in prison: Breaking the silence? *Theoretical Criminology,* 3(2), 147–173.

Linden, R. & Perry, L. (1983). The effectiveness of prison education programs. *Journal of Offender Counseling Services Rehabilitation,* 6(4), 43–57.

REFERENCES

Loader, I. & Sparks, R. (2010). What is to be done with public criminology? *Criminology and Public Policy*, 9(4), 771–781.

Lockard, J. & Rankins-Robertson, S. (2011). The right to education, prison–university partnerships, and online writing pedagogy in the US. *Critical Survey*, 23(3), 23–39.

Lockwood, S., Nally, J.M., Ho, T., & Knutson, K. (2012). The effect of correctional education of post release employment and recidivism: A 5 year follow up study in the state of Indiana. *Crime & Delinquency*, 58, 380–396.

Ludlow, A., Armstrong, R., & Bartels, L. (2019). Learning together: Localism, collaboration and reflexivity in the development of prison and university learning communities. *Journal of Prison Education and Reentry*, 6(1), 25–44.

Lumsden, K. & Winter, A. (2014). (Eds.) *Reflexivity in criminological research: Experiences with the powerful and the powerless.* New York: Palgrave Macmillan.

MacLean, B.D. (1991). Master status, stigma, termination and beyond. *Journal of Prisoners on Prisons*, 3(1/2), 111–118.

Malkin, M.L. & DeJong, C. (2019). Protections for transgender inmates under PREA: A comparison of state correctional policies in the United States. *Sexuality Research and Social Policy*, 16(4), 393–407.

Manheim J.B. & Rich, R.C. (1986). *Empirical political analysis: Research methods in political science* (2nd Edn). New York, NY: Longman.

Marquart, J.W. (1986). Doing research in prison: The strengths and weaknesses of full participation as a guard. *Justice Quarterly*, 3(1), 15–32.

Martin, C. (2000). Doing research in a prison setting, in Jupp, V., Davies, P., & Francis, P. (Eds.) *Doing criminological research* (pp. 215–233). Thousand Oaks, CA: SAGE.

Martin, G.E. (2017). From movement to movement: The urgency of formerly incarcerated individuals to lead decarceration efforts, in Epperson, M. & Pettus, D. (Eds.) *Smart decarceration: Achieving criminal justice transformation in the 21st century* (pp. 44–54). New York, NY: Oxford University Press.

Martinez, S.B. (2021). Grants support programming for Underground Scholars Initiative. *UC Riverside News*. https://news.ucr.edu/articles/2021/05/25/grants-support-programming-underground-scholars-initiative (accessed October 20, 2023).

Maruna, S. (2001). *Making good.* Washington, DC: American Psychological Association.

Maruna, S. & LeBel, T.P. (2003). Welcome home? Examining the re-entry court concept from a strengths-based perspective. *Western Criminology Review*, 4(2), 91–107.

Maruna, S. & Liem, M. (2021). Where is this story going? A critical analysis of the emerging field of narrative criminology. *Annual Review of Criminology*, 4, 125–146.

Mathiesen, T. (2015). *The politics of abolition revisited.* Abingdon: Routledge.

Matthews, R. (2017). False starts, wrong turns and dead ends: Reflections on recent developments in criminology. *Critical Criminology: An International Journal*, 25(4), 577–591.

Maxfield, M.G. & Babbie, E.R. (2014). *Research methods for criminal justice and criminology.* Belmont, CA: Cengage Learning.

Mays, L. & Ruddell, R. (2018). *Making sense of criminal justice*. New York: Oxford University Press.

McCleary, R. (1992 [1978]). *Dangerous men: The sociology of parole*. New York: Harrow and Heston.

McFarlane, R. (2019). *Student loans for those on long prison sentences, HEPI policy note 18*. Oxford: Oxford Higher Education Policy Institute.

McFarlane, R. & Pike, A. (2020). From prioner to student, in Earle, R. & Mehigan, J. (Eds.). *Degrees of Freedom: Prison Education at the Open University* (pp. 11–30). Bristol: Policy Press.

McMay, D.V. & Kimble, R.D. (Eds.) (2020). *Higher education accessibility behind and beyond prison walls*. Hershey, PA: Information Science Reference.

Moak, S.C. & Walker, J.T. (2014). How to be a successful mentor. *Journal of Contemporary Criminal Justice*, 30(4), 427–442.

Mobley, A. (2003). Convict criminology: The two legged data dilemma, in Ross, J.I. & Richards, S.C. (Eds.) *Convict criminology* (pp. 209–226). Belmont, CA: Wadsworth Publishers.

Mobley, A. (2009). Convict criminology: "Privileged information," and the authority of experience, in Powell, D.C. (Ed.) *Critical voices in criminology* (pp. 67–89). Lanham, MD: Rowman & Littlefield.

Mobley, A. (2010). Garbage in, garbage out? Convict criminology, the convict code, and participatory prison reform, in Maguire, M. & Okada, D. (Eds.) *Critical issues in crime and justice: Thought and practice* (pp. 333–349). Los Angeles, CA: SAGE.

Mohammed, S.K. (2023). *Adult learning and motivation of students previously involved in the US criminal justice system*. Doctoral dissertation, Walden University.

Morris, J.M. (1998). *Jailhouse journalism: The fourth estate behind bars*. New Brunswick, NJ: Transaction Publishers.

Murillo, D. (2021). *The possibility report: From prison to college degrees in California*. Los Angeles, CA: Campaign for College Opportunity. https://files.eric.ed.gov/fulltext/ED613716.pdf

Nellis, M. (2013). Review of *convict criminology*. *EuroVista: Probation & Community Justice*, 3(1), 237–240.

Nettler, G. (1970). *Explanations*. New York, NY: McGraw Hill.

Nettler, G. (1974). *Explaining crime*. New York, NY: McGraw Hill.

Nettler, G. (1982). *Explaining criminals*. Cincinnati, OH: Anderson Publishing.

Nettler, G. (2003). *Boundaries of competence: Knowing the social with science*. New Brunswick, NJ: Routledge.

Newbold, G. (2003). Rehabilitating criminals: It ain't that easy, in Ross, J.I. & Richards, S.C. (Eds.) *Convict criminology* (pp. 150–169). Belmont, CA: Wadsworth Publishers.

Newbold, G. (2013). The emergence of the supermax in New Zealand, in Ross, J.I. (Ed.) *The globalization of supermax prisons* (pp. 111–128). New Brunswick, NJ: Rutgers University Press.

REFERENCES

Newbold, G. (2017). Convict criminology, in Deckert, A. & Sarre, R. (Eds.) *The Palgrave handbook of Australian and New Zealand, criminology, crime, justice* (pp. 603–615). Cham: Palgrave.

Newbold, G. & Ross, J.I. (2012). Convict criminology at the crossroads. *The Prison Journal*, 93(1), 3–10.

Newbold, G., Ross, J.I., Jones, R.S., Richards, S.C., & Lenza, M. (2014). Prison research from the inside: The role of convict auto-ethnography. *Qualitative Inquiry*, 20(4), 439–448.

Newbold, G., Ross, J.I., & Richards, S.C. (2010). The emerging field of convict criminology, in Cullen, F. & Wilcox, P. (Eds.) *Encyclopedia of criminological theory* (pp. 2010–2012). Thousand Oaks, CA: SAGE.

Newbold, G. & Smith, M. (1996). Privatization of corrections in New Zealand, in Mays, G.L. & Gray, T. (Eds.) *Privatization and the provision of correctional services: Context and consequences* (pp. 75–86). Cincinnati, OH: Anderson Publishing.

Nichols, T. (2018). *The death of expertise: The campaign against established knowledge and why it matters.* New York, NY: Oxford University Press.

Ortiz, J. (2023a). Beyond the ivory tower: The need for collective activism in convict criminology. *Journal of Prisoners on Prisons*, 33(1), 76–86.

Ortiz, J. (2023b). Convict criminology 3.0: Envisioning a new future, in *Criminology with conviction* (pp. 6–8) [the official newsletter of the American Society of Criminology Division of Convict Criminology].

Ortiz, J. (Ed.) (2023c). *Critical and intersectional gang studies.* New York, NY: Taylor & Francis.

Ortiz, J., Cox, A, Kavish, D., & Tietjen, G. (2022). Let the convicts speak: A critical conversation of the ongoing language debate in convict criminology. *Criminal Justice Studies*, 35(3), 255–273.

Owen, B. (2003). Understanding women in prison, in Ross, J.I. & Richards, S.C. (Eds.) *Convict criminology* (pp. 227–246). Belmont, CA: Wadsworth Publishing.

Pastore, G. (2018). Inclusion and social exclusion issues in university education in prison: Considerations based on the Italian and Spanish experiences, *International Journal of Inclusive Education*, 22(12), 1272–1287.

Patenaude, A.L. (2004). No promises, but I'm willing to listen and tell what I hear: Conducting qualitative research among prison inmates and staff. *The Prison Journal*, 84(4 Suppl), 69–91.

Pelias, R.J. (1994). An autobiographical ethnography of performance in everyday discourse. *Journal of Dramatic Theory and Criticism*, 8(2), 163–172.

Pelligrino, V., Valenti, V., & Conte, C. (2021). The Convict University project and the autoethnography of the biographical changeover: A case study based on mutual narratives between external and convict students, in Ross, J.I. & Vianello, F. (Eds.) *Convict criminology for the future* (pp. 142–155). New York, NY: Routledge.

Pepinsky, H. & Quinney, R. (1991). *Criminology as peacemaking.* Bloomington, IN: Indiana University Press.

Piché, J. & Larsen, M. (2010). The moving targets of penal abolitionism: ICOPA, past, present and future. *Contemporary Justice Review*, 13(4), 391–410.

Piper, K. (2005). Activism, in Bosworth, M. (Ed.) *Encyclopedia of prisons & correctional facilities* (pp. 7–11). Thousand Oaks, CA: SAGE.

Pompa, L. & Crabbe, M. (2004). The inside-out prison exchange program: Exploring issues of crime and justice behind the walls, instructor's manual (Rev. Edn). Philadelphia, PA: Temple University.

Presser, L. (2017). Narrative criminology. *Oxford bibliography*. https://www.oxfor dbibliographies.com/display/document/obo-9780195396607/obo-978019 5396607-0171.xml (accessed January 25, 2023).

Presser, L. & Sandberg, S. (Eds.) (2015). *Narrative criminology: Understanding stories of crime*. New York, NY: New York University Press.

Prina, F. (2018). L'esperienza dei Poli universitari penitenziari italiani [The experience of Italian penitentiary universities], in Friso, V. & Decembrotto, L. (Eds.) *Universita e carcere. Il diritto allo studio tra vincoli e progettua-lita*. Milan: Edizioni Guerini Scientifica.

Project Rebound (2021). *Project Rebound*. Project Rebound Consortium. https:// www2.calstate.edu: 443/impact-of-the-csu/student-success/project-rebound (accessed October 20, 2023).

Ray, A. (2013). An "impossible profession"? The radical university in prison. *The Radical Teacher*, 95, 10–21.

Rhodes, C., Wright, C., & Pullen, A. (2018). Changing the world? The politics of activism and impact in the neoliberal university. *Organization*, 25(1), 139–147.

Richards, S.C. (2009). A convict criminology perspective on community punishment: Further lessons from the darkness of prison, in Ross, J.I. (Ed.) *Cutting the edge: Current perspectives in radical/critical criminology and criminal justice* (2nd Edn) (pp. 105–120). New Brunswick, NJ: Transaction Publishers.

Richards, S.C. (2010). John Irwin, in Hayward, K., Maruna, S., & Mooney, J. (Eds.) *Fifty key thinkers in criminology* (pp. 173–178). New York, NY: Routledge.

Richards, S.C. (2013). The new school of convict criminology thrives and matures. *Critical Criminology: An International Journal*, 21(3), 375–387.

Richards, S.C., Austin, J., Owen, B., & Ross, J.I. (2010). In memory of John Irwin. *Justice Policy Journal*, 7(2), 1–5.

Richards, S.C., Newbold, G., & Ross, J.I. (2009). Convict criminology, in Miller, J.M. (Ed.) *21st century criminology: A reference handbook*, Vol. 1 (pp. 356–363). Thousand Oaks, CA: SAGE.

Richards, S.C., Rose, C.D., & Reed, S.O. (2006). Inviting convicts to college: Prison and university partnerships. In *The state of corrections: (2005) Proceedings. ACA Annual Conferences* (pp. 171–180). Lanham, MD: American Correctional Association.

Richards, S.C. & Ross, J.I. (2001). Introducing the new school of convict criminology. *Social Justice*, 28(1), 177–191.

Richards, S.C. & Ross, J.I. (2003a). Ex-convict professors doing prison research, in *The state of corrections: 2002 proceedings ACA annual conferences* (pp. 163–168). Lanham, MD: American Correctional Association.

REFERENCES

Richards, S.C. & Ross, J.I. (2003b). Conclusion: An invitation to the criminology/criminal justice community, in Ross, J.I. & Richards, S.C. (Eds.) *Convict criminology* (pp. 347–353). Belmont, CA: Wadsworth Publishing.

Richards, S.C. & Ross, J.I. (2005). Convict criminology, in Bosworth, M. (Ed.) *Encyclopedia of prisons and correctional facilities* (pp. 169–175). Thousand Oaks, CA: SAGE.

Richards, S.C., Ross, J.I., & Jones, R.S. (2007). Convict criminology, in Barak, G. (Ed.) *Battleground criminal justice* (pp. 106–115). Westport, CT: Greenwood Press.

Richards, S.C., Ross, J.I., Jones, R.S., Lenza, M., Jones, R.S., Murphy, D.S., & Grigsby, R.S. (2012). Convict criminology, prisoner reentry, and public policy recommendations. *Journal of Prisoners on Prisons*, 21(1), 16–32.

Richards, S.C., Ross, J.I. Jones, R.S., Newbold, G., Murphy, D.S., & Grigsby, B. (2011). Convict criminology: Prisoner re-entry policy recommendations, in Ekunwe, I.O. & Jones, R.S. (Eds.) *Global perspectives on re-entry* (pp. 198–222). Tampere: Tampere University Press.

Rose, C., Reschenberg, K., & Richards, S.C. (2010). The inviting convicts to college. *Journal of Offender Rehabilitation*, 49(4), 293–308.

Ross, J.I. (1983). Jail dehumanizing say abolitionists. *Now*, June 2–8, p. 5.

Ross, J.I. (2003). (Mis) representing corrections: The role of our cultural industries, in Ross, J.I. & Richards, S.C. (Eds.) *Convict criminology* (pp. 37–58). Belmont, CA: Wadsworth Publishing.

Ross, J.I. (2008a). *Special problems in corrections*. Upper Saddle River, NJ: Prentice Hall.

Ross, J.I. (2008b). Analyzing contemporary introductory textbooks on correctional administration/management/organization. *Journal of Criminal Justice Education*, 19(3), 446–460.

Ross, J.I. (Ed.) (2009 [1998]). *Cutting the edge: Current perspectives in radical/critical criminology and criminal justice*. Westport, CT: Praeger.

Ross, J.I. (2010). Resisting the carceral state: Prisoner resistance from the bottom up. *Social Justice*, 36(3), 28–45.

Ross, J.I. (2012a). Varieties of prison voyeurism: An analytic framework. *Criminal Justice Review*, 95(3), 397–417.

Ross, J.I. (2012b). Why a jail or prison sentence is increasingly like a death sentence. *Contemporary Justice Review*, 15(3), 309–332.

Ross, J.I. (2012c). Deconstructing myths of American corrections. *Critical Criminology: An International Journal*, 15(3), 309–322.

Ross, J.I. (2016). *Key issues in corrections*. Bristol: Policy Press.

Ross, J.I. (2018). Prison activism, in Worley, R. & Worley, V. (Eds.) *American prisons and jails: An encyclopedia of controversies and trends* (pp. 5–9). Santa Barbara, CA: ABC-Clio Reference.

Ross, J.I. (2019). Getting a second chance with a university education: Barriers & opportunities. *Interchange: A Quarterly Review of Education*, 50(2), 175–186.

Ross, J.I. (2020). Dancing with the bomb throwers, December 20. https://jef
freyianross.com/dancing-with-the-bomb-throwers-amongst-us/ (accessed July
31, 2023).

Ross, J.I. (2021a). Context is everything: Understanding the scholarly, social, and
pedagogical origins of convict criminology, in Ross, J.I. & Vianello, F. (Eds.)
Convict criminology for the future (pp. 11–20). New York, NY: Routledge.

Ross, J.I. (2021b). Everything you wanted to know about convict criminology
but were afraid to ask. *Locali e Servizi Sociali*, 30(3), 615–629.

Ross, J.I. (2021c). Be mindful of the "lived experience fallacy" and its cousin,
"those who are closest to the problem are in the best position to change it."
March 23. https://jeffreyianross.com/be-mindful-of-the-lived-experience-fall
acy-and-its-cousin-those-who-are-closest-to-the-problem-are-in-the-best-posit
ion-to-change-it/ (accessed July 30, 2023).

Ross, J.I. (2021d). Won't you be my mentor? Understanding the challenges of
finding an appropriate graduate school mentor. October 21. https://jeffreyianr
oss.com/wont-you-be-my-mentor-understanding-the-challenges-of-finding-
an-appropriate-graduate-school-mentor/ (accessed July 30, 2023).

Ross, J.I. (2022). Training days: The challenges of providing higher education
in correctional institutions and how to overcome them. Keynote address.
Inauguration ceremony program 2021/2022, Casa di Reclusone Due Palazzi,
Padua, June 11.

Ross, J.I. (2023). Thinking critically about the next decade of convict criminology.
Journal of Prisoners on Prison, 33(1), 138–156.

Ross, J.I. & Copes, H. (2022). Convict criminology from here to there: A
content analysis of scholarship in a growing subfield. *Criminal Justice Studies*,
35(4), 442–457.

Ross, J.I. & Darke, S. (2018). Interpreting the development and growth of convict
criminology in South America. *Journal of Prisoners on Prisons*, 27(2), 108–117.

Ross, J.I., Darke, S., Aresti, A., Newbold, G., & Earle, R. (2014). Developing
convict criminology beyond North America. *International Criminal Justice Review*,
24(2), 121–133.

Ross, J.I. & Hornblum, A. (2009). No prison guinea pigs: President Obama
should act now to ensure prisoners aren't used for medical research. *Baltimore
Sun*, February 3 (reprinted in *Prison Legal News*, 20(2), 55).

Ross, J.I., Jones, R.S., Lenza, M., & Richards, S.C. (2016). Convict criminology
and the struggle for inclusion. *Critical Criminology: An International Journal*,
24(4), 489–501.

Ross, J.I. & Richards, S.C. (2002). *Behind bars: Surviving prison*. Indianapolis,
IN: Alpha Books.

Ross, J.I. & Richards, S.C. (Eds.) (2003). *Convict criminology*. Belmont,
CA: Wadsworth Publishing.

Ross, J.I. & Richards, S.C. (2005). Convict criminology, in Miller, J.M. & Wright,
R.A. (Eds.) *Encyclopedia of criminology* (pp. 232–235). New York, NY: Routledge.

REFERENCES

Ross, J.I. & Richards, S.C. (2009). *Beyond bars: Rejoining society after prison.* Indianapolis, IN: Alpha Books.

Ross, J.I., Richards, S.C., Jones, R.S., Lenza, M., & Grigsby, B. (2012). Convict criminology, in DeKeseredy, W.S. & Dragiewicz, M. (Eds.) *Handbook of critical criminology* (pp. 160–171). New York, NY: Routledge.

Ross, J.I., Richards, S.C., Newbold, G., Jones, R.S., Lenza, M., Murphy, D.S., Hogan, R., & Curry, G.D. (2011a). Knocking on the ivory tower's door: The experience of ex-convicts applying for tenure-track university positions. *Journal of Criminal Justice Education*, 22(2), 267–285.

Ross, J.I., Richards, S.C., Newbold, G., Lenza, M., & Grisby, R.S. (2011b). Convict criminology, in Dekeseredy, W.S. & Dragiewics, M. (Eds.) *Handbook of critical criminology* (pp. 160–171). New York, NY: Routledge.

Ross, J.I. & Sneed, V. (2018). How American-based television commercials portray convicts, correctional officials, carceral institutions, and the prison experience. *Corrections: Policy, Practice and Research*, 3(2), 73–91.

Ross, J.I., Tewksbury, R., Samuelsen, L., & Caneff, T. (2021). War stories? Analyzing memoirs and autobiographical treatments written by American correctional professionals. *Criminology, Criminal Justice, Law & Society*, 22(3), 1–13.

Ross, J.I., Tewksbury, R., & Zaldivar, M. (2015a). Analyzing for-profit colleges and universities that offer bachelors, masters and doctorates to inmates incarcerated in American correctional facilities. *Journal of Offender Rehabilitation*, 54(8), 585–598.

Ross, J.I. & Tietjen, G (2022). From fledgling network to the creation of an official division of the American Society of Criminology: The growth of Convict Criminology 2.0. *Social Justice*, 48(4), 85–102

Ross, J.I. & Tietjen, G. (2023). Every picture tells a story: Framing and understanding the activism of convict criminology. *Journal of Prisoners on Prison*, 33(1), 87–100.

Ross, J.I. & Vianello, F. (Eds.) (2021). *Convict criminology for the future.* New York, NY: Routledge.

Ross, J.I., Zaldivar, M., & Tewksbury, R. (2015b). Breaking out of prison and into print? Rationales and strategies to assist educated convicts conduct scholarly research and writing behind bars. *Critical Criminology: An International Journal*, 23(1), 73–83.

Ruggiero, V. (2010). *Penal abolitionism.* Oxford: Oxford University Press.

Salle, G. (2007). Une sociologie des "taulards": la convict criminology [A sociology of scoundrels: Convict criminology]. *Genèses*, 3, 132–144.

Sbraccia, A. (2021). Radicalization and experiences of detention, in Ross, J.I. & Vianello, F. (Eds.) *Convict criminology for the future* (pp. 170–185). New York, NY: Routledge.

Schlosser, E. (1998). The prison industrial complex. *The Atlantic Monthly*, December, 51–77.

Schlosser, J.A. (2008). Issues in interviewing inmates navigating the methodological landmines of prison research. *Qualitative Inquiry*, 14(8), 1500–1525.

Scott, J.W. (1991). The evidence of experience. *Critical Inquiry*, 17(4), 773–797.

Seigel, M. (2018). Critical prison studies: Review of a field. *American Quarterly*, 70(1), 123–137.

Shchukina, N.P. (2021). Kriminologiya osuzhdennykh v rossiiskom diskurse [Convict criminology in Russian discourse]. *Iuridicheskii vestnik Samarskogo universiteta* [*Juridical Journal of Samara University*], 7(4), 102–108.

Smith, H.P. (2013). Reinforcing experiential learning in criminology: Definitions, rationales and missed opportunities concerning prison tours in the United States. *Journal of Criminal Justice Education*, 24(1), 50–67.

Smith, J.M. (2021). The formerly incarcerated, advocacy, activism, and community reintegration. *Contemporary Justice Review*, 24(1), 43–63.

Smith, J.M. & Kinzel, A. (2021). Carceral citizenship as strength: Formerly incarcerated activists, civic engagement and criminal justice transformation. *Critical Criminology: An International Journal*, 29(1), 93–110.

Sokoloff, N.J. & Schenck-Fontain, A. (2017). College programs in prison and upon reentry for men and women: A literature review. *Contemporary Justice Review*, 20(1), 95–114.

Sorkin, M.D. (2015). Dave Curry dies: UMSL prof received presidential pardon for 34 year prison. *St. Louis Post-Dispatch*, May 14 (accessed January 3, 2023).

Sterchele, L. (2021). Can the "psychiatric prisoner" speak? Notes from convict criminology and disability studies, in Ross, J.I. & Vianello, F. (Eds.) *Convict criminology for the future* (pp. 156–169). New York, NY: Routledge.

Strayhorn, T.L., Johnson, R.M., & Barrett, B.A. (2013). Investigating the college adjustment and transition experiences of formerly incarcerated black male collegians at predominantly white institutions. *Spectrum: A Journal on Black Men*, 2(1), 73–98.

Sturm, S.P. & Tae, H. (2017). Leading with conviction: The transformative role of formerly incarcerated leaders in reducing mass incarceration. Columbia Public Law Research Paper, Rochester, NY.

Sudbury, J. (2004). A world without prisons: Resisting militarism, globalized punishment, and empire. *Social Justice*, 31(1–2), 9–30.

Swanson, C.G., Rohrer, G., & Crow, M.S. (2010). Is criminal justice education ready for reentry? *Journal of Criminal Justice Education*, 21(1), 60–76.

Sykes, G. (1958). *The society of captives: A study of a maximum security prison*. Princeton, NJ: Princeton University Press.

Taylor, J.M. (1994). Should prisoners have access to collegiate education? A policy issue. *Educational Policy*, 8(3), 315–338.

Taylor, J.M. (2002). *Prisoners' guerrilla handbook to correspondence programs in the United States and Canada* (2nd Edn). Brunswick: Audenreed Press.

Taylor, J.M. & Schwartzkopf, S. (2009). *Prisoners' guerrilla handbook to correspondence programs in the United States and Canada* (3rd Edn). Lakeland, FL: Prison Legal News.

REFERENCES

Taylor, J.M. & Tewksbury, R. (1995). From the inside out and outside in: Team research in the correctional setting. *Journal of Contemporary Criminal Justice*, 11(2), 119–136.

Taylor, J.M. & Tewksbury, R. (2002). Postsecondary correctional education: The imprisoned university, in Gido, R. & Allman, T. (Eds.) *Turnstile justice* (pp. 145–175). Upper Saddle River, NJ: Prentice Hall.

Terry, C. (2003a). From c-block to academia: You can't get there from here, in Ross, J.I. & Richards, S.C. (Eds.) *Convict criminology* (pp. 95–119) Belmont, CA: Wadsworth Publishing.

Terry, C. (2003b). *The fellas: Overcoming prison and addiction*. Belmont, CA: Wadsworth Publishers.

Tewksbury, R. & Mustaine, E.E. (2011). How many authors does it take to write an article? An assessment of criminology and criminal justice research article author composition. *Journal of Criminal Justice Education*, 27(1), 12–23.

Tewksbury, R. & Ross, J.I. (2019). Instructing and mentoring ex-con university students in departments of criminology and criminal justice. *Corrections: Policy, Practice and Research*, 4(2), 79–88.

Tietjen, G. (2017). In interviews with 122 rapists, student pursues not-so-simple question: Why? By Kamala Thiagarajan, *National Public Radio*, December. https://www.npr.org/sections/goatsandsoda/2017/12/16/570827107/in-interviews-with-122-rapists-student-pursues-not-so-simple-question-why (accessed October 20, 2023).

Tietjen, G. (2019). Convict criminology: Learning from the past, confronting the present, expanding for the future. *Critical Criminology: An International Journal*, 27(1), 101–114.

Tietjen, G. (forthcoming). *Justice lessons: The rise of system affected academic groups*. Berkeley, CA: University of California Press.

Tietjen, G., Burnett, J.L., & Jessie, B.O. (2021). Onward and upward: The significance of mentorship for formerly incarcerated students and academics. *Critical Criminology: An International Journal*, 29, 633–664.

Tietjen, G. & Kavish, D. (2021). In the pool without a life jacket: Status fragility and convict criminology, in Ross, J.I. & Vianello, F. (Eds.) *Convict criminology for the future* (pp. 66–81). New York, NY: Routledge.

Timor, U., Peled-Laskov, R., & Golan, E. (2023). Student mentors of incarcerated persons: Contribution of a mentoring program for incarcerated persons. *Criminal Justice Policy Review*, 34(1), 65–87.

Toch, H. (1967). The convict as researcher. *TransAction*, 4, 72–75.

Torrente, G. (2021). The reaction of the Italian prison administration in the face of a convict criminologist, in Ross, J.I. & Vianello, F. (Eds.) *Convict criminology for the future* (pp. 186–196). New York, NY: Routledge.

Tregea, W.S. (2003). Twenty years teaching college in prison, in Ross, J.I. & Richards, S.C. (Eds.) *Convict criminology* (pp. 309–324). Belmont, CA: Wadsworth Publishers.

Trulson, C.R., Marquart, J.W., & Mullings, J.L. (2004). Breaking in: Gaining entry to prisons and other hard-to-access criminal justice organizations. *Journal of Criminal Justice Education*, 15(2), 451–478.

Turnbull, S., Martel, J., Parkes, D., & Moore, D. (Eds.) (2018) *Critical prison studies, carceral ethnography, and human rights: From lived experience to global action*, Oñati Socio-legal Series, v. 8, n. 2.

Uggen, C. & Inderbitzin, M. (2010). Public criminologies. *Criminology & Public Policy*, 9(4), 725–749.

Unnithan, P. (1986). Research in a correctional setting: Constraints and biases. *Journal of Criminal Justice*, 14(1), 401–412.

Vacca, J.S. (2004). Educated prisoners are less likely to return to prison. *Journal of Correctional Education*, 55, 297–305.

Vegh Weis, V. (2021). It is time: Toward a Southern convict criminology, in Ross, J.I. & Vianello, F. (Eds.) *Convict criminology for the future* (pp. 112–126). New York, NY: Routledge.

Vianello, F. (2021). Developing convict criminology: Notes from Italy, in Ross, J.I. & Vianello, F. (Eds.) *Convict criminology for the future* (pp. 98–111). New York, NY: Routledge.

Vianello, F. & Ross, J.I. (2021). Conclusion: What does the future hold for convict criminology?, in Ross, J.I. & Vianello, F. (Eds.) *Convict criminology for the future* (pp. 211–217). New York, NY: Routledge.

Viren, S. (2021). The native scholar who wasn't. *New York Times Magazine*, pp. 26–32, 46, 49. https://www.nytimes.com/2021/05/25/magazine/cherokee-native-american-andrea-smith.html (accessed June 25, 2021).

Wacquant, L. (2002). The curious eclipse of prison ethnography in the age of mass incarceration. *Ethnography*, 3(4), 371–397.

Wakai, S., Shelton, D., Trestman, R.L., & Kesten, K. (2009). Conducting research in corrections: Challenges and solutions. *Behavioral Sciences & the Law*, 27(5), 743–752.

Walker, J.T. (2020). Mentoring faculty members. *The Criminologist*, 45(4), 28.

Warr, J. (2021). Many rivers to cross: Why I'm not a convict criminologist. *Criminology with Conviction*, Official Newsletter of the ASC Division of Convict Criminology, 1(1), 16–19.

Weaver, B. (2011). Co-producing community justice: The transformative potential of personalisation for penal sanctions. *The British Journal of Social Work*, 41(6), 1038–1057.

Weinbren, D. (2014). *The open university: A history*. Manchester: Manchester University Press.

Welch, M. (1996). *Corrections: A critical approach* (2nd Edn). New York, NY: Routledge.

Williams, D.J., Bischoff, D., Casey, T., & Burnett, J. (2014). "Mom, they are going to kill my dad!" A personal narrative on capital punishment from a convict criminology perspective. *Critical Criminology: An International Journal*, 22(3), 389–401.

REFERENCES

Williams, D.J. & Burnett, J. (2012). Interrelated problems of silencing voices and sexual crime: Convict criminology insights. *Journal of Prisoners on Prison*, 21(1–2), 132–138.

Williams, J.M. (2021). The division on convict criminology as a haven for radical racial exploration. *Criminology with Conviction*, Official newsletter of the ASC Division of Convict Criminology, pp. 12–14. https://concrim.asc41.com/wp-content/uploads/2021/07/2021-spring-newsletter.pdf (accessed January 6, 2023).

Woodall, D. & Boeri, M. (2014). "When you got friends in low places, you stay low": Social networks and access to resources for female methamphetamine users in low-income suburban communities. *Journal of Drug Issues*, 44(3), 321–333.

Wright, P. (2021). Language matters: Why we use the words we do? *Prison Legal News*, November, p. 18. https://www.prisonlegalnews.org/news/2021/nov/1/language-matters-why-we-use-words-we-do/ (accessed July 31, 2023).

Yeager, M.G. (2015). *Frank Tannenbaum: The making of a convict criminologist*. New York, NY: Routledge.

Zaldivar, M. (2013). How, why, and about what do federal prisoners complain: And what we can do about it. *Journal of Prisoners on Prison*, 22(2), 104–127.

Zaldivar, P. (2013). Pre-apprendi sentencing: Issues surrounding the retroactivity of an unconstitutional sentence. *St. Thomas Law Review*, 25, 392–418.

Zonn, S. (1977). Inmate unions: An appraisal of prisoner rights and labor implications. *University of Miami Law Review*, 32(3), 613–635.

Zoukis, C. (2013). *Inmates, prisoners, and convicts: What's the difference?* https://federalcriminaldefenseattorney.com/inmates-prisoners-convicts-difference/ (accessed September 14, 2022).

Zoukis, C. (2016). Tribute to Dr. Jon Marc Taylor, a prison education crusader. *HuffPost*, January 29. https://www.huffingtonpost.com/christopher-zoukis/tribute-to-dr-jon-marc-ta_b_9104560.html (accessed January 3, 2023).

Zwerman, G. & Gardner, G. (1986). Obstacles to research in a state prison. *Qualitative Sociology*, 9(3), 293–300.

Legal cases cited

Apprendi v. *New Jersey*, 530 U.S. 466, 490 (2000).

Blakely v. *Washington*, 542 U.S. 296 (2004).

United States v. *Booker*, 543 U.S. 220, 229 (2005).

Victor Hassine v. *Charles Zimmerman, The Attorney General of the State of Pennsylvania* (Civil Action 86-63-6315) (1997).

Index

References to endnotes show both the page number and the note number (167n2).

A

activism
definition of 123, 124
performative 21
and policies 53
see also activism in Convict Criminology;
prison activism
activism in Convict Criminology 123–124
activist scholarship 126–127
brief history of 126
competing demands, balancing 130–132
direct activism 128–130
essentiality 124–125
mentorship as activism 127
participating instructors and professors,
challenges for 130–132
Alexander, Elizabeth 117
Alinsky, Saul 27
allies, death of 33
American Civil Liberties Union (ACLU) 118
American Society for the Abolition of Capital
Punishment 122
American Society of Criminology
advantages and disadvantages of
joining 37–38
Atlanta meeting 2018 35–36
San Francisco meeting 2019 30–31, 37–38
Amnesty International 118
Aresti, Andreas (Andy) 30, 31–32, 41, 42, 58,
79, 80, 126, 142, 143
Argentina 30, 31–32, 41, 52, 126
Australia 9, 30, 38–41
Australian and New Zealand Society of
Criminology (ANZSOC) 39, 40
autoethnography 53, 56–58

B

Bachrach, P. 167n2
Ban the Box initiative 95, 129

Barak, Gregg 128
Baratz, M. S. 167n2
Belknap, J. 33, 96, 169n8
Bentham, Jeremy 120
Bernard, Thomas J. 111
Betts, Reginald Dwayne 12
Bint Faisel, A. 79
Biondi, Karina 32
Black Lives Matter 128, 129, 134
Black Panther Party 120
Boudin, Kathy 120
Bradley, Alexandria 170n12
Brazil 30, 31–32, 41, 126, 137, 142
British Convict Criminology 31
British Society of Criminology 31
Brotherton, David 139
Burnett, James L. 33, 76

C

Canada 40, 52, 138
Canadian Quaker Committee for Jails and
Justice 121
Carceral, K.C. 102
carceral citizenship 13, 115
Carey, Lukas 39, 40–41
Chessman, Caryl 116
Chiola, G. 82–84
chronology of Convict Criminology 147
Citizens United for Rehabilitation of Errants
(CURE) 118, 119
civil rights movement 120
Clark, Rod 77
Coates report 77
Colson, Charles "Chuck" 120
communication strategies 143
Condon, Jenny-Brooke 117
Conferenza dei Rettori delle Università
Italiane 83
constitution formation 35

convict criminologist 23–24
Convict Criminology 1.0 29–34
Convict Criminology 2.0 34–38
Convict Criminology for the Future 37, 50
"Convict Criminology for the Future"
    conference 36–37
co-production/participatory action research 19–20
correctional facilities
    classes 42
        see also education in correctional facilities
    goals of 64
    obstacles in 7–8
correctional reform, Convict Criminology's take
    on 134
correctional settings, changes in 43
corrections 15–16
COVID-19 pandemic 129, 135
Cox, Alison 44, 59, 143
criminal conviction 13
criminal justice system-contacted 24
criminal justice system-impacted 24
criminal justice system-involved 23–24
Criminologia dos Condenados e o Futuro, A 137
critical carceral studies 17
Critical Criminology 15–17, 30, 33, 54
critical prison studies 17–18
critical resistance 120
criticisms 43–44
    response to 44–45
cultural shifts 32
Curry, Glen David 34

D
Darke, Sacha 30, 31–32, 41, 42, 58, 79, 80,
    142, 143
Darrow, Clarence 116
Davidson, Howard 58
Davies, Bill 170n12
Davis, Angela 27, 120
death penalty, abolishing 122
desistance theory 15
direct activism 128
    American Society of Criminology Division
        of Convict Criminology's periodic public
        statements 129
    news-making criminology 128
    participating as prisoner
        representatives 128–129
    participating in contemporary progressive
        activist movements 129–130
    serving on editorial boards/reviewing papers
        for academic journals 129
distance learning 77

diversity and inclusion, lack of 32–33
Division of Convict Criminology (DCC) 37,
    70–71, 125, 129, 137–138, 144–145
    periodic public statements 129
doctorates, ex-convicts pursuing 40
Dolezal, Rachel 168n10
Doyle, C. 40, 41
Du Bois, W.E.B. 27

E
Earle, Rod 19, 27, 41, 78–79, 168n11, 168n14
education in correctional facilities 63, 65
    adequate resources to 70
    alternatives to face-to-face university
        instruction, lack of 66–67
    capable instructors, disinterest in teaching 67
    conducting empirical research on 71
    Convict Criminology resources, use
        of 70–71
    convincing politicians, news media, and
        public 72–73
    correctional workers and administrators
        distrust on educated prisoners 68
        distrust outside instructors 68
        providing evidence and arguments about
            university education utility 72
        utilization of appropriate resources 72
    difficult time registering for university
        courses 69
    distractions for convicts to study 68
    Division of Convict Criminology resources,
        use of 70–71
    dropping of classes and programs 66
    establishment of formal legal mechanisms 73
    existing programs, analysis of 71–72
    failure to provide, reasons for 65
    importance of 64–65
    in Italy 81–84
    labs and field trips 66
    learning difficulty in non-face-to-face
        situations 67
    limited non-classroom educational
        experiences 66
    master's and doctoral-level correspondence
        courses 73
    and nonprofit foundations and educational
        trusts 71
    outside instructors, bureaucratic obstacles to 67
    payment for college credit courses 69
    payment for post-secondary education in
        United States 69–70
    prison and university administrators,
        bureaucratic obstacles to 69

INDEX

security restrictions, impact of 68
substandard teaching modality 66–67
teaching on an ad-hoc basis 80
unaccredited institutions 73
undergraduate degree, predominance of 66
in United Kingdom 77–78
    Convict Criminology at Westminster University 80
    Learning Together program 79–80
    Open University program 78–79, 80
    recent challenges 80–81
in United States 73–74
    Inside-Out Prison Exchange Program 74–75
    Inviting Convicts to College Program 42, 74, 75–77
university-level instruction 64
Ekunwe, Ikponwosa (Silver) 30
Elijah, Soffiyah 117
Elliott, Liz 58, 59
Ellis, Adam 20, 79
Eskridge, Chris 36, 38
ethnography 56–58
European Group of the Study of Deviance and Social Control conference 31

F

failure of CC, reasons for 32–33, 35–36
fake allies, addressing 21–22
Fathi, David 117
female representations 33
Ferranti, Seth 102–103
Floyd, George 129
Flynn, N. 77
Folsom State Prison, California 120
formerly incarcerated person, labeling 12–13
founders health issues 33
founding period of CC 29–34
future of Convict Criminology 133–135
    battling misinformation 143–144
    better tracking of accomplishments 141
    boosting ongoing mentoring efforts 144
    communication technologies adoption 143
    conclusions of major books on CC 135–136
    continuous engagement in self-reflection 141–142
    critiques 136
    determination of 135–136
    importance of 135
    independent periodical conferences 142
    organizing special issues of relevant academic journals 143
    presence in other learned organizations 141
    regular release of relevant communications 142
    separate national Convict Criminology groups 143
    and written statements 135

G

Gaucher, Bob 58
Germany 142
Global Perspectives on Re-Entry 31
global scope, of CC 134
Gowdy, Bryan 117
Grigsby, Bob 30
Gupta, Vanita 117

H

Hassine, Victor 102–103, 111
Heurta, Adrian 129
higher education, and criminal recidivism rates 65
    see also education in correctional facilities
Huff, C. R. 120
Human Rights Watch 118

I

identities exposure 33
ideological debates 32–33
imposter syndrome 24–25, 92
incarcerated individuals narratives 9
incarcerated mothers 121
incarcerated reforms 10
incarceration lived experience
    importance of 5–7
    public presentation of 7–8
indirect mentorship 54–55
Innovator's Dilemma, The 45
Inside-Out Prison Exchange Program 74–75
"Insider Prison Perspectives in Europe & the Americas" symposium 41–42
Instead of Prisons: a Handbook for Abolitionists 19
Institutional Review Board (IRB) 107, 128–129
International Scientific Conference on Global Perspectives on Re-Entry 30–31
Inviting Convicts to College Program 42, 74, 75–77
Iowa State University 76
Irwin, John Keith 22, 27, 29, 56–57, 97, 168n17
Italy, education in correctional facilities in 81–84

J

jail activism *see* prison activism
Jewkes, Y. 127
Jones, Richard S. 30, 104, 110
Journal of Contemporary Ethnography 5, 56

Journal of Prisoners on Prisons 28, 47, 54, 58–59, 110, 140, 143

K
Kalica, Elton 37
Karam, Maria Lucia 137
Kavish, Daniel 37, 58, 129, 169n3
Khan, Usman 80
Knopp, Fay Honey 19, 121
Krippendorff, K. 50
KROM (The Norwegian Association for Penal Reform) conference 31
Krug, Jessica 168n10
Kuby, Ron 116
Kunstler, William 116

L
labeling 13–16
Lanier, Charles 102
leadership, lack of 34
Learning Together program 79–80
left-wing politics 123
Lenza, Mike 58, 143
life behind bars, realistic picture of 7–8
life course theory 15
Little Engine That Could, The 45
lived experiences 5–7, 9, 167

M
Malkin, M. L. 44
Marques, Olga 20
Mathiesen, Thomas 31
McCleary, Richard 102
McCord, Mary B. 117
McFarlane, R. 77, 78
Mehigan, J. 78–79
members, of Convict Criminology 10
mentoring 42, 85–86
   challenges with 96
      addressing 96–98
   definition of 86–87
   difficulty in find and retain a suitable mentor 98
   doubts about 99
   duties beyond the scope of 89
   duties of academic mentors 90–91
   helping formerly incarcerated people 92–96
   identification of suitable graduate mentor 91–92
   importance of 87
   individuals not amenable to being mentored, reasons for 87–88

mentorship 54–55
   as activism 127
   pathways in Convict Criminology 88–89
   process of 86
   and receptivity 88
   settings 87
   system of 44–45
#MeToo movement 134
minority representations 33, 43–44, 45
misconceptions 8–11
Moak, S. C. 87
Mothers Against Mandatory Minimums 118
movies, in prison settings 7–8
Murillo, D. 97
Murphy, Daniel 128

N
narrative criminology 19
National Conference of Rectors' Delegates for Prison Universities (CNUPP) 83
National Lawyers Guild 118
National Prison Project 118
Nellis, M. 168n18
Nettler, Gwynne 27, 28
New Zealand 38–41, 128
Newbold, Greg 39, 40, 127, 128
news media 42, 72–73
news-making criminology 128

O
open prisons 66
Open University program 78–79, 80
organizations competition 33
origin, of CC 4–5
Ortiz, Jennifer Marie 14, 139
Oshkosh Correctional 76
Oxford Handbook of Criminology 41

P
Padua, University of 36–37
panel of Convict Criminology 30–31, 42
participatory action research (PAR) 19–20
peacemaking criminology 18
Pell Grants 69–70, 121
Pepinsky, Hal 18
phenomenology 56
Philadelphia Prison System 74
Pike, A. 78
Piper, K. 116, 119, 122
policy debates, participation in 42–43
policy recommendations 25–26
political activism (examples) 125
politicians, convincing 72–73

INDEX

Pompa, Lori 74
Porter, Nicole 117
Portugal 137
prehistory era (1920–1999) 27–29
present stage 34–38
Presser, Lois 19
prison activism 115
 activists and organizations 116–119
 history of prison reform 120–121
 prison abolition 121
  movement 18–19
  and prison reform, distinguishing
   between 121–122
 and prisoner movements in the United
  States 115–116
 prominent lawyers in the United
  States 117–118
 sentencing reform 122
Prison Activist Resource Center 118
Prison Fellowship 120
Prison Legal News 12
Prison Moratorium 118
prison populations 40
Prison University Programs (PUPs), Italy 82–84
prisoner union 120
Prisoners' Education Trust (PET), UK 71, 77–78
Project Rebound 97
proximate leadership 6
public, convincing 72–73
Public Criminology 123
publication process 42

Q
Quaker 19
Quinney, Richard 18

R
Rapping, Jonathan 117
Reagan administration 120
Reed, Susan 75
research co-production 19–20
research methods
 training in 45
returning citizen 12–13
Richards, Stephen C. 22, 26, 29, 32, 35, 42, 51,
  58, 75, 125, 133, 136, 143
Rose, Chris 75
Rudovsky, David 117

S
San Francisco State University 97
scholarly research, collaborative
 and biases 105

challenges in conducting research behind
 bars 104–105
co-authoring with other educated inmates
 and outside scholars 110–111
constraints 107–109
dearth of insightful feedback or
 collaborators 109
developing a research to-do list 109
difficult time in gaining access to outside
 assistance 108
and exposition of criminal justice system 106
Institutional Review Board (IRB), approval
 from 107
and lack of appropriate published research
 materials 109
lack of research methods available 107
literature review 102–104
reasons for writing scholarly
 publications 105–107
resources and cost 107–108
serving as a reviewer for scholarly papers 110
shortage of fellow educated inmates 109
time factor 108–109
scholars 48
scholarship 50
 autoethnography and quantitative
  research 56–59
 changing policies and activism 55
 Convict Criminology content 54–55
 definition of 47–48
 formerly incarcerated individuals
  and Convict Criminology research 49–50
  and scholarly research 49
 impact of 53–54, 55–56
 lead researchers 52
 peer reviewed research 49, 50
 policy and activism 55
 publication of 52
 research methods 52–53
 Ross and Copes research 54–55
  conclusion 54
  method 50–56
 scientific research 48
 subject of mentorship, treatment of 53
scholarvism 127
Schools not Jails 118
self-aggrandizement 43
self-reflection, continuous engagement
 in 141–142
Sentencing Project 118
sentencing reform 122
Smith, Andrea 168n10
Society of Captives, The 57

Soros Foundation 118
South America 31–32
Stevenson, Bryan 117
Sullivan, Charlie and Pauline 119
SWOT analysis 136–137
   opportunities 139–140
   strengths 137–138
   threats 140–141
   weaknesses 138–139
Sykes, G. 57

T

Tampere conference 30–31
Tannenbaum, Frank 27, 28
Taylor, Jon Marc 102–103, 104
Temple University 74
tertiary influences 27–28, 168n2
Tewksbury, R. 104
theories aligned with Convict
   Criminology 15–17, 22–23
thug criminology 20
Tietjen, Grant 22, 32, 35, 59, 127, 129,
   143, 169n3
Tirant Lo Branch 137
tokenism 21
Trombley, J. Renee 59, 143

U

United Kingdom 77–78
   Convict Criminology at Westminster
     University 80
   Learning Together program 79–80
   Open University program 78–79, 80
   Prisoners' Education Trust (PET) 71,
     77–78
   recent challenges 80–81

United States 73–74, 86, 138, 142
   Citizens United for Rehabilitation of Errants
     (CURE) 118, 119
   Inside-Out Prison Exchange Program 74–75
   Inviting Convicts to College Program 42,
     74, 75–77
   payment for post-secondary education
     in 69–70
   payment for post-secondary education in
     correctional facilities 69–70
   prison abolition movement in 121
   prisoner movements in 115–116
   prominent lawyers who have attempted to
     change prison conditions 117–118
   toughest prisons in 7
   Violent Crime Control Act (aka the
     Crime Bill) 70

V

Vianello, Francesca 36, 81–82, 83, 127, 129, 136

W

Wacquant, Loic 57
Walker, J. T. 87
Wang, Cecillia D. 118
"White male" stigma of CC 96
Williams, D.J. 76
Williams, J. M. 130
Wisconsin–Oshkosh, University of 75
Women's Advocacy Ministry 120
Woodall, Denise 35
work in progress, CC as 146
Wright, Paul 12

Z

Zaldivar, Miguel 128